NUCLEAR WEAPONS,
THE BALANCE OF TERROR,
THE QUEST FOR PEACE

NUCLEAR WEAPONS, THE BALANCE OF TERROR, THE QUEST FOR PEACE

A.J.C. Edwards

State University of New York Press

First published
In U.S.A. by
State University of New York Press
Albany

For information, address State University of New York Press,
State University Plaza, Albany, N.Y., 12246

Typeset by TecSet Ltd, Surrey, England

Printed in Hong Kong

Library of Congress Cataloging-in-Publication Data

Edwards, A. J. C.
Nuclear weapons, the balance of terror, the quest
for peace.
Bibliography: p.
Includes index.
1. Nuclear weapons.   2. Nuclear warfare.   3. Nuclear
arms control.   I. Title.
U264.E39   1986   355'.0217   85–17383
ISBN 0–88706–185–0
ISBN 0–88706–186–9 (pbk.)

260282

Contents

List of Tables, Figures, and Appendix Figures

List of Abbreviations

ABM	Anti-ballistic missile
ACM	Anti-cruise missile
ADM	Atomic demolition munition
ALCM	Air-launched cruise missile
ASAT	Anti-satellite
ASW	Anti-submarine warfare
CEP	Circular error probable
CSCE	Conference on Security and Co-operation in Europe
CTBT	Comprehensive Test Ban Treaty
CW	Chemical warfare
C^3	Command, control and communications
ECM	Electronic counter-measures
EMP	Electromagnetic pulse
GLCM	Ground-launched cruise missile
IAEA	International Atomic Energy Agency
ICBM	Intercontinental ballistic missile
IISS	International Institute for Strategic Studies
INF	Intermediate-range nuclear forces
IRBM	Intermediate-range ballistic missile
KT	Kilotons (thousands of tons)
LOA	Launch on assessment
MARV	Manoeuvrable re-entry vehicles
MBFR	Mutual and balanced force reductions
MIRV	Multiple independently-targetable re-entry vehicles
MRBM	Medium-range ballistic missile
MRV	Multiple re-entry vehicles
MSMD	Mutual and stable minimum deterrence
MT	Megatons (millions of tons)
MX	American 'Peacekeeper' ICBM
NATO	North Atlantic Treaty Organisation

NEACP	National Emergency Airborne Command Post
NM	Nautical miles
NORAD	North American Aerospace Defense
NPT	Nuclear Non-proliferation Treaty
PTBT	Partial Test Ban Treaty
RV	Re-entry vehicle
SAC	Strategic Air Command
SALT	Strategic Arms Limitation Talks
SAM	Surface-to-air missile
SDI	Strategic Defence Initiative
SICBM	Single warhead, intercontinental ballistic missile
SIPRI	Stockholm International Peace Research Institute
SLBM	Submarine-launched ballistic missile
SLCM	Sea-launched cruise missile
SRAM	Short-range attack missile
SRBM	Short-range ballistic missile
SSN	Nuclear powered submarine
SS-	Prefix for Soviet ground-launched missiles
SS-N-	Prefix for Soviet sea-launched missiles
SSBN	SSN carrying ballistic missiles
START	Strategic Arms Reduction Talks
TERCOM	Terrain contour mapping
TNT	Trinitrotoluene
TNW	Theatre or tactical nuclear weapons

Preface

This book discusses from first principles, and as comprehensively as its moderate compass allows, some of the most fundamental issues of our time - peace and war in the nuclear era, deterrence and defence, nuclear strategy, world politics, disarmament and arms control, the balance of terror. It is intended for readers of all professions and persuasions, whether students of defence and politics, practitioners or laymen, supporters of nuclear deterrence or opponents, who believe that these issues cannot be wished away or laid on one side but need to be addressed with as much clarity, rigour, knowledge, understanding and realism as the human intellect can muster, even if this means thinking about the unthinkable or imagining the unimaginable.

Much of the discussion covers familiar ground. What I have tried to do is to bring more and less familiar arguments about the balance of terror together within a coherent system of thought. The early chapters recall what the balance of terror is and how it came into being. They suggest that, distasteful as it may be, there seems no practical alternative to it in the foreseeable future. Later chapters deal with the politics and, above all, the stability of the balance of terror, in both an intrinsic and a dynamic sense. The two final chapters discuss policies towards the balance of terror - the difficulties in policies which seek to reject it, the main threats to stability and the scope for improvements in policy which would enhance security and stability.

The endnotes and figures contain much factual information, particularly on the development of weapon systems, arms control agreements and the alliances. This is intended primarily for layman and student readers. An algebraic appendix presents a simple general equilibrium model of mutual deterrence: the reader who finds the language of algebra inconvenient is advised to turn a blind eye.

In writing the book I have received much help and encouragement from others. I began it during a year spent at the Royal College of Defence

Studies (1979). A preliminary draft for some of the early chapters appeared in Seaford House papers for 1979.

I am especially indebted to General Sir David Fraser, Commandant of the College during 1979, for his inspiring lectures and perceptive comments subsequently on an early draft of the book; to Brigadier General Robert H. Baxter of the US Air Force, who gave me many invaluable informal tutorials during 1979 on strike capabilities, stability and arms control; to John Wilberforce of the Foreign and Commonwealth Office, who gave me much useful advice on political aspects, extended deterrence and intermediate range nuclear forces; to Dr Christoph Bertram, then Director of the International Institute for Strategic Studies, who deepened my understanding of the role of politics in the balance of terror and helpfully identified lacunas in my early work on the subject; to Professor Lawrence Freedman, then at Chatham House, who gave me invaluable guidance both at the outset and in the middle stages of the project; and to Sir Michael Quinlan, formerly of the Ministry of Defence, who not only commented most penetratingly on the later chapters but also generously gave me access to several of his own writings. All of these saw my text in whole or in part at one stage or another and gave unstintingly of their knowledge and wisdom.

I am greatly indebted also to HM Government, who gave me permission to publish; to Air Vice-Marshal John Herrington, Rear Admiral Bryan Straker, Dr Roy Dean, Ian Cuthbertson, and others sadly too numerous to mention, who gave me much help on particular points; to Lieutenant-General Sir Maurice Johnston, Colonel John Friedberger and Aharon Nathan, who, perhaps unwittingly, gave me encouragement at critical times; to a whole succession of distinguished lecturers at the Royal College of Defence Studies in 1979, including Lord Brimelow, Sir Terence Garvey, Professor Michael Howard, Professor Lowenthal and Dr Edward Luttwak; to the Librarians and Assistant Librarians of the Royal College of Defence Studies, Ministry of Defence, Foreign and Commonwealth Office and Treasury; to the late Arthur Chilcot, who drew several of the diagrams; to the secretaries at the Royal College of Defence Studies and my own secretary, Mrs P. A. Hall, who typed and repeatedly retyped the text with extraordinary skill and good humour; to Muriel Calder, who read the proofs; and, not least, to my wife and family, who gallantly allowed me to complete a task whose scope and magnitude far exceeded my early expectations.

I hasten to add that none of those who have helped me so generously is in any way responsible for errors of fact or judgement which remain. The views expressed are my own and do not necessarily reflect government attitudes or policy.

I have two main anxieties as the book goes to press. The first is that some readers may be troubled by what they read in it. Peace, deterrence and nuclear weapons are subjects about which many people feel deeply. It is difficult to write about such subjects in a manner acceptable to all. The thrust of the argument may challenge convictions sincerely and passionately held.

If some readers are troubled, I ask them to forgive me. My defence is that the balance of terror is a crucial, if not a dominating, feature of today's world. Distasteful and controversial as it may be, the case for investigating it must correspondingly be overwhelming.

The second anxiety is that I am keenly aware how difficult it is to deal adequately with a subject of such magnitude and moment, and how presumptuous to seek a public audience. I have asked myself often: is the canvas too large for my untutored brush? Has zeal outrun discretion? Have I ventured,

Like little wanton boys that swim on bladders
This many summers in a sea of glory:
But far beyond my depth?

Some readers may think so. If they do, I offer no defence. I ask them, too, to forgive me.

Wimbledon
Easter 1985   A.J.C. EDWARDS

1   The Balance of Terror

More than a generation has passed since the United States dropped atomic bombs over Hiroshima and Nagasaki and President Truman is said to have declared: 'This is the greatest thing in history.'[1] Nuclear weapons have not so far been used again. But there is little question that their mere existence, unused and largely unseen as they have been since 1945, has profoundly influenced the course of history.

Local conflicts have been common since 1945, especially in Asia and Africa. The period between 1945 and the early 1980s has seen more than 160 such conflicts in which as many as ten million people may have been killed, compared with some six and a half million in the First World War and some fifty million in the Second World War.[2] But there has been no war in the continents of Europe or North America; no world war. Between East and West there has been a heavily armed peace - a nervous and precarious peace at times, and an expensive peace - but peace nevertheless.

To ascribe this peace to any single cause would be over-simple. In the early years of the post-war period, however, the peaceful intentions of the United States, then manifestly the strongest power in the world by virtue of its nuclear arsenal, were clearly crucial. More recently, few would doubt that a dominant factor, and the factor which distinguishes the present era from all previous eras, has been the so-called 'balance of terror' between East and West, which has resulted from the development of nuclear weapons by each side.[3] Coined in the mid-1950s, the phrase itself hints at a sea-change in the human story - an historic transformation from the balances of power of earlier periods.

The balance of terror has apparently succeeded up to now where earlier balances of power failed. The sheer scale and speed of the destruction which East and West are capable of inflicting on each other have enhanced the risks associated with war to the point where, fundamentally antagonistic though the two sides are, they have the strongest common interest in peace. The ability of each side to destroy a large proportion of the enemy's

1

population and industry in the space of a few minutes, with weapons launched from distances of thousands of miles, has transformed the calculus of risks in military conflict. Never before have the likely consequences of all-out warfare been so horrendous, so immediate, so altogether unacceptable, for winner and loser alike - if indeed there would be a winner and a loser.[4]

To suggest that the balance of terror has kept the world at peace is not to say that it has any merit in itself. On the contrary, it is clearly a dreadful expedient. How much better it would be if the world could manage without weapons of mass destruction - if a lasting peace could be assured without these hideous creatures of modern politics and technology.

But the balance of terror is almost certainly here to stay, for the foreseeable future at least. Distasteful as the prospect may be, the nuclear arsenals are likely to remain in being - not necessarily on their present scale - so long as the world's major powers remain fundamentally antagonistic towards each other. In the absence of mutual trust, peace between East and West is likely to continue to depend on mutual deterrence through a balance of terror.

Whether the balance of terror will in fact continue to keep the world at peace is an issue for consideration. It is a somewhat delicate balance. The avoidance of direct warfare between the major powers over a period of nearly 40 years, encouraging as it is, cannot offer a permanent guarantee of peace. History is not bound by precedent. And the factors which affect the balance of terror - political, economic, technological and military - are neither simple nor static: they have changed profoundly in recent years and will continue to change in the future.

Partly for this reason, and partly because of the intrinsic importance of the subject, the fundamental questions about the balance of terror between East and West need to be considered and reconsidered. How does it work? How and why has it come into being? Is it necessary? How does it affect world politics? Is it stable in an intrinsic and a dynamic sense? How secure is the prospect of a continuing peace on terms acceptable to both sides? Where are the main danger points? Are there practical alternatives to a balance of terror? What can the West do to maximise security and stability? What should the West's general strategy be?

The present study struggles towards some answers to this formidable list of questions, especially the critical questions concerning strategy and stability.

2 Basic Theory and the Evolution of Strategic Postures

INTRODUCTION

The theory of how mutual deterrence through a balance of terror would work, and of strategy in the nuclear age, was developed with remarkable speed in the latter part of the 1950s by a group of brilliant American thinkers which included Bernard Brodie, Herman Kahn, Oskar Morgenstern, Thomas Schelling and Albert Wohlstetter.[1] The basic ideas, discussed at greater length in chapter 6, are now familiar. The present chapter begins by summarising them. It then compares the balance of terror with earlier balances of military power and sketches the development of strategic postures in the period since 1945.[2]

BASIC THEORY

The first and fundamental requirement for preserving peace through a balance of terror is that each side must possess, and be seen to possess, a capacity to inflict horrendous damage on the other – damage on a scale which the other would find quite unacceptable. In addition, each side must remain, and be seen to remain, capable of inflicting such damage on the other even if the other has struck him first. Provided that these conditions are fulfilled, each side should perceive the risks involved in attacking the other, or provoking him beyond endurance, as being unacceptable, and should be deterred thereby from opening or provoking hostilities. In this way mutual conflict should be avoided. Whatever their other differences may be, the two sides will have a strong shared interest in avoiding conflict. At the price of massive expenditure on unused armaments, therefore, they are able to buy a considerable presumption of peace, or peaceful co-existence.

The phrase a considerable presumption' may sound a little grudging. But it reminds us that the avoidance of conflict cannot be totally guaranteed by any balance of power, not even by a balance of terror.

COMPARISON WITH EARLIER BALANCES OF POWER

The balance of terror over the period since the early 1960s has differed from earlier balances of military strength in the magnitude and immediacy of the mutual threat (see figure 2.1). As noted in chapter 1, the ability of each side to destroy a substantial proportion of the other's population and industry in the space of a few minutes with weapons launched from distances of thousands of miles has made war incalculably more dangerous. It is not surprising, therefore, that the balance of terror has preserved peace more effectively than past balances of military power.

In earlier times, before the advent of nuclear weapons, the use of warfare as a means of achieving political ends was frequently a tempting option for governments which perceived a good chance of victory. The expected benefits from victory often looked considerable in relation to expected costs. The possibility of defeat, terrible though it might be, typically looked less than catastrophic. For strong countries contemplating war against weaker brethren, the perceived surplus of benefit over cost could appear especially great. War against an equally strong opponent was a more serious prospect. But traditional balances of military power did not prevent wars between equals. Great as the perceived risks in military conflict might be, they were often not sufficient to deter. On the contrary, wars between equals have been a leitmotif of the human story.

For countries which participate in the balance of terror, all that has changed. With the advent of nuclear weapons, the risks in military conflict, and the potential costs, are manifestly out of all proportion to potential benefits except in the most extreme circumstances. It is not just that the prospect of defeat now looks so much more terrible than ever before. The sufferings of the victor, if any, are likely to be almost equally appalling. In no previous era has the common interest of fundamentally antagonistic nations in avoiding war been so great and so obvious.

UNILATERAL TERROR

For a decade and more after the Second World War the United States' territory was not vulnerable to massive damage by Soviet nuclear forces. There was consequently no balance of terror in that period, only unilateral

FIGURE 2.1 *Damage from nuclear weapons*

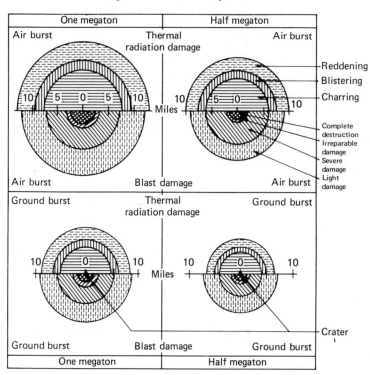

The circles show approximate ranges of thermal radiation damage to the skin (upper portion) and blast damage to buildings (lower portion) from one and half megaton bombs, airburst and ground-burst. Notice that doubling explosive power increases the areas of damage by only about 60 per cent. Notice also that the areas of damage from airbursts at an 'optimum' height are approximately double those from surface bursts. Surface bursts do however produce craters and radioactive fall-out.

For larger weapons at least, damage from initial nuclear radiation is unlikely to extend as far as damage from blast or thermal radiation. Residual radiation hazards from radioactive fall-out, on the other hand, are likely to extend over areas far exceeding those illustrated here.

Fire damage may also be extensive. In the case of heavy nuclear exchanges, smoke from the fires and dust from the craters could have devastating effects on the world's climate: see pp.168-9 and 257.

SOURCE: The diagrams are based on data from the Home Office and Scottish Home and Health Departments booklet, *Nuclear Weapons* (London: HMSO, 1974).

terror. Peace between East and West depended importantly on the combination in one nation, the United States, of massive and manifest nuclear superiority with peaceful intentions.

The United States did not use a single nuclear weapon in this period: the possibility is believed to have been considered and rejected on three occasions – during the Berlin crisis of 1948-9, the Korean War of 1950-53 and the Dien Bien Phu débâcle of 1954. But the American leaders let it be known that they had the capability to retaliate massively (by implication, with nuclear weapons) against any country which committed aggression against the United States or its allies. This was their chosen strategy for deterring Soviet aggression. The United States itself was self-deterred. It was doubtless deterred also by the massive local superiority of Soviet forces in the European theatre.

The classic statement of the 'massive retaliation' strategy was made by American Secretary of State John Foster Dulles as late as 1954.[3] The NATO alliance formally adopted the same strategy two years later.[4] By that time it was clear that the Soviets, too, would develop an arsenal of nuclear weapons and that the United States would have then to modify its strategic posture. For the time being, however, the threat of massive retaliation still carried a certain conviction. The posture of the United States government *vis-à-vis* the communist world in this early post-war period can be summarised, with a minimum of caricature, as follows:

> If you attack us, or provoke us too far, we reserve the right to retaliate immediately and massively, by means and at places of our own choosing, and the damage you suffer will outweigh any possible gains from aggression.

Mr Dulles saw the United States' heavy reliance on the deterrent power of its nuclear arsenal as providing 'more basic security at less cost'.

THE BALANCE OF TERROR

As the Soviets developed their nuclear and missile capabilities, the military balance between East and West changed, and with it the strategic posture of the United States. American analysts, including those mentioned at the beginning of this chapter, foresaw in the late 1950s that it was only a matter of time before Soviet capabilities would pose a massive threat to American territory comparable to that posed by American capabilities to Soviet territory. Once that happened, a new world order based on a balance of terror would supersede the existing order based on unilateral terror. Crude threats of massive retaliation would become empty. The United States would know that massive retaliation against the Soviet Union would provoke similarly massive retaliation against the United States itself. The best hope for preserving peace under the new world order would lie in a *stable* balance of forces between the United States and the Soviet Union, with each side possessing the capability to inflict unacceptable damage on the other even if the other had struck him first. Even in the short term - so the analysts argued - the threat of massive retaliation lacked credibility in relation to smaller-scale disturbances.

In the course of the 1960s these predictions were fulfilled. The Soviets succeeded, as expected, in developing a capability to inflict massive damage on the United States. By the early 1970s they had advanced so far that the balance of military strength between the United States and the Soviet Union could now be described, without undue violence to the facts, as approximate parity. Deterrence had become mutual and massive.

Again without excessive caricature, the message transmitted by each side to the other since the mid-1960s has run as follows:

> It would be insane for either of us to open hostilities or provoke each other too far. Once hostilities have begun, no one knows where they will end. But each of us knows that the consequences of nuclear conflict, for ourselves and the rest of the world, would be as unacceptable as they are incalculable.

The new message contrasts strikingly with the old. It is no longer a one-way message from strong to weak, but a mutual message from each side to the other. Its burden is no longer to threaten the other side with massive retaliation and defeat but rather to invoke the strong *shared interest* of both sides in avoiding war.

MUTUAL ASSURED DESTRUCTION

In the West the Kennedy/Johnson administration which took office in 1961 was greatly influenced by the new strategic thinking and added some distinctive glosses of its own. At the national level, the strategic doctrine of massive retaliation was replaced by a new policy, later known as 'assured destruction'.[5] In NATO the threat of massive retaliation was replaced by a new posture of 'flexible response'.[6]

Under the first of these concepts, the United States was seen as needing an 'assured destruction' capability to inflict unacceptable damage on the

Soviet Union even after absorbing a 'first-strike' by the Soviet Union. The emphasis was on retaliation against cities,[7] not military targets, and the required capability was defined in absolute terms. The new concept assumed that there was a certain level of damage to its cities which the Soviet Union would regard as totally unacceptable. The problem of quantifying this critical level was squarely confronted. In the mid-1960s the Pentagon is said to have considered 'roughly 25 per cent of the Soviet population and 45 per cent of Soviet industry as a cut-off point in targeting weapons'.[8] The United States' basic military requirement was seen as being to deploy 'second-strike' forces with an assured capability to survive a 'first-strike' by the enemy and then to inflict such a level of damage. Additions to nuclear strike power going beyond this 'flat of the curve' level would do little or nothing to enhance deterrence. In particular, attempts by the United States to maintain massive superiority would serve only to increase international tensions without adding to the basic security of the West.

In the judgement of the Johnson administration, the United States already possessed, by the early to mid-1960s, an assured destruction capability on the required scale. The task was to maintain it. With the rapid development of the Soviet Union's nuclear programme, such capabilities would shortly become mutual. Defence Secretary McNamara saw this, paradoxically, as being desirable as well as inevitable. The best prospect for peace between East and West was seen as lying in a world order based on 'mutual assured destruction' (originally a pejorative term) with approximate parity of nuclear arsenals.

The theory of 'mutual assured destruction' as propounded by American theorists in the mid-1960s contained several further paradoxes which distinguished it from earlier strategic theories – paradoxes which we shall discuss more fully in later chapters. In the first place it called for offensive weapons to be designed for use against civilian targets, not military. The theory's proponents feared that the development of 'counter-force' capabilities – weapons capable of destroying the more difficult military targets – could give each side dangerous incentives to launch pre-emptive strikes against each other's nuclear forces. Such developments were therefore better avoided. The weapon systems deployed by each side at the time carried single warheads and were not sufficiently accurate for use against military targets. The theory sought to make a virtue of these limitations and to perpetuate them.

A second paradox was that the theory sought to discourage both sides from defending their cities against nuclear attack. If cities could be defended successfully, then nuclear weapons would no longer be capable of inflicting unacceptable damage, and their deterrent power would be lost.

A third paradox - implicit in the doctrine that force requirements were to be measured in absolute, not relative, terms - was that the comparative strength of the two sides' forces was considered unimportant. The requirement was simply to have the capability to cause a specific absolute amount of destruction in the enemy's territory - an amount which he would find totally unacceptable.

These paradoxes of American thinking, to which the Soviets probably never subscribed, in no way altered the basic 'message' of mutual deterrence discussed in the preceding section. The point about limitation to civilian targets can, however, be seen as a kind of rider, or postscript, to earlier American versions of that message, as follows:

> The stability of mutual deterrence requires that all our cities should remain as vulnerable, and all our nuclear weapons as invulnerable, as possible. We shall be developing our weapon systems with these objectives in mind. We look to you to do likewise.

FLEXIBLE RESPONSE

In the European theatre, too, a new strategic concept known as 'flexible response', or 'effective deterrence', was developed to replace the earlier doctrine of massive retaliation. Formally adopted in December 1967 by all NATO countries except France, 'flexible response' and 'forward defence' have remained the basis of NATO strategy ever since.

With the growth of the Soviet nuclear arsenal, the old NATO policy of threatening massive retaliation with strategic nuclear weapons in response to aggression in any form, however small, had come by the mid-1960s to look like a recipe for escalating minor incidents into major nuclear wars. The threat of such retaliation, always somewhat crude, had lost all credibility. Hence NATO replaced this threat with a strategy of options - a warning to any potential aggressor that the alliance would respond to aggression in whatever way it thought necessary, the precise nature and force level of the response depending on the circumstances and in particular the force level used by the aggressor. The message transmitted by NATO to the Soviet Union under the flexible response concept can be summarised as follows:

> If you should attack us, or provoke us too far, we will respond in whatever way we judge necessary: we will not tolerate your securing even the smallest advantage by force of arms. The nature of our response

will depend on the circumstances, not least the nature and force level of your aggression. We are as anxious to avoid the insanity of nuclear war as you are. But we are prepared to use nuclear weapons if necessary and even, *in extremis*, to escalate any conflict to the strategic nuclear level.

Three aspects of this message call for special attention. First, 'flexible response' is, as mentioned earlier, a strategy of options. NATO's aim is to maintain a range of military options – conventional as well as theatre nuclear and strategic nuclear – which would enable it 'to meet aggression at any level with an appropriate response, while making it impossible for the aggressor to calculate in advance the nature of the response his attack will provoke, or how the conflict may develop thereafter'.[9] In contrast with the 'massive retaliation' strategy, the response is not pre-ordained. A potential aggressor might think it likely that NATO would respond at the same force level as he himself had used (see further below). But he could not be sure about this, still less about how the response might develop. The alliance reserves the right either to respond at the same force level – 'direct defence' – or to escalate if necessary to a higher force level, including *in extremis* the ultimate sanction of the United States' strategic nuclear forces.

Second, flexible response is nevertheless, in an important sense, a strategy of 'minimum force'. Without closing any options, it recognises that one of NATO's major concerns in the event of war breaking out would be to prevent unnecessary escalation. That is why strong conventional forces are so important to NATO as well as the other two elements in the 'triad' of forces – theatre nuclear and strategic nuclear. In the event of aggression at the conventional level, it is generally assumed that NATO would respond initially with 'direct' conventional defence. But the strategy also envisages that the alliance would be prepared to escalate the conflict by introducing nuclear weapons if necessary.

Finally, the 'flexible response' concept has been linked in practice with that of 'forward defence'. The phrase 'we will not tolerate your securing even the smallest advantage by force of arms' means what it says. The alliance is committed to preserving or restoring the territorial integrity of member countries right up to the border with the Soviet bloc. No country is to be treated as a buffer state. The security of individual members cannot be sacrificed so as to provide better defensive positions. Conventional forces must be 'strong enough to sustain a stalwart resistance in the forward areas'.[10]

SUBSEQUENT DEVELOPMENTS

The world has not stood still since the mid-1960s, when the 'assured destruction' and 'flexible response' doctrines entered the conventional wisdom. The 'assured destruction' policy has been partly overtaken by the development of 'counter-force' capabilities against military targets. 'Flexible response' has had to accommodate the build-up of Soviet nuclear forces.

The development of 'counter-force' capabilities in the United States has come about, partly as a by-product of general improvements in nuclear forces, and partly as a matter of policy. The administration felt obliged at the beginning of the 1970s to introduce multiple independently targeted warheads (MIRVs) in order to counter the Soviets' anti-ballistic missile defences and their superiority in numbers of missiles and explosive power of warheads. Improvements in target accuracy were likewise clearly desirable, especially at a time when the Soviets were making efforts to improve their target accuracy. These two technological advances, taken together, were reflected in growing 'counter-force' capabilities against land-based Soviet nuclear-forces.

The growth of such capabilities caused considerable heart-searching at first. It conflicted with the perception of the early 'assured destruction' theorists that stability required nuclear weapon capabilities to be limited to civilian targets. But the case for developing counter-force options has attracted increasing support over time. As early as 1970 President Nixon raised the question: 'Should a President, in the event of a nuclear attack, be left with the single option of ordering the mass destruction of enemy civilians, in the face of the certainty that it would be followed by the mass slaughter of Americans?'[11] Defence Secretary Schlesinger argued strongly in the early to mid-1970s, as did President Nixon himself, that the answer was no.[12] While firmly disowning any intention to develop a disarming first-strike capability which would leave the Soviets without effective means of retaliation, he argued that the United States needed options for a measured response to aggression, which must include capabilities against 'hard' military installations as well as 'soft' civilian targets. The argument gained force from the Soviet Union's evident intention to develop such capabilities. President Carter's 'Directive '59' of July/August 1980 went a stage further. This unpublished directive is reported to have stated that the United States must be prepared for the possibility of a sustained but limited nuclear war in which priority would be given to striking military as against civilian targets. The Reagan administration has likewise seen this as an essential capability.

A further consequence of the developing capabilities of each side against military targets (including the other side's nuclear forces) has been to enhance the importance of the relative numbers of delivery systems and warheads between the two sides, thus calling into question another tenet of the 'assured destruction' theorists. In a counter-city battle, relative numbers may, within limits, be unimportant. In a counter-force battle, they could be of the essence.

The evolution of 'counter-force' capabilities does not invalidate the mutual deterrence 'message' discussed earlier in this chapter. Neither does it invalidate the central thesis of the 'assured destruction' policy: the ability of each side to wipe out the other's cities remains the central and essential ingredient in the balance of terror. The advent of these capabilities has, however, made land-based nuclear forces vulnerable to attack. It has underlined the need to find ways of reducing this vulnerability and hence the military incentive to strike first (see further chapter 7). It also points to replacing our earlier 'assured destruction' postscript with a different one on the following lines:

> Let neither of us imagine that there could be advantage in striking pre-emptively at each other's military forces. Such a strike would not only be desperately dangerous in itself but could all too easily lead to extensive civilian casualties and full-scale war. We are both developing a capability to retaliate in kind against such an attack, as well as taking steps to make our weapon systems less vulnerable.

NATO's 'flexible response' posture has stood the test of time better than the early philosophies of 'assured destruction'. But it, too, has required a degree of updating. The warning that NATO is prepared *in extremis* to use nuclear weapons undoubtedly sounded more terrible in the mid-1960s, when the West retained a substantial nuclear superiority, than it does in the 1980s, when Soviet nuclear forces appear to be no less formidable than their American counterparts. The significance of the warning has changed in consequence. As with the transition from 'massive retaliation' to 'mutual assured destruction', the warning is no longer based on possession by NATO of greater ultimate strength but rather on NATO's readiness to escalate any conflict, if necessary, to a level which neither side could possibly want. It is as if a postscript has been added to the earlier 'flexible response' message, which reads:

> You may object that your nuclear arsenal is now as powerful as ours. That is not the point. What we are telling you is that we will not tolerate

aggression in any shape or form, and we reserve the right to escalate any conflict to the nuclear level if necessary, appalling though the consequences could be for us as well as you.

We discuss more fully in later chapters the properties of these and other strategic postures, their strengths and weaknesses.

SOVIET POSTURES

The Soviet Union has generally defined its strategic postures less explicitly than the United States and NATO.[13]

Up to the mid-1960s, Soviet military experts appeared united in the view that any conflict between East and West was bound to take the form of a full-scale nuclear war. They habitually emphasised the tactical importance of surprise and the practical possibility of victory.

Such philosophies always strained the credulity. For one would expect the Soviet Union, with its quantitative superiority in conventional forces in the European theatre, to perceive a strong military interest in limiting any conflict to the conventional force level as well as sharing the general interest in avoiding nuclear war.

Since the mid-1960s Soviet writers have moved gradually towards a more expected position. They do now appear to envisage that war between East and West might be limited to the conventional force level. They have also come increasingly to accept the paradox that there would, in some sense, be no winners in a nuclear war.

In June 1982, at the United Nations Special Session on Disarmament, President Brezhnev took the further step of appearing to commit the Soviet Union unilaterally not to use nuclear weapons first, though the Soviet Defence Minister assured the domestic audience subsequently that Soviet military options in time of crisis would not in practice be curtailed. The combination of the Brezhnev declaration and the Defence Minister's assurance can perhaps be seen as a Soviet postscript to the earlier mutual deterrence message, with a Shakespearian 'aside':

We would not expect to use nuclear weapons first and hope you would not do so either. *Aside*: But in times of crisis all our options would remain open.

We return in chapter 13 to the problems of 'no first use' undertakings.

3   How it Came To Be

INTRODUCTION

The balance of terror has come into being neither by accident nor by deliberate international arrangement. It has resulted, historically, from a combination of political tensions and advancing technology.

BIRTH OF NUCLEAR AGE[1]

The nuclear age was born on 16 July 1945, when the United States successfully exploded a nuclear fission device over the Alamogordo desert in New Mexico.[2] Less than a month later the United States dropped the only nuclear weapons ever used in war over Hiroshima (6 August) and Nagasaki (9 August), killing some 68 000 and some 38 000 people respectively.[3]

The production of these early weapons was made possible by remarkable scientific discoveries and hastened by the Second World War. Scientists from many nations, striving since the beginning of the century to understand the nature of matter, had helped unwittingly to prepare the way. The German scientists Hahn and Strassman had succeeded in December 1938 in splitting the uranium nucleus, and other scientists had diagnosed their results as nuclear 'fission' - the splitting of the nucleus of a heavy element into two positively charged nuclei of lighter elements which would repel each other and give off massive amounts of energy. This and subsequent discoveries - notably the confirmation that neutrons released during fission could produce explosive fission chain reactions in uranium and plutonium[4] - pointed clearly to the possibility of producing a nuclear fission weapon, or atomic bomb, with enormously greater energy and explosive power than the conventional weapons of previous eras (see figure 3.1). The new discoveries coincided with the advent of the Second World War. Not surprisingly, therefore, the governments of four major

---

FIGURE 3.1 *Fission chain reaction*

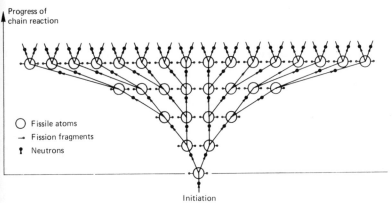

Progress of
chain reaction

○ Fissile atoms
→ Fission fragments
🌢 Neutrons

Initiation

Artist's impression of a developing fission chain reaction in which the neutrons released by each fissioned nucleus of uranium or plutonium cause two further nuclei to undergo fission.

In contrast with chemical reactions, which rearrange the atoms and their bonding electrons within explosive materials, nuclear reactions redistribute protons and neutrons from the nucleus of the atom to form different atomic nuclei, with the release of enormously greater amounts of energy.

One form of reaction used in nuclear weapons, and the only form used in the early atomic weapons, is 'fission' – the splitting of the nucleus of the heavy elements uranium 235 or plutonium into two nuclei of lighter elements. Fission is caused by the absorption of an unattached neutron into a nucleus and results in the liberation of further neutrons, typically two or three.

In any piece of fissile material, the process of atomic fission occurs naturally and continually. But below a certain 'critical' mass of material in relation to surface area the material does not explode: too many of the liberated neutrons escape from the surface, and too few remain within the fissile material itself, to sustain the build-up of an increasing chain of fissions. If, however, the ratio of mass to surface area is suddenly increased beyond a certain 'critical' point, the instantaneous liberation of neutrons which accompanies the fission process can produce a self-sustaining chain reaction (see figure) accompanied by the rapid release of enormous amounts of energy, and a nuclear detonation results.

To produce a massive explosion it is necessary to compress the fissile material suddenly and then to hold it together and prevent the liberated neutrons from escaping for as long as possible by means of a neutron-reflecting tamper. Otherwise the material will melt or explode weakly and prematurely (see also figures 3.2 and 3.3).

countries – Germany, Britain, the United States and the Soviet Union – decided to launch research and development programmes.

The existence, and ultimate success, of the Anglo-American programme are well known. In both countries the authorities long remained sceptical as to whether a nuclear bomb was feasible and in particular whether a sufficient number of atoms could be split in a sufficiently short space of time to generate an explosive fission chain reaction before the weapon blew itself to pieces. But they feared that Germany was trying to develop such a weapon, and these fears clinched the argument. Neither government could view with indifference the possibility, remote as it might be, of a Germany monopoly. Both governments provided accordingly for research to proceed, nationally at first and, from the end of 1943 onwards, in the joint 'Manhattan' project headed by Groves, Oppenheimer and others: Roosevelt and Churchill had finally agreed on collaboration at Quebec in August 1943. These decisions led directly to production of the first nuclear weapons.

In the event, the Manhattan project came to fruition too late to influence the war in Europe. With British consent, however, the United States administration decided to use the new weapon against Japan in August 1945, to compel an early surrender. Many of the scientists engaged on the project argued strongly that the bomb should not be used, and the President's advisers weighed carefully the possibility of inviting Japanese observers to a demonstration firing. But the prevailing view was that a demonstration was much less likely to achieve the key objective of shocking the Japanese into surrender. It would anyway not be easy to demonstrate the magnitude of the destruction, and there could be no assurance whatever of success in a demonstration: the fact that the first three atomic bombs all worked was truly remarkable (see further figures 3.2 and 3.3). For the Allied leaders themselves, the overriding priority was to end as quickly as possible a war which had already cost some 50 million lives. Truman and Churchill were especially anxious to avoid a full scale invasion of Japan in which many more Allied lives would have been lost and the Soviets, too, might have participated; and the full significance of the new weapon lay inevitably beyond the horizon of vision. So it was that the atomic bomb project continued after Germany was defeated and a weapon begotten of the war in Europe came to be used against Japan.[5]

Rather less well-known is the fact that Germany and the Soviet Union, too, launched nuclear programmes in the Second World War. The Germans had possibly the keenest interest in developing a nuclear weapon in further-ance of their war effort. But the domestic policies of the Nazi regime caused many of Germany's leading scientists to emigrate to Britain or the

United States, and German research concentrated on slow-neutron reactions as against the fast-neutron reactions which scientists in Britain and the United States saw to be essential for producing a bomb. By the spring of 1942, therefore, the German programme showed no promise of early results, and Hitler effectively stifled it.

In the Soviet Union nuclear physicists are known to have worked on nuclear energy from 1939 until the German invasion of 1941. Then in January 1943, after the victory at Stalingrad, the Soviet Government launched a programme under Kurchatov designed to produce a uranium bomb.

POLITICAL TENSIONS[6]

When once the United States had exhibited the possibility and power of nuclear weapons, certain other countries were virtually bound to want such weapons for themselves – especially if they foresaw the possibility of serious conflicts of interest with the United States or other potential nuclear powers. Conventional weapons on their own no longer looked adequate. No major country was likely to feel comfortable about letting other potentially hostile countries have a monopoly, overt or secret, of the new master-weapon. With the wisdom of hindsight, therefore, the spread of nuclear weapons, once invented, can be seen as very nearly a foregone conclusion.

The reason for the qualification 'very nearly' is that the development of the nuclear arsenals could undoubtedly have been more restrained, and might just conceivably have been avoided altogether, if the major powers of East and West had emerged from the Second World War as the best of friends – if the defeat of Nazi Germany and Japan had led to a new world order based on mutual trust and respect between the major powers, an absence of serious political tensions and a substantial measure of disarmament.

It was not to be. Like the giants in the story, the victors of the Second World War quarrelled over the spoils. The wartime hostility between Germany and the rest of the world was rapidly replaced by a deep antagonism between East and West. The Soviet Union and the West came to distrust each other keenly – more so than ever before. It is therefore hardly surprising that the United States maintained and developed its nuclear capability, while the Soviets gave the highest priority to acquiring a similar capability.

FIGURE 3.1 *Fission weapons: the 'atomic bomb'*

(A) THE GUN METHOD

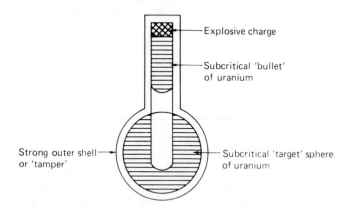

Artist's impression of the 'gun' method used to detonate the Hiroshima uranium 235 bomb.

The 'bullet' and the 'target' were individually subcritical. But when the 'bullet' was fired into the cavity in the target sphere, the ratio of mass to surface area in the sphere was suddenly increased, the critical mass was exceeded, and a fission chain reaction occurred. A neutron initiator was used to ensure that a sufficient density of neutrons was available at the moment of detonation.

This method was found suitable only for uranium-235 bombs. With plutonium, the spontaneous emission of neutrons was so strong that the full-scale chain reaction and explosion would have been pre-empted by a premature detonation and 'fizzle'.

FIGURE 3.3 *Fission weapons: the 'atomic bomb'*

(B) THE IMPLOSION METHOD

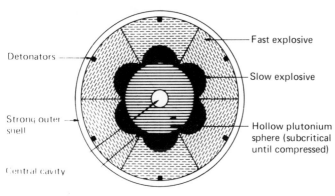

Detonators

Strong outer shell

Central cavity

Tamper reflector

Fast explosive

Slow explosive

Hollow plutonium sphere (subcritical until compressed)

Artist's impression of a cross-section of the implosion lens used to detonate the plutonium bombs at Alamogordo and Nagasaki, based, with permission, on a diagram in Peter Goodchild's *J. Robert Oppenheimer*, (BBC, 1980, with artwork designed by Quill).

A subcritical sphere or 'ball' of plutonium with a spherical hole at the centre was compressed suddenly, and thus made critical, by means of explosive charges directed against the surface of the sphere.

The implosion method, being faster than the gun method, solved the problem of premature detonation. It depended crucially on obtaining a symmetrical shock wave at the surface of the core by means of inward-pointing lenses and appropriate segments of fast and slow explosive. The method, once perfected, was far more efficient and controllable than the gun method, and is now used in virtually all nuclear warheads.

The story of the crescendo of tension and distrust between East and West after the Second World War is familiar. Initially, there were many in the West who genuinely admired the Soviets' achievements and the communist system. But the wartime honeymoon in East/West relations ended in disillusion. Even during the war relations were often strained, particularly over Poland and Austria. By 1947 the relationship had degenerated from wary co-operation into the profound distrust and antagonism, sometimes latent, sometimes overt, which have dominated world politics ever since.

From a Western point of view, the blame seemed to lie unequivocally with the Soviet Union and, later, China. The continuing evidence of the Soviets' territorial and ideological ambitions seemed to trample under foot the limited trust of the wartime years. In Iran and Manchuria, the Soviets failed to withdraw their forces after the war in accordance with the agreed timetable. In Europe their policies were even more disturbing. Not only were they clearly determined to hold on to the Baltic territories which they had absorbed early in the war. More serious still was their determination, stealthy at first but more open later, to impose the communist system as far as their armies marched – to establish throughout Eastern Europe a satellite empire of communist governments subservient to the Soviet Union. They seemed bent on dominating the rest of Europe as well to the maximum extent possible.

With President Truman's public commitment to the containment of communism in the 'Truman doctrine' of March 1947, the hostility between East and West was openly acknowledged. The period of 'cold war' began. Subsequent events were to deepen the West's distrust of Soviet intentions – the Soviets' brusque dismissal in June 1947, on behalf of the East European countries as well as themselves, of American finance under the Marshall Aid plan for economic reconstruction; their subsequent attempt to wreck implementation of the plan in Western Europe; Stalin's continuing attempts to bring Germany as a whole under Soviet domination; his blockade of Berlin in 1948-9; the Sino-Soviet plan to conquer South Korea and Taiwan in 1950, which led to the Korean war of 1950-53; and the simultaneous build-up of Soviet forces in Europe. Hardly less disturbing to the West than these acts of foreign policy were the Soviet Government's treatment of its own people and the people of Eastern Europe.

From a Soviet point of view there were likewise persuasive reasons for disliking and distrusting the West. The United States and other Western governments, having made their disapproval of Soviet activities in Eastern Europe progressively more clear, acted to prevent the further fulfilment of Soviet foreign policy objectives, both in Europe and elsewhere.

As implied above, the Soviets' chief objective in the early post-war period was evidently to consolidate Soviet control over Eastern Europe and to dominate the rest of the European continent as effectively as possible – an objective which depended importantly on getting rid of the United States' presence. Chastened by long experience of invasions from Western Europe, culminating in Hitler's 1941 offensive, the Soviet leaders were especially concerned to turn Germany into a communist state or, failing that, to keep it weak. They were likewise concerned to build up on their borders a reliable *glacis* of vassal communist states extending over as much of Europe as possible. The West might see the vassalage of Eastern Europe as intimidation, suppression and enslavement of the most blatant kind. Stalin claimed, at any rate, to see it differently: he was merely imposing his own social system on the territories which his armies had occupied, just as the Western powers were imposing their social system on the territories which they had occupied.

Greatly to Stalin's chagrin, the West moved progressively to frustrate Soviet ambitions, especially from the beginning of 1947 onwards. The Soviets succeeded in completing the vassalage of the occupied East European countries – surely a famous victory. But thereafter they made little headway. In defiance of Soviet wishes, the Western powers made plans for economic reconstruction and the establishment of parliamentary democracy in the Western zones of Germany. The Soviet riposte, in the form of the Berlin blockade of 1948-9, had the perverse effect of hardening and consolidating opposition to Soviet policies. In the spring of 1949, the North Atlantic Treaty provided for the United States to remain a European power, apparently on a permanent basis.[7] The new parliamentary democracy in West Germany had meanwhile opted unequivocally for the West and become the Federal Republic of Germany. The Federal Republic was admitted to the NATO alliance in 1954. The West had thus acted to prevent the Soviet Union from achieving its European objectives in full.

Since the death of Stalin in 1953, relations between the Soviet Union and the West have generally, but not invariably, been less strained than in the early post-war years. The two sides have acquiesced, substantially at least, in the status quo. They have broadly accepted the need for peaceful co-existence and the case for détente. They have talked almost continuously together. They have reached agreement on certain limited areas of international conduct where each side perceives a common interest – notably in the agreements of the early 1970s on crisis management and nuclear weapon deployments.

But the underlying tensions, geopolitical and ideological, have not disappeared. Relations have ebbed and flowed. The clash of wills may even have intensified as the Soviets have provided repeated confirmation of their commitment to a version of communist rule which is anathema to most people in the West; continued to suppress freedom in the East European countries; adopted more aggressive policies of subversion and intervention in the Third World; and built up armaments on a massive scale under cover of détente. The West has been repeatedly shocked by a succession of troublesome episodes – the invasion of Hungary in 1956, the Berlin crisis of 1958–62, the Cuban missile crisis of 1962, the invasion of Czechoslovakia in 1968, the Angolan and Ethiopian adventures of the 1970s, the occupation of Afghanistan at the end of 1979, the formidable build-up of SS-20 missiles from 1980 onwards and the pressures on Poland during the Polish crisis of 1980–82. At no time in the post-war period have the two sides approached anywhere near the point of trusting each other.

THE BALANCE OF TERROR

In this atmosphere of deep, endemic mutual distrust, each side has felt insecure, or potentially insecure, throughout the post-war period. Neither side has felt comfortable about ceding military supremacy to the other – either in force deployments or in technology. Both have consequently felt it essential to build up enormous reserves of military strength, including large arsenals of nuclear weapons and delivery systems. The process has been aggravated by asymmetries of geography and force structures between the two sides and by uncertainties, particularly in the West, as to the scale of future force deployments by the other side.[8]

   In the early post-war years the United States enjoyed a monopoly of nuclear weapons. Responding to powerful domestic pressures, the Truman administration rapidly demobilised most of the American armies in Europe, leaving the Soviets with a massive superiority in conventional forces in the area.[9] American policy relied on the American nuclear monopoly to counter the Soviets' geographical advantages in the European theatre and their local superiority in conventional forces. The administration came to regard atomic bombs, delivered by manned bomber aircraft, as the primary weapon in the American military arsenal – the ultimate guarantee of national security and the security of Western Europe. The United States proceeded, accordingly, to build up a massive arsenal of atomic bombs and heavy bombers.

The American monopoly of nuclear weapons disturbed the Soviet authorities deeply. Stalin responded by determining to catch up with American nuclear capabilities as quickly as possible, while maintaining a massive superiority in conventional forces in the European theatre. After hearing from Truman at Potsdam in July 1945 about the success of the American bomb project, he immediately accelerated Soviet nuclear research and ordered a crash programme. Thus began the notorious 'action–reaction cycle' of the post-war arms race.

For a short period there seemed a chance, at least, that competition in nuclear terror between East and West might be avoided. The major countries agreed to talk together about disarmament and international control of atomic energy.[10] On a joint proposal from the United States, the Soviet Union and Britain, the newly-founded United Nations set up in January 1946 an international Atomic Energy Commission and charged it with making proposals for exchanging basic scientific information and eliminating nuclear weapons from national arsenals. But the major powers could not agree on how this should be done. The commission had therefore to admit failure, and progress towards a balance of nuclear terror became inevitable.

With the wisdom of hindsight, the commission was virtually bound to fail. Any agreement to forswear national production or use of nuclear weapons would have required a degree of mutual trust which plainly did not exist. In the dark days of the Cold War, the United States could hardly have accepted the Soviet proposal for a treaty banning forthwith the production and use of the nuclear weapons on which the West depended for offsetting Soviet superiority in conventional forces in Europe. It is difficult enough to see how the United States could even have carried out its own proposal, which called for the surrendering of nuclear weapons to an international control authority, once properly established, and would have required the United States at that stage to abjure, Prospero-like, the rough arts of nuclear weapon construction. The Soviets, similarly, could hardly have been expected to call off their own nuclear weapons programme, thus leaving the United States with a monopoly of the technology. Even if the political will had been there on both sides to make major concessions, the crucial problems of verification and enforcement remained intractable, especially as the Soviets were equivocal about on-site inspection. It is therefore hard to see how either side could have felt comfortable about subscribing to agreements of the kind discussed – or how either side could have trusted the other not to cheat when the consequences of cheating were potentially so devastating.

FIGURE 3.4 *Fission and fusion weapons: the 'hydrogen bomb'*

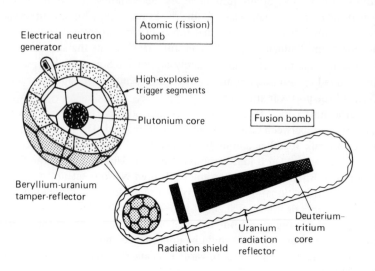

Artist's impression of a thermonuclear warhead, reproduced by kind permission of *The Economist*. By combining fusion with fission reactions, scientists have been able since the early 1950s to produce warheads of far greater explosive power and flexibility than would have been possible with fission reactions alone.

At the temperature of several million degrees centigrade reached in the detonation of a fission weapon, atoms are stripped of most of their surrounding electrons and the nuclei move at very high speeds and collide with each other. In these conditions the nuclei of the hydrogen isotopes deuterium and tritium have enough energy of motion to overcome the repulsive forces between the positive electrical charges of their single protons and are able to fuse together, releasing enormous amounts of energy. Because of the very high temperatures, fusion reactions are called 'thermonuclear'. The main products of such reactions are helium and a high speed neutron.

A thermonuclear warhead consists accordingly of a fission ball or 'primary', as in figure 3.3, and a 'rod' or 'core' of deuterium and tritium atoms (DT), placed in a cylinder about one and a half feet in diameter and five feet long. Detonation of the fission ball releases powerful X-rays which are focused and reflected by a lining of uranium reflectors and a shield so as to impact evenly on the DT rod. Fusion occurs during the fraction of a second between arrival of the X-rays, which travel at the speed of light, and of the slower blast wave, which blows the rod to smithereens. An unenriched uranium tamper for the DT rod will produce a further fission reaction as the rod explodes.

The complete fission of one pound of uranium or plutonium would release as much explosive energy as 8000 tons of conventional TNT (though not all the material in a weapon does in fact undergo fission). The complete fusion of all the nuclei present in one pound of deuterium would release as much energy as about 26 000 tons of TNT.

As the disarmament negotiations ran into the sand, the 'action-reaction' cycle of nuclear weapons development proceeded apace. Soviet scientists shocked the West by successfully testing their first atomic bomb in August 1949. The Americans, uncertain as to what the Soviet Union would do next, responded in the early 1950s by expanding their own development programme to encompass the vastly more powerful hydrogen bomb, using thermonuclear fusion as well as fission,[11] larger fission bombs and smaller nuclear warheads for tactical use. President Truman launched the 'super-bomb' or 'hydrogen bomb' programme in January 1950.[12] Initial tests were made in November 1952 at Eniwetok Atoll and full-scale tests in March 1954 at Bikini Atoll. The Soviets pursued a similar programme, with an initial test in August 1953 and larger tests in November 1955.[13]

In the meantime work proceeded in both the Soviet Union and the United States on the development of long-range missiles – ballistic missiles based on the German V2 and X7, and cruise missiles based on the German V1.[14] Neither side felt it could rely on the continuing ability of its heavy bombers to penetrate enemy air defences and deliver nuclear warheads. Both saw the solution as lying in the development of long-range 'inter-continental' missiles, especially ballistic missiles, effective defences against which seemed virtually impossible of achievement. Such missiles would enable nuclear warheads to be delivered against targets thousands of miles away.

The Soviets shocked the West again in 1957 by testing an intercontinental ballistic missile (ICBM) and launching a man-made satellite ahead of the Americans.[15] In the United States these spectacular indications of advancing Soviet technology led to fears of a 'missile gap'. The United States government responded by accelerating their missile and nuclear programme. Still uncertain as to Soviet intentions, they deployed massive forces of land-based and submarine-launched ballistic missiles (SLBMs) at remarkable speed in the late 1950s and early 1960s. These deployments completed, they proceeded to consolidate their forces at their existing levels in the belief that deterrence called for an absolute level of destructive power, or 'assured destruction', which had now been reached and indeed exceeded.[16] With certain important updatings and upgradings, the deployments of the late 1950s and early 1960s have formed the backbone of the American nuclear forces into the 1980s: 1054 land-based ICBMs, mainly 'Minuteman'; 656 SLBMs in 41 submarines; and about 450 strategic bombers, mainly B52s.[17]

The Soviets took longer to build up their nuclear forces but proceeded inexorably over the 1960s and 1970s to match and even overtake the American deployments (except for heavy bombers), while simultaneously building up a massive navy and airlift capability to project the Soviet presence world-wide and counter Western influence. By the end of the 1970s the Soviets had deployed 2504 strategic nuclear delivery systems as against the Americans' 2141; the total yield of Soviet warheads exceeded that of American warheads by a ratio of possibly 5: 2; and the area of destruction they were capable of causing exceeded that of American warheads by a ratio of possibly 5: 3. With improved target accuracy the Soviets probably have the capability to destroy a substantial proportion of the United States' land-based ICBMs in a first strike.

The United States has responded to these Soviet advances, not by matching increases in its own deployments of delivery systems, but by updating and upgrading its capabilities. On the defensive side, some progress was made with the development of anti-ballistic missile (ABM) systems in the late 1960s. The two superpowers undertook in the SALT 1 agreement of 1972 to limit severely the deployment of such systems.[18] But research work on defensive systems has continued. On the offensive side, the United States developed and deployed multiple independently targeted warheads (MIRVs) for its ICBMs[19] and increased the yield of some of the Minuteman warheads. Target accuracy has been raised substantially by means of improved guidance systems. These developments, taken together, have increased the 'counter-force' capability of the United States' nuclear forces against military targets; and this trend will be carried further in the new MX ICBM, Trident II SLBM and air-launched cruise missile (ALCM) systems.[20] The Soviets have upgraded and improved their strategic nuclear forces in broadly similar ways.

Below the strategic level, the Soviets have deployed large numbers of triple-warhead SS-20 intermediate-range missiles targeted on Western Europe and China: some 414 at the time of writing. NATO responded with the 'twin-track' decision of December 1979 to deploy new intermediate-range nuclear forces in Western Europe – 108 Pershing II ballistic missiles and 464 ground-launched cruise missiles – and to seek talks with the Soviet Union about the control of intermediate-range nuclear forces (INF).[21] Deployments began in November 1983.

CONCLUSION

So it is that profound distrust and advancing technology have combined to produce a balance of terror between East and West, based on the possession by each side of massive forces, nuclear and conventional. On each side, the habit of vast expenditure on defence – both force deployments and the development of new weapon systems – has become deeply ingrained. Military expenditure, though it fell perceptibly as a proportion of Gross National Product (GNP) during the 1970s, has generally continued to rise in real terms.[22] As a result, the most powerful armies the world has ever seen face each other in Europe, while the destructive power of the super- powers' nuclear arsenals is on a scale to dwarf all previous experience. These massive military forces have themselves contributed to the tensions between East and West which gave rise to them.

It is doubtless idle to speculate whether the balance of terror had to develop in the way it has – whether what has happened, had to happen; whether what is, has to be. The more urgent question, discussed in the next chapter, is whether a balance of terror will continue to be necessary in the future.

There are, however, two impressions which linger in the mind after study of the post-war years. The first is that, given the deep distrust between East and West, the development of a balance of terror based on nuclear weapons was probably inevitable once these weapons had been invented. No other guarantee of national security has since looked adequate. The second is that the *scale* of the present nuclear arsenals is probably not inevitable: with better luck and management, they might have been a great deal smaller.

4   Is It Necessary?

To suggest that the development of a balance of terror since the Second
World War has probably been inevitable is not to suggest that a balance
of terror will necessarily remain inevitable for the rest of time. There is
no *a priori* reason why two superpowers on a single planet should continue
indefinitely, and at huge expense, to maintain the means of obliterating
each other's main centres of population several times over.

The existing balance of terror is the product (so we have argued) of
deep distrust between nations and a remarkable scientific invention. The
invention cannot be disinvented. But the deep distrust could, in principle
at least, be replaced over time by a new relationship of mutual trust. If
such a consummation could be achieved, the need for a balance of terror
would certainly diminish and might just conceivably disappear. If there
remained no fundamental antagonism between East and West – no clashes
of belief and interest in areas perceived by each side to be of the highest
importance – thee it is possible, at least, that the two sides might agree that
it was no longer necessary to retain massive arsenals of horrendous weapons
for the sake of mutual deterrence. If the two sides no longer felt even
remotely threatened by each other, they might just conceivably feel able,
in the fullness of time, to gather their swords together and turn them into
ploughshares.

In practice there seems, sadly, no prospect of such a consummation in
the foreseeable future. Both superpowers have come to regard nuclear
forces as their ultimate deterrent – the ultimate guarantee of their security
and independence. A truly remarkable degree of mutual trust would be
needed before they would feel secure about disbanding these forces
altogether, as opposed to reducing them. Without such trust, each side
would be afraid of cheating by the other. It would be relatively easy,
especially for the authoritarian Soviet government, to retain secret stock-

piles. Each side would worry that the other was poised to rebuild its nuclear arsenal at short notice.

The question is, therefore: how likely is it that East and West will come to trust each other to the extent required? The answer has to be that it looks most unlikely in the foreseeable future. Trust of the order required lies far beyond the horizon of vision. Both sides *do* feel threatened by the other in areas which they perceive to be of the first importance. Their mutual antagonism and distrust *do* run deep. And there seems, unhappily, no early prospect of any significant convergence of interests or philosophies which might open the way to building mutual trust.

A further consideration is that, even in the unlikely event that the Soviet Union and the United States could achieve a remarkable bilateral rapport, they could well perceive other risks which would preclude disbandment of their nuclear arsenals. Both would feel uncomfortable about forswearing a nuclear capability if other countries, such as China, retained such a capability or the potential to acquire it quickly. The Soviets in particular could hardly be expected to contemplate such a momentous step unless France and Britain, as well as China, were to do likewise. They might anyway feel that forswearing the nuclear option would weaken unacceptably their hold over Eastern Europe.

For all these reasons, a world order based on a balance of terror looks to be inescapable for the foreseeable future. Reduction of the nuclear arsenals is one thing; disbandment, quite another.

Familiar as such judgements may be, however, their importance is such that they should not be taken for granted. Hence we devote the rest of this chapter to considering whether the mutual distrust and antagonism which have produced the existing balance of terror are indeed likely to persist. How inevitable are they? Why does each side still perceive itself to be threatened by the other? Must these perceptions continue?

WESTERN PERCEPTIONS OF THE SOVIET THREAT

The West's perception of the threat from the Soviet Union is rooted partly in what the Soviets have said, and still say, and partly in what they have done, and still do. The Soviets have repeatedly conveyed to Western countries, by word and deed, the impression that they nurse longer-term political and ideological ambitions world-wide, whose fulfilment would be totally unacceptable to the West – in particular, an ambition to spread across the globe irremovable communist governments, based on the Soviet model and friendly (or subordinate) to the Soviet Union, together with the accompanying Marxist/Leninist ideology. They have also repeatedly given the impression that they are willing to use without scruple whatever means and opportunities may be available to that end, provided that the risks to the Soviet Union itself are not too great. The West's perception of the threat has been heightened in recent years by the Soviet Union's progressive build-up of vast military power – including colossal nuclear forces and the continuing deployment in Eastern Europe of massive conventional forces in what the experts describe as a classic offensive posture.

WORDS

Interpretation of what the Soviets *say* is complicated by their practice of expounding their policies, and their view of world history, in the language of Marxism/Leninism. It is a matter for debate whether Marxism/Leninism is a creed which inspires Soviet policy or a linguistic idiom designed to justify policies otherwise difficult to defend. Probably it has become a convenient habit of both speech and mind. Interpretation is further complicated by the Soviet practice of applying words with an agreeable connotation, such as democratic, to their own system, and words with a disagreeable connotation, such as imperialist, to Western systems, irrespective of the words' original descriptive content.

   Such difficulties of interpretation cannot, however, obscure the serious challenge to the West which is contained in Soviet language and the Marxist/Leninist philosophy as the Soviets expound it. The Marxist/Leninist creed, combining as it does the determinism of Marx with the opportunism of Lenin, is deeply provocative to non-believers. Especially disturbing for the West is its international 'missionary' dimension, which infects East/West relations with an antagonism comparable to that of religious wars in earlier eras. The Marxist prediction of the ultimate triumph world-wide of the communist revolution and the collapse of 'capitalism' (as practised by the Western democracies) leaves no room for compromise. The Leninist prescription for seizing all opportunities to advance the communist cause by encouraging internal revolution in other countries is blatantly aggressive. The Marxist/Leninist philosophy sees relations with non-communist countries as a continuous struggle, part of the world-wide class struggle. The cognoscenti may debate whether this is a genuine article of faith or a cover for Soviet expansionism. On either interpretation, the challenge to the West, and to all countries which believe in freedom and self-determination, is unmistakable.

It is true that the Soviets' language could be more explosive, and more aggressive in the short term, than it is. In the first place there is, paradoxically, some comfort for the West in the familiar Marxist/Leninist doctrine that, although there may be setbacks from time to time, the tide of history, or 'correlation of forces', is flowing inexorably in favour of communism and the Soviet Union and the final outcome is beyond doubt. It is plainly less dangerous that the Soviets should believe that time is on their side than that time is on the side of the Western democracies.

Second, there is some comfort in Marxist/Leninist doctrines of caution in the use of force. The traditional doctrine prefers subversion to overt military action. Force is seen as an extension of foreign policy, easier to begin than to end and therefore to be used with caution. It may, however, be used to further Soviet aims where it is safe to do so.

The practice of Soviet leaders has accorded well with this doctrine of military caution, and the development of nuclear weapons has so far clearly reinforced their caution. Around the time of Stalin's death in 1953 the Soviet leaders dropped earlier beliefs that total war was inevitable and adopted instead the policy of 'peaceful co-existence'. They are probably as conscious as are Western countries of the horrendous consequences of nuclear war. Khruschev made the point in characteristic style when signing the friendship pact of June 1964 with East Germany: 'Nuclear war is stupid, stupid, stupid! If you reach for the push button, you reach for suicide.'[2]

Another factor which has made the Soviets' posture and language seem less aggressive in recent years, especially the late 1960s and the 1970s, was the policy of détente. Especially significant within that policy was the Soviets' willingness to negotiate with the United States about major interests which the two sides have in common, in particular arms control and crisis management. The pursuit of détente since 1963, fitful as it has been, has undoubtedly reduced the tensions between East and West and mitigated fears of mutual conflict, though relations have deteriorated markedly since 1973 and, even more, since the Soviets' invasion of Afghanistan in December 1979 and their SS-20 deployments.

In all these ways, the posture and language of the Soviet leaders has often in recent years been less immediately aggressive than it might have been, and than it has been at times in the past. They have evidently accepted that the world-wide triumph of the communist revolution will be a longer haul than they once liked to think. They have adapted their strategy and tactics to events, in particular the development of nuclear weapons.

But it is important not to overrate the significance of these changes. There is no evidence of a change in the Soviets' underlying political ambitions, either in Europe or world-wide, which feed the antagonism between East and West. As the Soviet leaders themselves have implied, peaceful co-existence is no more than a strategy, and détente, when, they pursue it, than a tactic. The Soviet Union has much to gain from both (and Mr Brezhnev's successors surely erred in pouring so much frost on East/West relations). The softening of mutual tensions through détente lessens in some degree the risk of a disastrous nuclear war and makes it easier for the Soviets to pursue subversive activities in other countries. The diverting of attention from the communist threat tempts Western governments to spend less on defence and hardens the task of justifying a high level of defence expenditure to Congress or electorate. The thaw in relations enables the Soviet Union to buy much-needed technology from the West, and even grain. None of this implies a change in basic political aims. Mr Brezhnev expressed the point very clearly in his address to the Soviet Union's 25th Party Congress in March 1976 when he described détente as being, in effect, a cover for advancing the communist cause world-wide[3]:

> It could not be clearer, after all, that détente and peaceful coexistence have to do with inter-state relations . . . Détente does not in the slightest abolish, nor does it alter, the laws of the class struggle . . . We make no secret of the fact that we see détente as the way to create more favourable conditions for peaceful socialist and Communist construction.

DEEDS

Important as words are, Western perceptions of the Soviet threat depend even more heavily on what the Soviets have *done* over the years than on what they have said. The previous chapter touched on the Soviets' European objectives and on the post-war episodes which have disturbed the West. Suffice it here to recall once more the Soviets' large territorial acquisitions in the Second World War; their acquisition after the war and subsequent retention of a satellite empire in Eastern Europe; their brinkmanship in the Berlin and Cuban missile crises; their interventions in Third World countries, notably Angola, Ethiopia and Afghanistan, where the unstoppable tide of the Marxist revolution appeared to need a helping hand; their subversive activities in Western countries, including their attempts to wreck the Marshall Aid programme; their support for local communist parties such as the Portuguese party in 1974-5 and the suspicion of Soviet involvement in the terrorism which has afflicted many Western countries in recent years; and their massive build-up of armaments in recent years. These are among the activities which have moulded Western perceptions of Soviet political and ideological ambitions world-wide.

Western perceptions of the Soviet threat have been intensified by the Soviets' treatment of people under their own control – their purges of their own citizens in the 1930s and early 1950s; their suppression of basic human rights; their massive deployments of secret police; their treatment of dissidents; and their subjection of the East European countries, including the invasions of Hungary and Czechoslovakia in 1956 and 1968 respectively and their military encirclement of Poland in 1981. Such activities are bound to make the threat of Soviet political ambitions world-wide seem the more terrible.

For West European countries, the Soviets' treatment of Eastern Europe has the special significance of allegory. It seems plausible to suppose that, if the Soviets had succeeded after the Second World War, or were to succeed in the future, in obtaining suzerainty over Western as well as Eastern Europe, their aim would have been, or would be, to control the countries of Western Europe in the same way as those of Eastern Europe. The Soviets have done little in recent years to conceal the vassal status of the latter countries. Their limited independence was publicly acknowledged in the 'Brezhnev doctrine' of 1968, enunciated at the time of the invasion of Czechoslovakia. Countries inside the Soviet bloc are required to be friendly towards Moscow; to maintain a rigid, single-party system; and to permit no internal opposition which could threaten the supremacy of the communist party. The Soviets claim the right to intervene as necessary to safeguard their communism; and other countries in the bloc are expected to join the fight against enemies within the gates, as defined by the Soviet Union, as well as enemies outside.

The invasion of Czechoslovakia and the 'Brezhnev doctrine' will surely continue to influence Western perceptions of the Soviet threat for years to come. Even the communist parties of Western Europe found the medicine rather strong. The events of 1968 hastened the evolution of 'Euro-communist' parties which purported, at least, to accept the basic institutions of democracy, including free elections, and rejected the Soviet model of single-party rule.

A further factor which has influenced Western perceptions is the propensity of successive Soviet leaders to make false statements, as at the times of the Cuban missile crisis, the invasion of Afghanistan and the shooting down of the Korean airliner in September 1983. This too is inevitably destructive of mutual trust.

The catalogue of Soviet activities since 1945 is such that it is perhaps surprising that Western countries have felt able to co-operate with the Soviet Union to the extent that they have. There seems no prospect that they will come to trust the Soviet Union to any significant extent in the foreseeable future. On the contrary, the West seems bound to continue to feel threatened by the Soviet Union's formidable combination of world-wide political ambitions and massive military strength.

SOVIET PERCEPTIONS OF THE WESTERN THREAT

It is easy for Western observers to blame the underlying antagonism between East and West on the political ambitions and opportunism of the Soviet Union. But the Soviet leaders undoubtedly feel threatened as well, both externally and internally. To a significant extent, moreover, their perception of external threats appears to reflect traditional Russian preoccupations which date from long before the present régime and may well outlast it.

In the last two centuries, and most recently in the Second World War, the Russians have suffered terribly from external invasions. To this day they are said to nurse a sense of isolation and encirclement – by a hostile climate to the north and mainly hostile countries to the west, south and east. In the world outside they have few friends, and their declared distrust of the West, especially the United States, is doubtless genuine. After an interlude of softness at the end of the Second World War, the United States and other Western countries have repeatedly demonstrated their opposition to Soviet expansionism and the communist system, and they have been concerned to thwart the international ambitions of the Soviet leaders. What appears to Western leaders a defensive posture probably looks offensive to the Kremlin. Particularly in the early cold war years, with the surprise of Hitler's invasion fresh in the memory, the combination in the United States of clear military superiority and vehement opposition to communism must have looked as threatening to the Soviet Union as the Soviet Union's reaction-testing behaviour looked to the West. The massive build-up of the Soviet Union's armed forces has doubtless been intended, among other things, to counter this perceived threat.

Closer to home the Soviet leaders are beset by problems which likewise probably appear as threats. They can have no illusions that for the most part the restive European satellite countries on their borders are bound to the Soviet Union by fear rather than friendship. They are conscious that the West would like to see these countries liberated from the Soviet yoke, if that could happen without a major conflagration. Occasional talk by Western statesmen of detaching the satellite countries from the Soviet Union must sound highly provocative to Soviet ears. The Soviet leaders' sense of isolation is doubtless deepened by the estrangement between the Soviet Union and the other major communist power, China.

It seems likely that problems at home must enhance the Soviet leaders' sense of insecurity and vulnerability. In the first place the régime is in effect a military autocracy, depending for its survival on its hugely powerful army and ubiquitous secret police. Like any régime which depends on force rather than popular support it must ultimately be vulnerable. That is not to say that a putsch is likely in the foreseeable future, still less that the victors in any power struggle would be anti-communist. On the contrary, the Soviet leadership takes unique precautions to integrate the army with the Communist party leadership: the armed forces are well represented in all the supreme organs of the State; 90 per cent of the officer corps are party members; and KGB informers are assigned to every military unit. In the very long term, nevertheless, the support of the people provides the best assurance of survival for any system of government, and military might is no substitute: witness the collapse in 1979 of the Shah's régime in Iran.

The dependence of the Soviet régime on force rather than popular support is not purely an internal problem. It also means that the Soviets cannot afford to have normal relations with other, non-communist countries. The borders of the Soviet bloc have to be firmly sealed, and a wall built across Berling, to prevent an exodus of emigrants. Overseas visits by Soviet citizens have to be strictly limited and controlled. Within the Soviet Union there can be no freedom for visitors from overseas, any more than for Soviet citizens themselves, to travel or trade as they please: they have to be closely monitored and controlled. The Soviety people have to be shielded from outside influences and monitored by secret police. The Soviet leaders could not afford to reach a genuine accommodation with the West, or to have normal country to country relationships, without risking a major loss of control and ultimately undermining the whole system of government. The threat would be too great. Much the same points apply, moreover, to the satellite countries. In these circumstances, the prospects for creating mutual trust between the Soviet Union and the West, and removing fundamental antagonisms, cannot at present be considered bright.

A further problem for the Soviet leadership is that their political system has moved far away from the Marxist ideal. The moral ascendancy of the most powerful communist state in the world has been severely compromised. In place of a dictatorship of the proletariat, there is dictatorship by an oligarchy of party leaders chosen by co-option from a party membership which includes under 6 per cent of the population. In place of equality there is striking inequality, though in general affluence is publicly financed. Disbelief in the communist ideology is reported to be widespread, and dissidents have succeeded in making their voices heard. China and other communist countries have joined Yugoslavia in rejecting the Soviet Union's erstwhile moral ascendancy. So too have the major communist parties of Western Europe. These developments can only have increased the régime's sense of isolation and vulnerability.

Other chinks in the armour of the Soviet leadership include the growing proportion of Asians in their population and a disappointing economic performance in recent years. The economic dimension could in time become very important. In no sense has Khrushchev's boast that the Soviet economy would overtake the Western economies by 1970 been fulfilled. The Soviets have shown themselves extremely good at developing priority sectors, notably the military sector. But the experts are agreed that, in the economy as a whole, output per head is low relative to most Western economies, and economic growth has been slowing down in recent years. Living standards in some of the satellite countries, though disappointing by Western standards, are perceptibly higher than in the Soviet Union.

In the face of all these problems it would not be surprising if the Soviet leaders felt themselves surrounded by threats, from without and within. As shown by their strong reaction to President Carter's emphasis on human rights in 1977, they are highly sensitive to the danger that the West may seek to exploit their domestic problems. It seems likely, therefore, that problems within must reinforce their sense of being threatened from without; and there seems little prospect that their perception of the threat from without will diminish in the foreseeable future.

As has often been observed, the Soviet Union has been run for many years by a gerontocracy of aged, conservative and generally predictable men. Since the death of Mr Brezhnev in the autumn of 1982, after 18 years at the helm, the direction of Soviet policies has become less predictable. Perhaps the most likely outcome, after a period of transition, is a return to Brezhnev-style policies. Be that as it may, the changes are unlikely to affect the fundamental antagonism between the Soviet Union and the West.

CONCLUSION

We concluded in chapter 3 that the mutual distrust between East and West in the years since nuclear weapons were invented has been such that development of a balance of terror has probably been inevitable – though not necessarily at existing levels of armaments. To this sad conclusion we have now to add the even sadder conclusion that the balance of terror is probably here to stay for the foreseeable future – once again, not necessarily at existing levels of armaments. Distasteful as the prospect may be, peace between the two sides is likely to continue in the foreseeable future to depend on mutual deterrence through a balance of terror.

The reasons for this gloomy prognostication are twofold. First, nuclear weapons cannot be disinvented. Second, there seems no prospect whatever in the foreseeable future of that transformation in relations between East and West which alone could encourage the two sides to take the enormous risk of discarding their nuclear weapons. The legacy of mutual distrust is too profound. The factors which have caused this distrust will not change quickly. There seems little prospect of a convergence of political systems. Even the lesser goal of a genuine rapprochement is seemingly ruled out by the Soviet Union's continuing political and ideological ambitions world-wide – ambitions which Western countries are bound to perceive as deeply provocative – and by the apparent impossibility for the Soviet régime, relying as it does on force, secret police and isolation, to move towards 'normal' relations with Western countries.

There are certain schools of thought which by implication do not accept the conclusions of this and the preceding chapters. They argue instead for policies based on rejecting the balance of terror. We consider the feasibility of such policies in chapter 13.

5   Nuclear Weapons and World Politics

INTRODUCTION

In the two preceding chapters we have discussed how political tensions, interacting with technological advance, have created the balance of terror and seem likely to preserve it. The present chapter considers how the balance of terror has in its turn affected international political relationships,[1] even though neither side has used a nuclear weapon since the Second World War, or even threatened overtly to use one.[2] We consider first what extra political power individual countries can derive from the possession of nuclear weapons and then the global effects of nuclear weapons on world politics.

MILITARY STRENGTH AND POLITICAL POWER

Enormously strong as is the shared interest of East and West in avoiding nuclear war, that interest is not so overriding that nothing else matters. As discussed in chapter 4, there is an actual political struggle between East and West as well as the risk of a military struggle. The two sides are concerned not just to avoid a military struggle but also to win (or not to lose) the political struggle – not just to preserve peace but to preserve it on acceptable terms. Both sides are deeply committed to maintaining their own political and social systems and territory; each side is concerned to prevent the other from imposing his politics and ideals on third countries.

In the political struggle between East and West military strength, and in particular the nuclear arsenals, play a role which is often misunderstood or underestimated. More than a century and a half ago Clausewitz pointed out that war was 'nothing but a continuation of political intercourse'.[3] In just the same way, the mere *possession* of military power is a dimension of political intercourse – an instrument which may enable countries to

38

achieve, without actually going to war, political objectives they could not have achieved from a state of military weakness. The possession of nuclear weapons, in particular, is likely to strengthen a country's political muscle, possibly in an 'offensive' sense and certainly in a 'defensive' sense.

In an 'offensive' sense, a nuclear country may, depending on circumstances, gain an enhanced ability to influence, intimidate or dominate other countries without resort to military force – to make them behave in ways they would not have chosen for themselves. Even if these other countries rather doubt that the strong country would actually use his military might against them, there are some risks which are simply not worth taking.

The Soviet Union's relationship with Eastern Europe provides a striking example of how military strength can be exploited for 'offensive' political purposes. The Soviets have relied heavily on their vast military power for preserving political control over their satellite empire in Eastern Europe. Were it not for the Soviets' massive military superiority, it is doubtful whether any of the East European countries would still be run by communist governments under a single-party system with a foreign policy of subservience to the Soviet Union. The Soviets' deployments of conventional forces in the East European countries have played a key role in preserving their control, as has their willingness (demonstrated in Hungary in 1956, and again in Czechoslovakia in 1968) to invade these countries in case of trouble. The Soviet nuclear arsenal has been crucial as well. It is this that ultimately rules out as hopeless any thought that the people of Eastern Europe might entertain of throwing off the Soviet yoke by fighting the Soviet armed forces. Such a project could succeed, if at all, only with help from the West, and the existence of the Soviet nuclear arsenal makes it virtually certain that such help would never be forthcoming. Mr Nagy discovered as much in 1956. Mr Dubcek knew it in 1968. The people of Poland have had to face the fact in the early 1980s.

The Soviets have also used the political weight of their vast military might from time to time to bring pressure to bear on neighbours outside the Warsaw Pact such as Finland and Yugoslavia. These countries cannot ignore the Soviet dimension in forming their policies.

With regard to countries further from home, the scope for using vast military strength as a basis for political offensives, is much more limited. In no sense does the possession of such strength make a country all-powerful – least of all if another country or countries, too, possess similar capabilities. Later sections of this chapter will discuss the limitations on the 'offensive' political power of nuclear countries.

In a 'defensive' sense, the role of nuclear arsenals in strengthening a country's political muscle is likely to be much more decisive, even in a world which contains several nuclear countries. A nuclear country may not be able to influence, intimidate or dominate others. But he should at least be able to resist attempts by others to influence, intimidate or dominate *him*. Since nuclear weapons were invented, moreoever, no alternative guarantee of national independence has looked really adequate.

These comments apply especially to the superpowers. Even small nuclear forces, however, should be able to confer substantial protection against political intimidation, provided that they are capable of inflicting damage on a scale which others would find unacceptable. Therein lies part of the reason why Britain, France and (one may suspect) China decided to acquire nuclear capabilities – and why certain other countries are tempted to follow their example.

From a Western standpoint, the nuclear 'shield' or 'umbrella' which the United States holds over Western Europe through NATO provides a striking example of how a nuclear capability can protect countries against political intimidation or domination. This nuclear umbrella has contributed, and continues to contribute, decisively to the independence of Western Europe. If the West had possessed no nuclear deterrent to counter the massive military capabilities of the Soviet Union, the countries of Western Europe would have been seriously exposed to political pressure and intimidation from the Soviet Union; their independence would, at best, have been severely compromised.

The Soviets, for their part, can be assumed to see their massive nuclear arsenals, similarly, as protecting them against political pressures from the West, and especially the United States. Such pressures are probably perceived as a serious threat by a ruling oligarchy which maintains a system of government commanding little public support and holds neighbouring countries in a state of subordination.[4]

LIMITATIONS ON POLITICAL POWER OF STRONG COUNTRIES

The scope for using military strength as a basis for applying political pressures in an 'offensive' sense is subject in practice to many limiting factors, including the strength of will of the countries against whom the pressures are directed, the strength of will of the strong country itself, and other countries' perceptions of that will. The latter perceptions are likely to be influenced in turn by the range of the strong country's military capabilities, the existence, attitudes and relative strengths of other strong countries, especially nuclear countries, and general attitudes to the use of military force.

WILL-POWER OF WEAKER COUNTRIES

The political efficacy of a strong country's superior military strength *vis-à-vis* weaker countries will obviously depend in part on the extent to which the latter countries are prepared to be bullied or intimidated. The more they are prepared to stand up to the strong country, to discount the risk of military aggression, to call the strong country's bluff, the less potent the strong country's political influence will be.

It goes without saying that some weaker countries are better placed than others to stand up to bullying. Smaller nuclear countries are especially well placed, and likewise countries which acquire the benefits of a nuclear shield by voluntary participation in an alliance with a nuclear power such as NATO.

The neutral countries of central and northern Europe – Austria, Switzerland, Sweden and Finland – are relatively well placed as well, though Finland's movements are inevitably constrained by its territorial tangency with the Soviet Union. These countries know that aggression by one stronger country would be vigorously challenged by other stronger countries. This gives them a considerable degree of political independence. The significant armed forces and reserves which some of the neutral countries maintain, notably Sweden and Switzerland, make them less of a sitting target: would-be aggressors could not count on achieving a quick and total victory before other strong countries had time to react. Relatively small as they are, these forces help to reinforce the political independence of the neutral countries.

The ability of Third World countries to stand up to bullying by a strong country will depend on a wide range of considerations including their size and strength, their proximity to the strong country which wants to bully them, and their ability to enlist support from another strong country.

Even the East European countries can resist Soviet political influence in some degree by declining to be bullied in areas where the risk of Soviet reprisals is small. As recent events in Poland have again demonstrated, however, their scope for such resistance is limited. In contrast with the neutral countries and most Third World countries, the Soviets can intervene too easily. Their determination to retain control of Eastern Europe is well known. Their local military superiority is overwhelming. The countries themselves are full of Soviet servants, including soldiers and secret police. Above all, there is no serious fear of Western challenge.

WILL-POWER OF STRONG COUNTRIES

The will-power of the strong country itself is no less important than that of the weaker countries which might fall under its influence. For military might to be reflected in political muscle, the government which controls the military might must be willing to make its position of strength felt in international bargaining situations. It must also convince others that it has the will to use its military might if necessary, and in particular to win political support at home for such a step.

An example may help to illustrate the point. If one of the superpowers were repeatedly to decline to intervene in any way to help Third World friends in trouble, whether because of high aversion to risk or political difficulties at home or for any other reason, its political muscle would be weakened, and likewise the political muscle of its friends in Third World countries.

PERCEPTIONS AND SIGNALS

A strong country's political muscle depends not just on its actual will and capabilities but also (and crucially) on how others perceive that will and those capabilities. As with deterrence, so with the conversion of military into political power, the perceptions of others are all-important

How are such perceptions moulded? The short answer is that all the information reaching country B about country A, whether true or false, is likely to affect in some degree B's perception of A. Even palpably biased propaganda from country C may have some effect: the number of people in country B who actually believe C's propaganda may be small, but C may succeed nevertheless in planting seeds of doubt where none is justified or in making well-founded judgements seem controversial.

That said, there is no doubt that what country A actually does, and what the leadership (and others) in country A actually say, must be especially important in moulding other countries' perceptions of country A. Everything that a country does, especially in the field of foreign policy and defence, and everything that is said in public – or even in private, yet reported to other countries – is significant not just in itself but also because of the signal which it will transmit to the rest of the world. This applies to internal debates quite as much as to inter-government communications. Country B may well rate what person 1 has said to person 2 in country A as a more significant signal than what country A's leadership has said directly to country B's leadership. Particularly in Western countries, statements by political opponents of government policies may affect the signal transmitted to the rest of the world by influencing expectations as to the development of those policies.

The importance of signals and perceptions is strikingly illustrated by the Cuban missile crisis of 1962 and the Korean War of 1950–53. Relatively happy as the outcome was, it is remarkable that the Cuban missile crisis should have occurred at all – remarkable that Khruschev should ever have thought he could get away with setting up a forward missile base in Cuba.[5] It is said that his perception of likely American reactions was influenced by the low opinion of Kennedy's resolution which he had formed from the Bay of Pigs episode in Cuba, the Vienna Summit meeting of 1961 and the muted American response to the building of the Berlin wall. Be that as it may, the United States clearly failed to transmit an effective signal ahead of the crisis. The President had to place the American strategic nuclear forces on full combat-readiness before the message was understood in the Kremlin.

The decision of the communist powers to launch the Korean war in 1950 seems likewise to have been based on a complete miscalculation of how the United States would react. The communist powers appear to have considered the risk of American intervention as negligible. In this they were encouraged by false signals from the United States – not only the withdrawal of American troops from South Korea in 1949 but also hints by the United States administration that Korea and Taiwan were 'expendable': neither Korea nor Taiwan were included in the American 'defense perimeter' as defined by Secretary of State Dean Acheson in January 1950.

We return in chapter 14 to the importance for the West of sending the right signals to the rest of the world.

CONVENTIONAL CAPABILITIES WORLD-WIDE

Perceptions of a strong country's will, and hence the voltage of its political electricity, are certain to be influenced by the range and capabilities of its conventional as well as nuclear forces. Massive megatonnages of nuclear weapons are often no substitute for an ability to intervene or help conventionally in particular trouble spots. In many circumstances the threatened use of nuclear weapons by any of the major powers would manifestly lack

credibility, and indeed it is most unlikely that such threats would be made
at all. When East and West are supporting rival Third World factions, for
example, the ability to convey practical help to the parties on the ground
is likely to be the most important military factor. Hence a superpower who
wishes to exercise political muscle across the globe, or to prevent a rival
superpower from doing so, needs a world-wide capability to intervene or
give support conventionally, as well as a nuclear capability.

Both East and West have recognised the political importance of conventional capabilities in developing their over-all military capabilities. The
United States, in particular, has argued frequently for strengthening NATO's
conventional capabilities in Europe and has begun to deploy a world-wide
rapid deployment force.

On the Soviet side, similar considerations have loomed large in the
massive build-up over recent years of the Soviet navy under Admiral
Gorshkov, and in the development of a large airlift capability comprising
several airborne divisions. The Soviets have doubtless felt the need for a
strong navy to give them effective deterrence and war-fighting capabilities
– to carry their submarine-launched ballistic missiles (SLBMs), to try to
monitor movements of American submarines and to disrupt shipment of
supplies and reinforcements across the Atlantic in the event of a conflagration
in Europe. But another major purpose of the world-wide deployment of
the Soviet navy has been to enhance the Soviet Union's ability to intervene, or give logistical help, in Third World situations in support of their
political offensives in the Third World. The airlift capacity doubtless has
a similar purpose. The Soviet navy may be unable at present, for logistical
reasons, to support overseas operations as efficiently as it might. But the
Soviets have proved themselves indefatigible in the progressive improvement
of their capabilities, and there is no question of their ability to get in the
way of naval operations by the United States or other Western powers.
The build-up of the Soviet navy has weakened the political muscle of the
West.

OTHER NUCLEAR COUNTRIES

As implied earlier, the most important limitation of all on the 'offensive'
political muscle which a country can derive from its nuclear arsenal is
the existence of other nuclear arsenals, owned by other countries. A
nuclear country's political muscle will be greatest if it has a monopoly
of nuclear weapons, or massive superiority; weakest, if its nuclear arsenal
is massively inferior to those of other nuclear countries; and of inter-

mediate strength, if its nuclear arsenal is broadly comparable with that of another country.

Taking these cases in turn, if a country has a *monopoly* of nuclear weapons, or overwhelming superiority, its political muscle must potentially be very strong. The range of its foreign policy options, though still subject to significant constraints, must be vastly increased. Such a country will not necessarily behave in an aggressive way, but its potential for intimidating and dominating weaker countries will clearly be very considerable.

The only country which has ever enjoyed a nuclear monopoly, or massive superiority, is the United States in the early post-war years. The Americans did not, however, exploit the massive political power which this nuclear privilege gave them, except for defensive purposes. For all their faults, the American administrations of the early post-war years were inspired by high ideals of freedom, self-determination and anti-colonialism. They had no desire to use their political power aggressively, though they did rely on their nuclear strength to neutralise the West's conventional inferiority in the European theatre. This nuclear strength was also useful to them in other contexts, such as the Cuban missile crisis of 1962. Part of the reason why President Kennedy was able to take the stand he did in that crisis, and to resolve it, was that he knew, and Khruschev knew too, that the United States could still harm the Soviet Union more than the Soviet Union could harm the United States.

To obtain a better idea of the political power potentially conferred by nuclear monopoly, we need look no further than the Soviet Union and Eastern Europe. The Soviet Union's political domination and subjection of Eastern Europe depends importantly on the presence of vast Soviet conventional forces in the East European countries themselves and close to their borders. As noted earlier, however, the ultimate and fundamental reason why the East European countries cannot take up arms against their Soviet masters, or go too far in flouting Soviet political orders, is that the Soviet Union possesses in its nuclear arsenal a master weapon which the East European countries do not possess. In the last analysis, it is the Soviet nuclear arsenal that underwrites the subjection of Eastern Europe by making physical support for East European countries too dangerous for the West to contemplate.

It requires no great leap of the imagination to extrapolate from the example of the Soviet Union's domination of Eastern Europe to the scope for wider international domination by an unscrupulous country with a nuclear monopoly. If the Soviet Union, or any other country, possessed a large nuclear arsenal and a world nuclear monopoly, that country could hold a larger area than Eastern Europe in a state of subjection, and bring intense political pressure to bear on other countries as well. The efficacy of the nuclear monopoly country's political control would depend on other factors including those described earlier – its perceived will to make use of its nuclear strength, its deployment of conventional forces and its underlying economic strength – but a large area of the world could in principle become like Eastern Europe, writ large.

A country with a *small* nuclear arsenal cannot expect, in the presence of a superpower or two superpowers, to derive from it any great political influence of an 'offensive' kind. The possibility of bilateral nuclear use by such a country is credible, if at all, only in circumstances where its own independence or even survival are threatened. On the other hand, possession of a small arsenal can give a country highly effective political defences, even against a much stronger superpower, in a way that nothing else can do. Provided that the arsenal is reasonably invulnerable and is capable of inflicting a level of damage on the stronger country which the stronger country is not prepared to risk, the country with the small arsenal should be able to resist political pressures and call the bluff of stronger countries if the latter should attempt political intimidation. France and Britain are in approximately this position, bilaterally, *vis-à-vis* the Soviet Union, as well as having the American nuclear shield.

There remains the important intermediate case where two rival nuclear powers are evenly matched and share an ability to devastate each other's population and territory. This has been the position of the United States and the Soviet Union since the late 1960s. In such a case neither country will be able to use his nuclear capability as a basis for political blackmail against the other. The scope for aggressive or interventionist foreign policies will likewise be much circumscribed. This certainly applies to political relationships with countries recognised to be in the other side's sphere of influence. It applies also to a considerable extent in Third World situations. The two countries may still be prepared to risk political or even military offensives in Third World theatres on the assumption that the rival country will be deterred by the fear of escalation or other considerations from becoming involved. But in a world order based on approximate parity between two nuclear superpowers, the launching of such adventures becomes much more risky. These risks are plain, moreoever, for others to see, as well as the superpowers themselves. Hence other countries may be quite well placed to resist political pressures from the nuclear superpowers. The political influence which results from the diplomatic anticipation of active involvement by a strong country is much diluted by the existence of another equally strong country which would oppose the involvement of its rival.

RELATIVE MILITARY STRENGTHS

Even within a context of approximate parity between the superpowers, perceived changes in the nuclear balance can have political impact. Such changes can influence not only direct political dealings between the two superpowers but also, potentially at least, Third World situations. Even here, nuclear capabilities and the ultimate nuclear balance may be important as well as conventional military capabilities. If one superpower is perceived to have ceded military supremacy to the other, his wishes are less likely to command respect. His will to make sure that they are respected may also be weakened. For in all situations of international bargaining or tension, the leaders of the superpowers are likely to ask themselves: 'If the worst came to the worst and, against all expectations, this crisis escalated into a nuclear confrontation, could we hurt the enemy as much as the enemy could hurt us?' If the answer to this question is yes, the leader is likely to be more willing to hold out for a better bargain, or to increase aid to his own faction, even if that means provoking the other superpower. If the answer is no, he is likely to be more cautious and to feel inhibited in the pursuit of political goals. The side which feels that in the ultimate analysis he is weaker is likely to suffer a degree of political debilitation. Imagine the psychological impact on the leader of one superpower if at the end of any ultimatum which he directs at the rival superpower he has to add an unspoken gloss in the Shakespearian manner:

> *Aside* . . . though it must be admitted that if the worst came to the worst we should probably suffer a great deal more than you, and your options are significantly greater than ours.

It is not even necessary to imagine. We know from those who have surrounded leading statesmen how powerful these considerations can be in practice.

ATTITUDES TO USE OF MILITARY FORCE[6]

A further factor which may limit the political leverage which strong countries can derive from military power is that such power may now be less usable, and be seen to be less usable, than in earlier times. The reasons for postulating a decline in the usability of military power are many and various. First, war is now so much more terrible than ever before and the dangers in escalation so much more devastating. Second, the development of 'people's war' techniques, guerilla warfare, and terrorism, has made traditional military force less effective in many real-world situations. Third, the moral standards used to assess whether the use of force is justified have become more exacting: gone are the days when the glory of acquiring extra territory, or the profits from securing extra trade, could be held to justify a war. Fourth, the spread of Western-style democracies, coupled with the remarkable acceleration of news transmission, has led to a far greater mobilisation of public opinion than ever before, in the West at least. The signs are that public opinion generally has little enthusiasm for the use of force against other countries, except when deeply stirred or provoked. Lastly, the influence of world opinion, as expressed by 'floating voters' in the United Nations and elsewhere, has probably increased over time: such opinion generally condemns those who initiate the use of force.

TAUNTING GOLIATH[7]

The ability of smaller countries, especially in the Third World, to criticise and flout the superpowers, especially the United States, interestingly illustrates several of the points made above about the limitations on the political muscle of nuclear countries. This intriguing phenomenon was especially prominent in the 1960s and early 1970s. American diplomats in particular had to learn then how little influence their massive military and economic might gave them with the rulers of some Third World countries. The governments of these countries were quick to learn that they could taunt Goliath with impunity.

It is beyond question that the superpowers have the strength to reduce the civilisations of these countries to rubble. But the leaders of Third World countries will often judge, quite rightly, that they are running no serious risks in criticising the superpowers – that the United States in particular would not have the will to use its military strength against them and would anyway be deterred from doing so by concern as to the reactions of the Soviet Union and fears of criticism at home and abroad, or simply by a desire not to become too deeply involved. Criticism of the superpowers may, however, serve a politically useful purpose. It may help the government of a small country to rebut domestic charges that it is dependent on another country. Since many more such governments do in fact depend on the United States than on the Soviet Union, the United States has tended to be the chief target for such criticisms.

GLOBAL POLITICAL EFFECTS

From the relationship between the nuclear capabilities and political muscle of individual countries, we turn to the global political effects of a balance of nuclear terror. The most important such effect – so we shall argue in later chapters – is to increase the probability of peace. But there are others as well. We touch on these under four headings – bipolarity, the status quo, conventions of international behaviour and the incentive to bargain.

BIPOLARITY

The massive military superiority of the United States and the Soviet Union compared with other countries, coupled with the antagonism between them, gives world politics a bipolar aspect. The United States and her democratic allies confront the Soviet Union and her communist subjects. Third World countries are critical spectators who sometimes become involved in the drama.

This bipolarity is politico-strategic rather than economic. The West, including Japan, relies heavily on the United States for protection against the political and military threat posed by the Soviet Union, while the allies of the Soviet Union live in a state of military and political subordination to the Soviet Union. With limited exceptions, the United States represents the Western interest in Third World problem areas, and the Soviet Union represents Soviet and communist interests. China and the European ex-colonial powers play a role as well. But the superpowers predominate.

In politico-economic terms there is again a polarity between East and West. The free-market, highly developed economies of the United States and her principal allies contrast with the centrally planned and comparatively under-developed economies of the Soviet Union and her subjects. The other actors in the drama, however, have larger roles than on the politico-strategic stage. Each important country grouping has a special role to play – industrial countries, oil producers, producers of food and other raw materials and the centrally planned economies. Within each group no single country predominates to the same extent as the superpowers within the military and political groupings.

THE STATUS QUO AND SPHERES OF INFLUENCE

A second, powerful effect of the balance of terror is to preserve the international geopolitical status quo, based on mutually recognised territorial spheres of influence.

Since the early post-year years, each side has had territorial spheres of influence which it regards as its own and which are tacitly recognised by the other side – the East European satellite countries (and perhaps Afghanistan) in the case of the Soviet Union, and the NATO countries and Latin America in the case of the United States. These spheres of influence are based partly on geographical proximity, partly on history.[8] Their existence is confirmed in most cases by alliances and deployments of armed forces. Each side knows that interference in the other's spheres of influence would be regarded as deeply provocative and that a change in the status quo would require a war. Because of the nuclear dimension, however, war would be potentially disastrous, and the two sides have a strong common interest in avoiding it. Hence, with the possible exception of Cuba, neither side has overtly interfered to a significant extent in the other's spheres of interest. For these areas at least, the status quo has become entrenched.

In contrast with these acknowledged spheres of influence, there are many other countries, especially Third World countries, which neither side acknowledges to lie in the other's sphere. Rivalry between the superpowers is less dangerous in such countries, and the Third World has thus become the main arena for overt conflict of political systems. Even here, however, the superpowers have treated each other with considerable circumspection and have gone out of their way to avoid direct confrontations between their own forces.

Between these two groups there lies a third group of countries about whose political status and allegiance there is no clear understanding between East and West. The main countries in this category are Yugoslavia and Finland. Yugoslavia has been formally non-aligned since Tito's break with Stalin and has been careful to maintain relationships with both East and West; but the Soviet leaders have never accepted Yugoslavia's non-aligned posture as permanent. Finland is a democratic country with strong Western connections and definitely on the western side of the Iron Curtain but tied to its Soviet neighbour by a military treaty. In these potentially explosive areas the effect of the balance of terror is once again to preserve the status quo, ambiguous as it is, and to discourage unilateral attempts to change it. Similarly, too, with Austria, the existence of a balance of terror tends to entrench the status quo of military neutrality, despite Austria's broadly Western political orientation.[9]

CONVENTIONS OF INTERNATIONAL BEHAVIOUR

A third characteristic of a world order based on a balance of terror is the existence of certain tacitly agreed conventions, or traffic rules, of international behaviour. These conventions reflect the shared recognition of the geopolitical status quo in large areas of the globe. Each side accepts that there are certain categories of action, notably intervention in each other's sphere of influence, which they cannot contemplate. Such actions would be too risky in a world which contains massive nuclear arsenals.

For the people of Europe and America these accepted conventions of international behaviour do much to take the sting out of the balance of terror. True, the Soviets probably have nuclear warheads targeted on all the major cities of America and Western Europe. True, the Americans probably have nuclear warheads targeted on all the major cities of the Soviet Union. True, these warheads could reach their targets within minutes of the orders being given. Yet ordinary people do not live in daily fear of being overrun or obliterated. On the contrary, most people living in the developed world today probably feel safer than their ancestors used to feel.

The risks faced by the ordinary citizen under a balance of terror are genuine and ever-present. But they are conditional risks for the most part – risks which *would* arise *if* the country concerned were to depart from the tacitly agreed conventions of international behaviour and take some course of action which it need not take. They are not like the risks which a soldier faces on the field of battle; they are more like those which face a pedestrian in a street with moving traffic. He knows that it would be certain death to step in front of the traffic. He therefore takes special care to obey the traffic rules. He also knows that if vehicles go out of control he may be run over. But he does not therefore live in a state of perpetual terror.

THE INCENTIVE TO BARGAIN AND DÉTENTE

Finally, the balance of terror gives the nuclear countries a stronger incentive to bargain and negotiate together than any previous balances of military power. Their enhanced incentive to bargain with words rather than violence is the obverse of their shared interest in avoiding military conflict in the presence of nuclear weapons. Both East and West have a stronger interest than the rival powers of earlier periods in resolving differences without resort to force and in preventing such differences from arising in the first place. Both have an interest in reducing tensions and co-operating within circumscribed areas.

Events since 1945 have amply confirmed this enhancement of the incentive to negotiate. More than ever before international politics has become a continuous process of bargaining, sometimes overt, sometimes tacit. In no other period of history have implacable enemies negotiated so continuously and comprehensively. In no other period have rival countries put so much effort into achieving and maintaining the reduced tensions and limited co-operation which have come to be known as détente.

Especially since the early 1960s, the world's leading powers have concluded a large number of agreements on subjects which are potential sources of tension and conflict, notably arms control and crisis management. These agreements, to which we return in chapter 9, have been less far-reaching than one would wish. But the fact that they have been reached at all is important. The chief credit for them must go to the United States, on whose initiative most of them have been negotiated. Also important has been the habit of international discussion of world issues fostered by the United Nations, likewise an American invention.

In addition to formal agreements and negotiations, direct bilateral bargaining, overt as well as tacit, has taken place between the superpowers on occasions of world tension and crisis, notably in the Berlin and Cuban missile crises and at the time of the 1973 Arab-Israeli war. It seems possible, at least, that these crises may show the characteristic form, or paradigm, of conflict between the superpowers in the nuclear era – direct bargaining accompanied by episodes of limited action after prior warning. In the presence of nuclear weapons, the political leaders of both superpowers have the strongest incentive to bargain together rather than launch hostilities, either conventional or nuclear. Never before in history has Clemençeau's dictum that 'war is too important to be left to soldiers' been more pertinent; nor Clausewitz's dictum that 'the subordination of the military point of view to the political is, therefore, the only thing which is possible.'[10] The possibility cannot be excluded that one side or the other may abandon the idiom of bargaining, break off communications and proceed to all-out war. But it is arguable, at least, that the more likely pattern is one of Cuban-missile-style crises, possibly writ large and accompanied by demonstrations of force, with politicians rather than generals in leading roles.

CONCLUSION

In this chapter we have considered the balance of terror as an element in the totality of political relations between countries whose objectives are not just to preserve peace but to preserve it on acceptable terms. We took as our starting point Clausewitz's dictum that war is 'nothing but a continuation of political intercourse'. At the risk of oversimplification, our principal conclusions can be recreated in the form of six axioms in further elaboration of this famous insight:

1. The mere *possession* of military strength is likewise a dimension of political intercourse, which may enable a country to achieve political ends without a shot being fired – especially if the military strength includes a nuclear capability.

2. These political ends may be *offensive or defensive*: they may include influence, intimidation or subjection of other countries, or they may be confined to resisting such intimidation by other strong countries.

3. The ability of even a superpower to convert military strength into effective political *offensives* is in practice limited, especially in the presence of a rival superpower. The Soviet Union has succeeded famously in imposing political hegemony on Eastern Europe. But countries against whom political offensives are directed may be in a position to refuse to be intimidated; they may doubt the superpower's will to use his military might; they may count on support from the other superpower, *in extremis*; they may calculate that the aggressive superpower would be deterred by this and other considerations from using force in support of his political offensive.

4. There are no comparable limits on the *defensive* value of military strength, including nuclear capabilities. A perceived ability to inflict unacceptable damage in retaliation if attacked provides the best available defence against attempts at political blackmail or intimidation based on the possession of massive military strength. Even a small nuclear arsenal may be quite effective in providing such a defence.

5. From a *global* standpoint, a balance of nuclear terror between two strong countries, or blocs of countries, introduces a bipolar aspect into world politics, entrenches the geopolitical status quo based on tacitly recognised territorial spheres of influence, and sets tacitly agreed limits on political and military behaviour within which countries can feel reasonably secure.

6. A balance of terror also enhances the incentives towards the kinds of *bargaining* and limited co-operation, on the basis of shared interest, which have come to be known as détente.

6 Intrinsic Stability

INTRINSIC AND DYNAMIC STABILITY

The preceding chapters have touched on the basic theory of the balance of terror, the factors which have brought it into being and its effects on world politics. The formidable task which lies ahead is to consider how stable a balance of terror is likely to be. In a world where, for better for worse, peace between East and West depends so heavily on mutual deterrence through a balance of terror, questions such as 'how safe are we?' and 'how secure is the prospect of peace in our time?' reduce ultimately to questions about the stability of the balance of terror. How reliable is it? How durable? How dependable?

It is convenient to consider this question of stability under two headings 'intrinsic' and 'dynamic'.

Under the first heading we will consider what conditions are likely to make the balance of terror intrinsically stable (or unstable) and inherently likely (or unlikely) to keep the world at peace – what combinations of political attitudes, strategic postures and weapon systems. We will consider also to what extent the conditions for maximising stability are fulfilled in practice and how serious the threats to stability are. Chapters 6 to 9 address these issues. The Appendix presents an algebraic summary.

Under the second heading, we will move beyond the static analysis and consider how war might in practice occur, or be prevented from occurring, in dynamic, real-world situations. We will touch on conflict scenarios, escalation, crisis management, extended deterrence and the possibility of limiting nuclear war. Chapters 10 to 12 address this group of dynamic issues.

PRELIMINARY EXPOSITION

If a system of mutual deterrence is to be intrinsically stable, each side must effectively deter the other from opening hostilities. Correspondingly, each side must perceive the risks involved in opening or provoking hostilities himself as outweighing decisively any risks he might avoid, or advantages he might obtain. Effective deterrence by the one side consists precisely in causing the other side to perceive the risks in this way: such perceptions are the medium of deterrence. If each side succeeds in creating the necessary perceptions of risk by the other, then both should be deterred from opening hostilities.

Consistently with this, the minimum requirements for stability can be summarised as follows:

(i)   Each of the two sides must be risk-averse.
(ii) There must exist for each of them a level of damage which they regard as totally unacceptable.
(iii) Each must believe that, if he himself were to open hostilities, the enemy would still have the ability, and possibly the will, to inflict this unacceptable level of damage on him in retaliation.
(iv) Each must also believe that the risks involved in opening hostilities, even in the form of a pre-emptive strike, decisively exceed those involved in *not* opening hostilities.

In theory the system should work even if the beliefs at (iii) and (iv) above are false. In practice there can be little assurance of stability through time unless each side actually possesses the capabilities which the other side ascribes to him and has reasonably reliable means of monitoring and assessing the other's capabilities.

These minimum conditions for stability depend on the perceived capability of each side to inflict an *absolute* level of damage which the other side would find unacceptable – a capability which has come to be known as an 'assured destruction' capability.[1] In a rational world, they might also be sufficient conditions. But in the real world behaviour is more complex. Especially in situations of international tension, governments may be prepared to take risks which are strictly irrational. Their behaviour may be influenced, not just by the absolute amount of damage which they would risk suffering, but also by their perception of the *relative* amounts of damage which the enemy and the home country would suffer in a full-scale conflict, by deeply entrenched rivalries and suspicions, by wounded pride and loss of face, and by sheer misunderstanding. Hence there can never be a watertight guarantee that hostilities will be avoided – just a higher or a lower probability – and other factors which tend to enhance stability may be of the utmost importance as well as the minimum conditions at (i) to (iv) above. The following factors, in particular, are likely to be important:

(v) The total military strengths of the two sides, offensive and defensive, and their over-all war-fighting capabilities, should broadly balance each other: neither side should be confident of winning a conflict, in the sense of emerging from it in a significantly stronger position than the enemy.

(vi) There should be well-established procedures for communication and consultation between the two sides, especially at times of tension and crisis, and preferably an established tradition of negotiation as well.

The conditions set out above are in practice more complex, and more exacting, than may appear at first sight. The rest of this chapter and the next chapter discuss the main elements at some length – risk aversion, unacceptable damage, perceptions, the will to retaliate, intelligence, communications and military aspects, including the incentive to strike first.

We note first an important gloss which applies to the whole of the analysis in these chapters. Just as there can be no absolute guarantee of avoiding war, however intrinsically stable the balance of terror may be, so it is by no means inevitable that war must break out if the balance of terror should become unstable, or contain unstable features. The two sides may be 'self-deterred': they may simply have no wish to strike each other, or they may feel inhibited by moral and political considerations, quite apart from the system of mutual deterrence. Thus the Soviet Union chose not to strike at China when the Chinese nuclear programme was in its infancy, even though the ability of the Chinese to retaliate has so far been limited and relatively few Soviet weapons might have sufficed, at an earlier stage, to decimate the Chinese nuclear forces. It seems more than possible that the United States and the Soviet Union would in practice feel similarly inhibited from striking each other, even if the system of mutual deterrence between the two superpowers did become unstable and neither side felt deterred by the other from opening the striking. We must hope that this is so. For in that case destabilising developments in the balance of terror need not necessarily lead to the disaster of war, and the world can only be a safer place.

Be that as it may, the importance of preserving stability in the balance of terror can hardly be exaggerated. To say that instability *need* not lead to war is not to say that it *will* not lead to war; and there is no question that the likelihood of war must be enormously reduced by a stable balance of terror in which each side believes that policies of aggression are far too risky to contemplate and far more risky than policies of non-aggression.

RISK-AVERSION AND UNACCEPTABLE DAMAGE

As noted already, deterrence depends on perceptions of risk and on judgements as to what levels of damage would be unacceptable. If either side were prepared to suffer, or run a considerable risk of suffering, damage on the massive scale implied by strategic nuclear conflict, there would be no assurance that he would be deterred from opening hostilities. There would likewise be no assurance that the balance of terror would work. In short, the system would be unstable. The danger of conflict would be especially acute if the side in question thought he would emerge from a conflict in a stronger position than his opponent.

The attitude of each side towards risk has two principal dimensions. The first is the level of damage to the home country which each side is prepared to contemplate. The greater that level is, the less stable the system of mutual deterrence is likely to be. History suggests that countries may be willing to suffer very considerable amounts of damage provided that the causes at stake are perceived to be major ones. Equally, however, there are likely to be for most, if not all, countries levels of damage which they regard as totally unacceptable, whatever the issues at stake.[2] It will usually be difficult to define the borderline between acceptable and unacceptable levels of damage precisely, regardless of surrounding circumstances. But most countries, if not all, would probably regard damage on the scale they would be liable to suffer in a full-scale nuclear attack by a superpower as being totally and unequivocally unacceptable, either to suffer or to risk significantly. It is this that distinguishes the present balance of terror from earlier, less effective, balances of power between nations. It is this that brings, correspondingly, a far greater presumption of stability.

The second dimension is the pure 'risk-aversion' of the two sides – the extent to which they are prepared to run the risk of suffering any given degree of damage, and in particular 'unacceptable' damage. Different countries may have similar views on what levels of damage are unacceptable and yet differ in their willingness to gamble. One country may be more willing than another to discount what he perceives to be a small probability of suffering unacceptable damage. 'Pure' risk-aversion, in this sense, is of great importance. The more willing either side is to take risks, to call bluff to gamble on the other's unwillingness to retaliate, the greater will be the danger of war by miscalculation. Contrariwise, the greater the risk-aversion of each side, the more stable the system will be.

Fortunately there is no evidence to suggest that either the United States or the Soviet Union regard the level of damage likely to result from a full scale nuclear conflict as acceptable, or that they would be prepared to run significant risks of sustaining such damage. Hence the present balance of terror probably has a high degree of built-in stability. But it remains possible that one side or the other (or both) may at some time perceive the risks involved in opening hostilities to be less than those involved in leaving to the other side the option of opening hostilities; and herein lies potentially at least, a considerable threat to stability which will loom large in later chapters.

PERCEIVED WILL TO RETALIATE

If either side were convinced that the other did not have the will to use his nuclear weapons, even in retaliation, then once again the system of mutual deterrence could break down. The side in question might in theory be tempted to launch an offensive.

It is fortunate that such a complete breakdown in the system is unlikely. The side which contemplates aggression might think it rather improbable that the other side would retaliate with nuclear weapons. But the risks involved in nuclear conflict are so appalling that he would need to feel virtually certain that the other side would not retaliate in this way before he could rationally decide to open the striking; and in the nature of things it is difficult to conceive how any side could ever have this degree of certainty about the enemy's reactions.

Much more would be required than a few ill-judged remarks of a pacifist nature by a President of the United States, for example, to give the Soviets the necessary degree of conviction about American responses. It is just about possible to imagine a situation where a new President of the United States had been elected on a pacifist platform and the Soviets received confirmation through covert intelligence reports that the new policy was genuinely one of non-retaliation, whatever the provocation might be. Even in an unlikely scenario of this kind, however, the Soviets could hardly count on non-retaliation. The American President himself would not know for sure what his actual reaction to a Soviet attack would be, bearing n mind all the political pressures upon him. Short of such an unlikely scenario, moreoever, the side contemplating aggression is virtually bound to retain a degree of uncertainty about the reactions of the other side which should more than suffice to deter him from opening the striking. Herein lies another great strength of the balance of terror.

A more realistic possibility, which chapter 7 discusses at some length, s that one side might conclude from his assessment of the enemy's will (or lack of it) that, provided that he himself refrained from using nuclear weapons, he could launch a political offensive, possibly accompanied by use of conventional military force, without provoking the other side to use nuclear weapons. This belief might embolden him to push his quest for unilateral advantage beyond tolerable limits and thus provoke an escalation of crisis which could end in a major conflict.

From the standpoint of intrinsic stability, there are two important points to be made about such a scenario. The first is that provocative acts will be deterred, and stability consequently enhanced, if each side succeeds in conveying to the other that he has the necessary will and resolution to fight, and in particular to use his nuclear weapons, if sufficiently provoked; and contrariwise stability will be reduced if either side gives an impression of doubting whether there are any circumstances in which he would be prepared to use nuclear weapons. That is not to say that deterrence will be most effectively achieved, and stability most effectively enhanced, by a posture of maximum belligerence: on the contrary, such a posture could increase the other side's fear that war is inevitable and hence his incentive to strike pre-emptively so as to deny the home country the advantages of striking first. The best posture must be one which indicates maximum firmness of purpose and willingness to retaliate if attacked or provoked, without at the same time conveying an undue impression of bellicosity.

> HAMLET : I prithee take thy fingers from my throat;
> For, though I am not splenitive and rash,
> Yet have I in me something dangerous,
> Which let thy wiseness fear.

We noted in chapter 5 the importance of sending the correct signals to the enemy and the dangers involved if Western leaders leave doubts in the enemy's mind about their will and resolution.

The second point is that a country's will to fight, both actual and perceived, and in particular its willingness to retaliate against an enemy who has struck first, must depend on its military capabilities, both in absolute terms and relative to those of the enemy. The military dimension is thus crucial, not only in its own right, but also because of its effects on political will.

INTELLIGENCE

Since mutual deterrence depends directly on each side's perceptions of the other side's intentions and capabilities, rather than his actual intentions and capabilities, the ability of each side to monitor and assess developments on the other side has a special importance.

There may be circumstances in which false beliefs about the other side's capabilities will enhance stability. In general, however, provided that each side in fact has the capability to inflict damage which the other would find unacceptable, stability is likely to be enhanced if each side is well informed about the other.

That is not to say that each side should be perfectly informed. A degree of uncertainty can sometimes enhance perceptions of risk and hence deterrence and stability. But if one side is extremely uncertain about the other's capabilities and intentions, and has no means of finding out about them, the resulting fears and suspicions are more likely to upset than enhance stability. Periodic 'discoveries' about the enemy's dispositions, whether true or false, will tend to be unsettling and destabilising.

Surveillance by reconnaissance satellites has enabled each side in recent years to obtain a good knowledge of the numbers and location of the other's land-based forces and bases. Such surveillance has also made it difficult for either side to prepare a surprise attack on the other without being detected. All this has contributed powerfully to stability. Deployment of 'killer' satellites and other developments which reduce the effectiveness of surveillance would undoubtedly detract from stability. There may in principle, therefore, be scope for the United States and the Soviet Union to agree not to interfere with each other's reconnaissance satellites, difficult though it would be for either side to trust the other to honour such an agreement in the event of conflict.

Invaluable as they are, reconnaissance satellites reveal little or nothing about such crucial matters as weapons performance, strategy and political intentions. Hence other forms of intelligence – public and clandestine – are important for stability as well. Clandestine intelligence activities can be a source of friction and distrust between countries; but neither East nor West are likely in practice to abandon such activities and the ignorance and distrust which would result from having no reliable information on the other side's counsels and dispositions would probably be even more dangerous.

COMMUNICATIONS

The importance of good channels of communication between the two superpowers has been generally recognised since the Cuban missile crisis of 1962. Stability is likely to be significantly enhanced by satisfactory arrangements for communication, consultation and the general conduct of relations between the two sides.

One of the great lessons of history is that wars can all too easily begin from misjudgements of the other side's intentions and false beliefs as to his capabilities, exacerbated by poor mutual communications. Hence the great leaps forward which have been made in these areas in recent years are to be welcomed – the agreement after the Cuban missile crisis to establish a 'hot line' between the United States and the Soviet Union, the agreements on procedures in the event of nuclear accidents, and the agreements of the 1970s on consultation in times of tension and confidence building measures, including exchanges of observers on military exercises.[3]

For the West any such agreements have dangers, as indeed does the whole environment of peaceful coexistence and détente. An ambience of détente may breed complacency. And complacency may lead to under-provision for defence and deficiencies of military preparedness. On balance, however, the reduction in overt belligerence, the tradition of direct negotiation with the other side and the improvements in mutual communications have contributed powerfully to stability in recent years.

7 Military Capabilities

FIRST AND SECOND STRIKES, COUNTER-FORCE AND COUNTER-CITY[1]

We come now to the military dimensions of the balance of terror. It may be helpful to begin by recalling the distinctions between 'first strike' and 'second strike', between 'counter-force' and 'counter-value' or 'counter-city'.

The side which attacks first with nuclear weapons is said to make the 'first strike'. The other side's response is described as the 'second strike'. We shall use the word 'strike' throughout to refer to attacks with nuclear warheads and in particular with warheads delivered by long-range 'strategic' ballistic missiles, cruise missiles or bombers (see figures 7.1 and 7.2).[2]

A strike directed against military targets, such as nuclear bases and silos, is called 'counter-force'. A strike directed against civilian targets, such as cities, industrial complexes, power stations or bridges, is called 'counter-value' or 'counter-city'. For convenience, we use the latter term throughout.

Counter-force weapons need to be more accurate and to carry warheads of greater explosive yield[3] than counter-city weapons. Military targets are relatively small, and are often protected, or 'hardened', by silos or other forms of concrete shelter (hence the term 'hard' targets): they are therefore more difficult to destroy than unprotected 'soft' targets, such as cities or industrial complexes. The degree of 'overpressure' in the vicinity of the target created by the blast wave from the exploding warhead needs to be much greater than in the case of civilian targets.[4] Overpressure is a decreasing function of distance from the point of detonation and an increasing function of warhead yield: hence the critical importance, in a counter-force strike, of target accuracy in conjunction with warhead yield.[5] For counter-city strikes, accuracy is less crucial and large warhead yields are 'uneconomic' in terms of areas of damage caused.[6]

The distinction between counter-force and counter-city, like that between first and second strikes, will play a prominent part in the analysis which follows. In the real world, however, the distinction will typically be less clear-cut than in the world of theory. Missile silos and bases, for example, may be located close to towns, so that 'counter-force' strikes might well damage civilian communities as well as military targets. In addition, strikes against centres of government, or command and control centres, would be likely to present the attacker with some of the same kind of military problems as counter-force targets; but the victim would be quite likely to perceive such attacks as counter-city strikes and react accordingly. None of this invalidates the analysis; but it complicates the practical applications in ways which we shall discuss.

SECOND-STRIKE CAPABILITY TO INFLICT UNACCEPTABLE DAMAGE

From a military standpoint, stability in a balance of terror between two rival nuclear powers requires, first and foremost, that each must perceive the other to be capable of inflicting an unacceptable level of damage on him, not only in a first strike but also, and more importantly, in a second strike. Just as there must be for each side a level of damage which he regards as unacceptable (see chapter 6), so each side must possess, and be seen to possess, the military and technical capability to inflict that level of damage on his opponent, even if he has previously suffered a full-scale attack by his opponent. If this minimum requirement is fulfilled, the perceived risks in opening hostilities, or 'striking first', should more than suffice to deter both sides.

The unacceptable damage with which we are here concerned relates primarily to civilian and industrial, not military, targets. The more able each side is to inflict unacceptable damage on such targets, the more catastrophic a full-scale conflict would be and the less inclined either side should be to risk provoking such a conflict.

The ability of the two sides to inflict unacceptable damage on each other's cities in a second strike can be seen to comprise two key elements. Both sides need nuclear forces which are capable of:

(a)   surviving a first strike by the other's nuclear forces, and then
(b)   penetrating the other's defences and inflicting a level of damage on his cities which he would find unacceptable.

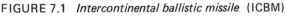

FIGURE 7.1 *Intercontinental ballistic missile* (ICBM)

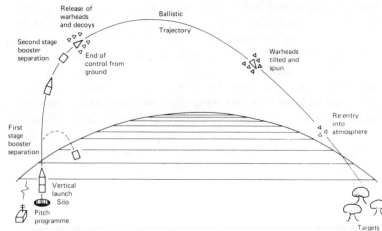

Artist's impression of a two-stage, land-based ICBM, with inertial guidance. One rocket is superimposed on another to boost velocity (maximum, about 15 000 mph) and range (7000-8000 nautical miles). Maximum height above the earth is about 700 miles; time spent above the earth's atmosphere, about 20 minutes; total flight time, about 30 minutes.

Ballistic missiles use inertial guidance systems based on gyroscopes and accelerometers, which sense changes in direction and velocity in three axes – roll, pitch and yaw. Target accuracy has improved markedly in recent years: the circular error probable (CEP) of the American MX ICBM is expected to be only some 300 feet.

Launch is vertical. After four minutes, about 55 miles up, the missile is tilted towards the target in accordance with a pre-planned flight path. When the required velocity and direction are achieved, the final-stage rocket engine shuts down, the nose-cone falls away, and the post-boost vehicle or 'bus' pushes off its cargo of independently targeted warheads or re-entry vehicles (RVs) and decoys. The warheads then follow free-fall, ballistic trajectories to their targets during the remaining 'mid-course' and 'terminal' stages of the flight. Ground control can influence ICBMs for only the first 10 per cent or thereabouts of their total flight time. They contain no 'destruct' mechanism for fear of vulnerability to electronic counter-measures (ECM).

In submarines, information on starting positions and direction is necessarily less precise than in land-based systems. To improve accuracy, therefore, the new-generation American SLBMs will have mid-course guidance systems based on star-sighting. The latest intermediate-range ballistic missiles have terminal homing systems which use radar and on-board computers to guide missile to target.

FIGURE 7.2 *Ground-launched cruise missile (GLCM)*

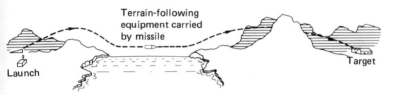

Artist's impression of a ground-launched cruise missile. In contrast with ballistic missiles, cruise missiles travel slowly (usually below the speed of sound) and at low altitudes (usually between 50 and 300 feet) beneath conventional radar cover. As the name suggests, they cruise in the atmosphere like pilotless aircraft and breathe air into their small, turbofan jet engines instead of using rocket fuel with its own oxidising agent. For any given amount of thrust, they need only a third of the weight of fuel of ballistic missiles and are much cheaper. New-generation American cruise missiles are mobile and are capable of delivering single warheads over ranges of upwards of 1500 miles.

A navigation system of 'terrain contour mapping' (TERCOM), developed in the United States, has produced remarkable target accuracy: a circular error probable of only some 50 feet. The system comprises an inertial platform, altimeters to measure heights above the surface and above sea level, and an on-board computer. Information about the starting point, the target and checkpoints on the way is fed into the computer. With the aid of the inertial guidance platform and the altimeters, the computer then ensures that the missile follows the contours associated with the correct flight path. From the final checkpoint the missile proceeds to target by inertial guidance, but digital scene-matching terminal guidance is under development.

It is clear that if either of the two sides lacked either of these capabilities the balance of terror would no longer be stable. There would no longer be any presumption that they would be deterred from opening hostilities. Thus, if the second-strike forces of either side were so vulnerable that the other side felt confident of wiping them out in a first strike, then (for reasons discussed below) both sides would have positive incentives to strike first. Similarly, if either side felt confident of his ability to protect his cities against attack, he would no longer be deterred from opening hostilities by the fear of suffering unacceptable damage: there would indeed no longer be a balance of terror.

In practice no country has yet found any effective means of defending its cities against enemy missiles carrying nuclear weapons. In addition, submarine-launched ballistic missiles (SLBMs) have turned out so far to be near-perfect second strike weapons, combining substantial 'survivability', or invulnerability to attack, with highly effective counter-city (but not counter-force) capabilities.[7] Since SLBMs were developed, therefore, it has been comparatively easy for nuclear countries to have an assured capability to inflict unacceptable damage on each other's cities in a second strike. The United States and the Soviet Union (and, on a smaller scale, Britain and France) have possessed such capabilities for a considerable period of years[8] and there is a high probability that they will continue to do so (see below). The first, crucial military requirement for stability in the balance of terror has therefore been fulfilled so far and will probably continue to be so in the foreseeable future.

ALTERNATIVE FORMULATIONS

The key requirements for stability discussed above – the possession by each side of second-strike forces which can survive, penetrate and destroy cities – can be alternatively formulated in terms of offensive or defensive capabilities. In terms of *offensive* capabilities, stability will be maximised if the two sides combine:

(a) weak counter-force capabilities, such that the other side's nuclear forces would survive a first strike in sufficient numbers to inflict unacceptable damage in retaliation, with

(b) strong counter-city capabilities, providing an assured ability to penetrate the other's defences and destroy his cities.

The eschewing of counter-force capabilities was a central tenet of the 'assured destruction' theories developed in the 1960s.[9]

In terms of *defensive* capabilities, the position is the obverse, or 'dual', of that on offensive capabilities. Stability will be maximised if the two sides combine:

(a)   a strong capability to defend their nuclear forces against attack, with

(b)   a weak capability to defend their cities.

In other words, cities should be vulnerable; nuclear forces, invulnerable. The eschewing of city defences was another central tenet of the 'assured destruction' theories.[10]

One corollary of the key principle that each side must be able to inflict an unacceptable level of damage on the other's cities, even in a *second* strike, is that neither side must have a decisive advantage in a *first* strike, such that he could destroy the other's capacity to deliver unacceptable damage in retaliation. A second corollary is that neither side should be able to protect his cities against unacceptable damage. The remainder of this chapter will discuss in some depth these critical questions of first-striker's advantage and city defences.

FIRST-STRIKER'S ADVANTAGE AND THE INCENTIVE TO STRIKE FIRST

Of all the threats to stability in a balance of terror, none is more potentially serious than first-striker's advantage. If either side judged that by striking first at the other side's nuclear forces he could incapacitate the other side to the point where he would be unable or unwilling to deliver unacceptable damage in retaliation, the balance of terror would become highly unstable. The side in question would not only not be deterred from opening the striking; he could also have positive incentives to strike first – both the 'offensive' incentive of gaining ascendancy over the other side and the 'defensive' incentive of enhancing his own security by preventing the other side from striking him first.

It may be useful to consider these incentives, and the interactions between them, a little further. Let us suppose, first, that side A possesses a decisive advantage in a first strike (against B's nuclear forces), while side B does not. In this case, both A and B may be tempted to strike first. B may be tempted to forestall a first strike by A which would leave him at A's mercy and powerless to retaliate; while A may be tempted both to gain ascendancy over B and to forestall any such forestalling strike by B.

If B, too, has the ability to cripple A in a first strike against A's nuclear forces, then the situation will be even more unstable. For each side will have two incentives for striking first – not only the incentive of crippling the other side but also the even more powerful 'damage-limitation' incentive of forestalling, or pre-empting, a crippling strike by the other side. In situations of international tension the temptation to launch a pre-emptive strike could be powerful: a point could be reached where war (or nuclear war) seemed inevitable and the risks involved in *not* striking first appeared to outweigh those involved in striking first.

Implicit in the above analysis are two points of importance about first strikes. The first is that they are virtually certain to be directed against military, not civilian, targets (counter-force, not counter-city). The second is that the side which strikes first will have a strong incentive to deliver as devastating and incapacitating a strike as he can muster (though that is not to say that he will necessarily do so).

Taking these points in order, the first-striker's incentive to strike first turns exclusively on his ability to destroy the enemy's offensive forces without using up all of his own in the process. His primary concern must be to alter the balance of power decisively in his own favour and/or to prevent the other side from reaping a corresponding advantage. This points unequivocally to striking the other side's military strike forces, rather than his cities. The first striker will want, in addition, to achieve these objectives with minimum damage to his own country. In particular, he will be anxious to do all he can to prevent escalation of the conflict to civilian targets, since his own cities will then be at risk. This again points to directing a first strike against military targets with the aim of removing the other side's ability to retaliate, or at least weakening it to the point where he will feel compelled to negotiate. In the hope of keeping the conflict clear of civilian targets, the first striker is likely to be as scrupulous as he can be about confining his strike to military targets. He may include field command and control centres among these targets; but he will probably avoid attacks on centres of government (as well as counter-city attacks generally) since these would be likely to be perceived by the other side as counter-city strikes and provoke retaliation in kind against the first striker's own cities.

In contrast with the above there is little incentive, and indeed considerable disincentive, to strike first against civilian targets: little incentive, because the enemy would retain his means of retaliation; and considerable disincentive, because he would be virtually bound to retaliate in kind against the first striker's own cities.

It is just about possible to conceive of a situation in which one side might be tempted, albeit as a second best policy, to strike first against civilian targets. Thus, to develop the first of the scenarios outlined earlier, side A might possess the capability to destroy side B's nuclear forces altogether. B, on the other hand, might have no significant counter-force capability and yet be able to inflict massive damage on easier, civilian targets. B might then be persuaded that A was on the point of destroying both his (B's) nuclear forces and his cities as well. In such circumstances B might decide to launch his own forces before A could eliminate them, with a view to destroying as many of A's cities as he could. It would arguably be irrational, however, for B to react in this way. For attacking A's cities would maximise the risk that A would destroy his (B's) cities. The scenario anyway bears no resemblance to the actual strategic configurations of the superpowers: neither of them is as powerful as A, or as vulnerable as B.

The analysis confirms our earlier conclusion that strong counter-force capabilities may detract from stability (by providing all parties with an incentive to strike first), while effective defence of nuclear strike forces should enhance stability (by reducing or removing the incentive to strike first). In contrast with this, stability will be enhanced by strong counter-city capabilities (which increase the risks associated with war) and reduced by effective city defences (which would lessen these risks).

Our second point about first strikes was that a first striker will have a strong incentive to make his strike as devastating and incapacitating as he can. As suggested earlier, he is likely to perceive his interest to lie in reducing as much as possible his opponent's capacity to retaliate. He would be defeating his own object if he were to deliver a less than full-scale strike and thus leave the enemy with an ability to retaliate greater than it need have been.

The above is not intended to imply that the first striker is *bound* to launch a massive, all-out, counter-force strike. He will be keenly conscious of the consequences for his own country if his first strike should fail to incapacitate the other side. He may also be deeply fearful of the climatic consequences of a large-scale nuclear exchange for his own and other countries (see the discussion of the 'nuclear winter' hypothesis in chapter 13). In the dynamic conditions of crisis, it is much more likely that the side introducing nuclear weapons would begin in a scrupulously circumscribed way. He might have suffered serious reverses in conventional fighting. He might decide to respond to these by using a strictly limited number of smaller 'tactical' nuclear weapons with the aim of signalling readiness to escalate the crisis to the highest levels of force, rather than submit to defeat, and thus compelling the enemy to stop and think again.[11] Even in such a scenario, however, a really powerful first-striker's advantage at the strategic level could heighten the dangers. The greater the advantage to the first striker at the strategic level, the more tempted each side might be to escalate quickly to an all-out strike and deny this advantage to the other side.

For all the reasons discussed, a *strong* incentive to strike first at the strategic level, based on a *decisive* first-striker's advantage, would seriously threaten the stability of the balance of terror. It would tend both to make nuclear conflict more probable and to hasten escalation to the highest force level in conflicts which have begun at lower force levels. The potential dangers are clearly enormous.

The actual dangers should not, however, be exaggerated. The words 'strong' and 'decisive' are important. The first-striker's advantage would need to be really decisive before the threat to stability would become acute. If one of the superpowers were convinced that he could incapacitate the other totally, by destroying all his ICBMs on land, all his SLBMs in the oceans and at port, and all his bombers in the air and at their bases, with only minor exceptions, he might then feel that he could strike first without serious risk to his own cities. If both superpowers were so convinced, the dangers would be mutliplied. But neither superpower possesses anything remotely resembling such capabilities at present – even against Britain and France, much less against each other. Both have massive SLBM forces capable of surviving a first strike and destroying each other's main centres of population. Neither could reckon to wipe out the other's SLBM forces in a first strike. Neither could even reckon to wipe out more than a substantial proportion of the other's land-based ICBMs and bombers.

Looking ahead, the prospects that either side will develop a genuinely incapacitating first-strike capability in the foreseeable future likewise look extremely remote. There are many steps which could be taken, if necessary, to reduce or negate first-striker's advantage. A limited degree of first-striker's advantage, moreoever, need not be especially dangerous. It may even, paradoxically, contribute to stability by reinforcing deterrence against conventional attack. The next few sections examine these matters in more detail.

COUNTER-FORCE EXCHANGE RATES

The existence or otherwise of first-striker's advantage depends on the numbers and properties of the weapon systems of each side. More specifically, it depends on the number of missiles which the first striker possesses; on their ranges, success rates and accuracy; on the number, size and targeting possibilities of the warheads which they carry, including the scope for hitting several targets simultaneously; and on the number, properties, deployment and defences of the other side's missiles.[12]

All these properties can be summarised in terms of (a) the total numbers of weapons possessed by each side and (b), the *exchange rates* between the number of missiles or warheads used by the side which strikes and the number of enemy missiles or warheads destroyed. If the first striker can reckon to destroy on average only one enemy missile with each missile he launches (an exchange rate of unity), he will have no incentive to strike first unless his total arsenal of nuclear weapons significantly exceeds that of the enemy or he wants to pre-empt a first-striker's advantage possessed by the enemy. If, on the other hand, he can reckon to destroy on average as many as three enemy missiles with each missile he launches (an exchange rate of three), his incentive to strike first may be considerable. In practice, given the multiple, independently-targeted or manoeuvrable warheads (MIRVs or MARVs) of modern missiles and their extraordinary accuracy, the expected exchange rate for an attack against land-based weapons is likely, over the next few years at least, to be favourable to the attacker (greater than unity) and thus provide a certain incentive to strike first.

The exchange rate on which attention is usually focused is that which applies for a first strike by each side. Also important, however, is the exchange rate which would apply for a second strike by each side, after absorbing the enemy's first-strike. The SLBM second-strike forces of the two sides have not in the past been sufficiently powerful or accurate for a counter-force role. They have been primarily counter-city weapons. But that is likely to change in the future.[13] Moreover, neither side could possibly rely at present, or in the foreseeable future, on being able to destroy the whole of the other side's land-based counter-force capability in a first strike (see further below). The calculation by each side of his first-striker's advantage needs therefore to take account of the counter-force potential of the other side's surviving strike capabilities.

THE DEVELOPMENT OF COUNTER-FORCE CAPABILITIES

Historically, neither the United States nor the Soviet Union have in recent years possessed anything approaching an overwhelming first-striker's advantage in the sense of an ability to incapacitate the other side totally in a first strike and remove his means of retaliation. On the other hand, the two sides have developed and are continuing to develop, significant counter-force capabilities against fixed-point targets – notably, each other's land-based ICBMs and bomber and submarine bases – and these capabilities have given them a considerable, and increasing, degree of first-striker's advantage.

In the United States, the 'assured destruction' theorists foresaw the problem of first-striker's advantage in the mid-to-late 1960s. They hoped to prevent it from ever arising by means of a mutual understanding between East and West, overt or tacit, to eschew the development of counter-force capabilities. They argued that the United States should forswear development of counter-force capabilities and that the Soviets might then follow suit. They looked with disfavour on any developments in weapon systems which increased target accuracy, weapon yield or the number of independently targeted warheads per missile, on the grounds that such developments would increase the weapons' counter-force potential.

With the wisdom of hindsight, it was doubtless wishful thinking to imagine that, in deference to a strategic theory which the Soviet Union, at least, has probably never accepted, the two sides would forswear by tacit agreement the important improvements in weapon systems made possible by continuing technological progress. As time has passed, it has become increasingly clear that such agreements will not solve the problem. Neither the Soviets nor, in practice, the Americans themselves have abstained from technological improvements which would increase the counter-force potential of their nuclear arsenals.

The Soviets have clearly felt no inhibitions about developing a counter-force capability. In the latter part of the 1960s they had already begun to deploy SS-9 ICBMs with warheads of enormous yield – far greater than required for civilian targets and far greater than the American Minuteman.[14] They then proceeded, like the Americans, to improve target accuracy and to develop multiple warheads (MRV), followed from 1973 onwards by independently targeted warheads (MIRVs) for the SS-9 and its successors. The Soviets have thus achieved a potentially formidable counter-force capability against American land-based ICBM silos and other fixed-point targets in the United States and elsewhere.[15]

In the United States the assured-destruction philosophy, which sought in the interests of stability to restrict strike capabilities permanently to civilian targets and frowned on the development of counter-force capabilities, as well as on city defences, has exercised a powerful but diminishing influence on successive administrations. The Minuteman and Polaris systems developed by the Kennedy/Johnson administrations in the early 1960s were specifically tailored to the counter-city role: warhead yields were relatively low; delivery systems, inaccurate.[16] By the end of the 1960s these forces no longer looked adequate in comparison with the SS-9s and other Soviet systems, with their enormously greater explosive power; and the deployment of anti-ballistic missile (ABM) defences around Moscow raised anxieties as to the ability of American missiles to penetrate Soviet defences. Successive administrations perceived, accordingly, a need to upgrade the United States' capabilities. As noted in chapter 2, President Nixon raised the further question in 1970: should the mass destruction of enemy cities be the President's only option for retaliating against a nuclear attack?[17] Defence Secretary Schlesinger's answer was that the President must not be faced with a stark choice between destroying enemy cities and doing nothing in response to such an attack, but must have other options as well. Successive administrations came increasingly to recognise the need for a broader range of nuclear targeting options – and in particular for a spectrum of capabilities for more limited responses to aggression, including capabilities against military installations and hard targets – while still denying any deliberate intention to develop an incapacitating first-strike capability.

In response to these anxieties and changing perceptions of need, the United States has carried out substantial programmes for upgrading its nuclear forces since the end of the 1960s. These upgradings have taken three main forms – the introduction of multiple independently-targeted warheads (MIRVs), improvements in target accuracy, and higher explosive yields in MIRV warheads. The first generation ICBMs and SLBMs carried large single warheads. Polaris missiles were then equipped in the mid-1960s with triple warheads (MRV) aimed at the same target.[18] Much more significant was the introduction of independent targeting of multiple warheads (MIRVs) from the early 1970s:[19] this increased many times the number of targets which could be covered by any single missile. The Minuteman 3 has 3 MIRV warheads per missile; Poseidon, 10 per missile; Trident I, 8 per missile. The new MX 'Peacekeeper' ICBM[20] has 10 warheads per missile, and the new Trident II or D-5[21] is expected to have up to 14. Increases in target accuracy have been hardly less important. Improved guidance systems have reportedly reduced the 'circular error probable' of the Minuteman 3 to around 600-700 feet, and the corresponding figures for MX and the D-5 are expected to be some 300 and 400 feet respectively.[22] In other words, there is estimated to be a 50 per cent chance that the centre of the area destroyed by the warhead will be within 600-700, 300 and 400 feet, respectively, of the target point. As to explosive yields, the latest Minuteman 3 warheads are reported to yield about 350 kilotons,[23] and MX warheads about half a megaton. The new D-5 SLBM warheads are variously reported as yielding 150 or 350 kilotons. The higher explosive yields of the latest warheads and the improved target accuracy of the missiles are giving the United States a formidable counter-force capability. The combination of this with multiple independently-targeted warheads (MIRVs) has opened up the possibility of knocking out several Soviet missiles with every missile launched from the home country. This in turn implies a favourable counter-force exchange rate for a first strike against fixed point military targets, and a degree of first-striker's advantage to match that already obtained by the Soviets. In theory, but probably not in practice, each side should be able in the second half of the 1980s to destroy virtually all the other's land-based missiles in a first strike.

For the reasons discussed earlier, a really decisive first-striker's advantage would make the balance of terror highly unstable. Hence it must be a matter for concern that both sides should have developed or be developing a substantial first-striker's advantage. That is not to say, however, that the balance of terror is likely to be particularly unstable by the late 1980s. For neither side is likely to develop in this period – or indeed at any time in the foreseeable future – anything like an overwhelming advantage.

The reasons for this are twofold. The first is that the first-striker's advantage of each side will relate primarily to land-based forces. Each side would be likely to retain most of its SLBM and bomber forces after absorbing a first strike, and these surviving forces would provide a more than ample capability to inflict unacceptable damage in a second, retaliatory strike.

The second is that neither side could be confident of anything like total success in wiping out even the other's land-based ICBMs in a full-scale first strike. Such an operation would be both gigantic and unrehearsed. Neither side has practised sending even a single missile against the other's homeland, much less a barrage of missiles more or less simultaneously. There must be a high probability that performance, in both delivery systems and warheads, would fall well short of specification. One recent study has concluded that, on present technology at least, Soviet planners could not be confident of destroying significantly more than half of the current American ICBM force.[24] Some missiles (or warheads) would probably fail altogether, while others would be likely to fall wide of target. A particularly serious hazard is that some of the warheads, as they exploded, would be likely to destroy or deflect others ('fratricide') while climatic conditions would deflect others. Even in the unlikely event that the whole operation went perfectly, the other side would probably retain a significant capability to strike back against military targets (thus reducing the first-striker's advantage). In the far more likely event that much went wrong, the other side's capability to strike back against military targets could be very substantial indeed.

For all these reasons, neither side is likely to see himself in the foreseeable future as possessing the kind of overwhelming and incapacitating first-striker's advantage which would make the balance of terror seriously unstable. There is thus no particular cause for alarm. But still less is there cause for complacency. Even a less than overwhelming first-striker's advantage has its dangers. One cannot rule out the possibility that, in the fraught conditions of international crisis, one side or the other might convince himself that nuclear war was inevitable sooner or later. In such circumstances the existence of even a less than overwhelming advantage could encourage him to open the striking. The world is therefore likely to be safer if the extent of first-striker's advantage can somehow be limited. The question is how this could be done.

WAYS OF REDUCING FIRST-STRIKER'S ADVANTAGE

As the possibilities of agreement, overt or tacit, to forswear technological progress have receded, it has become increasingly clear that the problem of limiting first-striker's advantage will need to be tackled in other ways. The solution must in principle lie in:

(a) reducing missile vulnerability (protecting missiles more effectively against attack, either by means of anti-ballistic and anti-cruise missile defences (ABM and ACM) and air defences, or by more effective 'hardening' or dispersal, or by making them mobile, or by relying on the relatively invulnerable SLBMs); or

(b) second-strike counterforce capabilities (developing an invulnerable 'second-strike' capability which would enable the victim of a first strike to respond by inflicting corresponding damage on the enemy's remaining ICBMs and other offensive missiles); or

(c) a 'launch on warning' policy (being prepared to launch nuclear weapons as soon as monitoring devices indicate an enemy attack and before his warheads reach their targets);

or in some combination of these.

To take these possible approaches in turn, deployment of ABM, ACM and air defences systems to protect land-based nuclear forces is in principle an attractive solution. If these missiles and bases were not vulnerable to attack, the problem of first-striker's advantage would disappear. But the technical problems in providing reliable protection for even a relatively small area, such as a missile site, are formidable. ABM systems as conceived

in the 1960s and 1970s called for a sophisticated combination of radar to
track incoming warheads, interceptor missiles to destroy them and computer
systems to analyse the data and control the launching of the interceptor
missiles. The costs of such systems would have been enormous; their
effectiveness, strictly limited. A sophisticated attacker would have little
difficulty in attacking or saturating the ABM radars or exhausting the
interceptor missiles by means of multiple MIRVed or MARVed warheads
and decoys. After much heated argument, and in response to strong
Congressional pressure, the Johnson administration decided in September
1967 to produce a light ABM system called 'Sentinel' for the protection
of cities against a small-scale attack from China. The Nixon administration
proposed, and Congress finally approved, in 1969, a more ambitious system
called 'Safeguard' for defending missile sites rather than cities. But American
experts became increasingly convinced at that time that ABM defences
in general were a 'mug's game'.[25] By 1972 both superpowers were willing
to agree on a treaty limiting their ABM deployments to two spatially
limited missile-defence complexes each, with no more than 100 non
reloadable interceptor missile launchers. In 1974 they agreed to reduce
the limit from two to one, and the United States is not, in practice
deploying the system to which it is entitled under the treaty. The Soviet
Union's system is deployed to protect Moscow, as being the national
command and control centre. Moscow is thus the only place in the world
to be served by a fully operational ABM system.

Looking ahead, there must continue to be serious doubts as to whether
really effective ABM defences will ever be possible. For the foreseeable
future, therefore, it is virtually certain that other means will need to be
found for protecting missiles and reducing first-striker's advantage. The
United States administration has launched a major programme of research
the 'Strategic Defence Initiative' (SDI), into a new, advanced technology
defensive system which would use lasers (and possibly particle beams) as
well as interceptor missiles to destroy incoming missiles. President Reagan
has spoken publicly in his 'star wars' speech of March 1983 and subsequently
of his hope that such systems will rid our planet of the scourge of nuclear
weapons. But it is far from clear, at the time of writing, how effective or
reliable such systems could be.[26] In times past the human mind has been
no less fertile in devising ways of overcoming defensive systems than in
devising the defensive systems themselves, and there must be a strong
chance that history will repeat itself. If, against the odds, President Reagan's
vision did come true – if really reliable ABM defences could be devised
for cities, as well as missile silos and bases – the consequences would be
far-reaching. The deterrent power of nuclear weapons would be largely

removed. East and West would need to find other ways of keeping the peace. We discuss these matters further in a later section of this chapter and in later chapters.

A second way of protecting land-based missiles would be through more effective 'hardening'. Proposals have been made in the United States for strengthening concrete silos with massive amounts of resilient reinforcing steel and even for building a giant missile base deep underground. It looks unlikely, however, that such approaches would provide a total solution.

A third means of reducing the vulnerability of land-based ICBMs (but not bases) to enemy attack is to make them *mobile* and thus more difficult for the enemy to target. This approach too has its problems. Mobility, and a multiple aim point system, were intended by the Carter administration to be key features of the new American MX ICBM. The plan was to construct no less than 4500 hardened shelters for 200 missiles and to move the missiles between the shelters without detection by enemy satellites.[27] The Soviets would not then know exactly where the missiles were at any particular time, and they would need to destroy all 4600 shelters in order to be sure of destroying all 200 missiles. As both the Carter and Reagan administrations have discovered, however, such a system would be extravagant in cost and use of land as well as being ineffective in the absence of an arms control agreement limiting warhead totals. The Reagan administration has adopted accordingly the 'second best' expedient of deploying the first 50 MX missiles in vulnerable Minuteman silos.

Mobility is likewise a feature of one version of the proposal for a single-warhead ICBM (SICBM), the so-called 'Midgetman', also under discussion in the United States.[28] The idea would be to place a small, light ICBM, with a single 350 kiloton warhead, on a hardened transporter. This mobility would make the missile much less vulnerable. Even a successful strike against the transporter would, moreoover, knock out only one warhead rather than a cluster of MIRVed warheads: as both sides have discovered, MIRVing may improve the home side's counter-force exchange rate but it has the disadvantage of improving the other side's counterforce exchange rate as well, by offering him richer targets. A rival school of thought, clearly influenced by the Carter administration's original plans for MX, argues for placing SICBMs in ordinary silos and having many more silos than missiles – an approach which would depend critically on preserving the secret of which silos contained the missiles and which did not. Other possibilities, again, which have not so far found favour, would include placing small ICBMs on merchant ships or in fixed point silos so widely spaced that an aggressor would need to use up one or more of his own missiles (or warheads) for each missile (or warhead) he destroyed and would therefore have no incentive to strike first. Yet another variation on the theme of mobility would be to develop an air-launched ballistic missile. None of these approaches, however, is free from technical or cost problems.

The Soviets, too, appear to see mobility as providing a likely solution to the problem of ICBM vulnerability. They are known to be testing a new, 10-warhead missile, the SSX-24, which would be transported on railway wagons. They are reportedly testing another new missile as well, in defiance of the SALT 2 provision – the lighter, 4-warhead SSX-25, which might be deployed on trucks.

The second broad approach to negating first-striker's advantage which we identified was the development of an invulnerable second-strike counter-force capability which would make it possible to retaliate in kind after absorbing a first counter-force strike by the enemy, and cripple his offensive forces to a similar extent. As discussed earlier, such an approach would require a combination of invulnerability and accuracy in missile systems which has not yet been achieved. The present second-strike forces of the United States and the Soviet Union are based mainly on submarine-launched ballistic missiles (SLBMs), though strategic bombers and air-launched cruise missiles (ALCMs),[29] surviving ICBMs and possibly intermediate range ballistic missiles would also play an important role. Submarines hiding on the ocean floor are much less vulnerable to attack than other missile launchers and, barring a major technological breakthrough in underwater detection, are likely to remain so. But their accuracy has not so far been sufficient for counter-force strikes, and this has limited their potential use to strikes against civilian targets, which cannot offset the first striker's advantage.

Present indications (see the preceding section) are that the new generation second-strike forces *will* have much greater accuracy and a significant counter-force capability – especially the American air-launched cruise missiles (ALCMs) and probably also the new generation of SLBMs. This should help to reduce first-striker's advantage. It would be difficult to offset the advantage altogether by these means. For the second striker would lack the benefit of surprise and would use up some of his second-strike force in the process of attacking what remained of the enemy's first-strike force. But the existence of second-strike counter-force capabilities should considerably reduce the potential first-striker's expectation of net advantage, and his perception of the risks involved in letting the other side strike first.

A system which depended on second-strike counter-force capabilities to offset first-striker's advantage would have several drawbacks compared with a system of effective missile defences. First, it would be less effective in removing first-striker's advantage. Second, it would give each side an incentive to build large numbers of weapons. The present system has a similar disadvantage. Third, it might also weaken deterrence by encouraging each side to expect that the other would respond to a first counter-force strike with a second counter-force strike, rather than a counter-city strike. The resulting 'exchange of Queens', though preferable to counter-city strikes, would far better be avoided. On the other hand, deployment of fully effective systems to protect ICBM installations seems unlikely in the foreseeable future. Second-strike counter-force capabilities are therefore likely to play a useful role for a considerable time ahead.

A more radical solution to the problem of first-striker's advantage would be to abandon land-based ICBMs altogether and rely exclusively on the less vulnerable bombers with ALCMs and, particularly, on SLBMs. If, as seems likely, SLBMs can be developed so as to provide the desired range of counter-force as well as counter-city options, this solution would provide simultaneously for protection of strike forces and for a second-strike counter-force capability.

The main objection to such a solution is that it would oblige the super-powers to rely to an uncomfortable extent on SLBMs and bombers. Strategic planners attach importance to maintaining a 'triad' of launcher categories – land-based ICBMs, SLBMs and bombers. They would fear being left seriously exposed if they had abandoned land-based ICBMs and then, against expectations, a breakthrough were made in antisub-marine warfare (ASW) or the locations of their submarines were betrayed through espionage. There would, moreover, be substance in such fears. SSBN submarines typically carry between 150 and 200 independently-targeted warheads. An enemy who found a way of locating and destroying submarines could destroy all of these with a single warhead of his own. His advantage in a first strike could be truly decisive.

The abandonment of land-based ICBMs would be especially difficult for the Soviets. Their strategic nuclear forces are more heavily concentrated on such ICBMs than are the American forces, and the United States is believed to have greater ASW capabilities. In general, however, the problems discussed in this section are common to both sides.

To sum up, then, there no longer seems any realistic prospect that the problem of first-striker's advantage will be solved by agreement between the two sides, overt or tacit, not to develop counter-force capabilities. Other solutions will be needed. The two obvious ones – more effective protection of missiles and development of second-strike counter-force capabilities – have their problems, not least the constraints of technological feasibility. From the standpoint of stability, the effective protection of missiles outpoints the development of second-strike counter-force capabilities. Yet another solution might be for both sides to abandon their land-based ICBMs and rely exclusively on SLBM and bomber forces. But none of these approaches is likely to provide a total solution in the near future.

LAUNCH ON ASSESSMENT

The third approach to limiting first-striker's advantage which we identified earlier was a policy of 'launch on warning' or 'launch on assessment' (LOA). A side with such a policy would reckon to launch a retaliatory strike against the enemy more or less automatically, as soon as his radar screens, or other monitoring devices, indicated an enemy attack, and before his nuclear forces were destroyed. His justification would be that he simply could not afford to wait until his nuclear forces had been eliminated. The net result might be an 'exchange of Queens', and the expectation of such a result might deter the opposing side from opening the striking in the first place.

At first sight a policy of launch on warning may seem highly attractive as a means of negating first-striker's advantage. It offers the enticing prospect of solving the problem 'at a stroke', without recourse to expensive programmes for the development of missile protection systems or second strike counter-force capabilities. The trouble is, however, that the dangers in such a policy are probably even more serious than the dangers against which it is directed.

Under a launch on warning system, the danger of war by accident or miscalculation, is enormously increased. The problem lies partly in the all too real possibility of misreading specks on radar screens and other monitoring devices, with all the associated possibilities for mischief by personnel in critical positions; and partly in the terribly short period of time which political leaders would have to reach the launching decision – a maximum of 15 minutes, if indeed they had time to weigh the decision at all. It strains the credulity to imagine that the leaders of any country would be willing to take such a momentous decision without the certainty that they were actually being attacked; and about the reality and scope of the attack there could be no absolute certainty until the missiles had actually landed. It strains the credulity no less to imagine that the leader would be willing to take such a decision in so short a space of time, much less to leave the counter-strike to be delivered automatically.

In addition to these major problems and anxieties, it is not even obvious whether a policy of launch on assessment would be advantageous from a military point of view. As a long-term policy it would make national security depend to an uncomfortable extent on the efficient functioning of the monitoring devices. Even as a short-term expedient, it would be of questionable military value. True, some of the home-country's missiles would be used against the enemy rather than destroyed in their silos. But would they be used against the right targets? How many of them would be wasted on empty silos in the enemy's country? And if some were targeted on cities, would this escalation of the conflict from counter-force to counter-city necessarily be in the home country's best interests? The better course, even from a narrowly military point of view, might be to ride out the first strike and re-target the home-country's surviving missiles before striking back.

For all the reasons given, there must be severe doubts as to whether it would ever be rational, or realistic, to carry out a policy of launch on warning. Moreover, the fact that each side would be fully aware of the difficulties would tend to reduce the credibility of the policy and hence its deterrent effect. But that is not to say that there would be no deterrent effect at all. If side B were to convey to side A that it had a launch on warning system in position and did not rule out the possibility of using it, side A might feel relatively certain that B would not in fact use it when it came to the point; but he might also be more uncertain than before about B's reactions and more anxious about the likely consequences of opening the striking. These doubts could contribute to deterring him. Be that as it may, a launch on warning policy is plainly no substitute for more secure and stable means of removing first-striker's advantage.

COUNTER-CITY SECOND-STRIKE CAPABILITIES AND THE 'STRIKE AND BARGAIN' SCENARIO

We have been concerned in the previous sections to identify possible ways in which first-striker's advantage might be negated. It is at least possible, however, that the next few years will see a rapid and continuing improvement in first-strike counter-force capabilities without a comparable degree of progress in the development of missile protection or second-strike counter-force capabilities. It is possible, in other words, that the advantage to the first striker will become more significant, and that second-strike capabilities will continue for the time being to be confined mainly to the counter-city role. The question arises, therefore: how stable would a system be where each side had a first striker's advantage, based on counter-force capabilities, coupled with a second-strike capability limited to civilian targets?

The short answer to our question is that possession by each side of large and relatively invulnerable second-strike capabilities confined to the counter-city role, though it cannot *negate* the other side's first-striker's advantage, is still likely to deter him from exploiting that advantage and does, therefore, offer a very considerable presumption of stability. For the risks involved in launching a first, counter-force strike against an enemy who possesses such a capability are at once daunting and obvious.

To elaborate this a little, the side contemplating a first strike (side A) is bound to recognise the terrible risk that the other side (B) may retaliate by using his second-strike capability to strike his (A's) cities. Side A may take the view that B is unlikely to retaliate in this way because B's primary concern will be to protect his own cities and he will judge that a strike against A's cities would provoke A to strike against B's cities. But it is unlikely that A will feel entirely confident about this judgement, and he will be keenly aware of the appalling consequences for his own cities if it proves wrong.

There is another consideration which is likely to undermine any confidence A may have in such a judgement about B's response. A is likely to recognise that his first strike, though intended as a counter-force strike, is likely to cause extensive damage to local civilian communities in B's country as well as military targets. (Estimates of American casualties in the event of an all-out Soviet attack on the United States' ICBMs range from 300 000 to 40 million dead.)[30] Hence B would be likely to perceive A's strike as being, in part at least, a counter-city strike, and to feel that the damage done to his cities demanded nothing less than retaliation in kind against A's cities. More generally, A is likely to recognise that he cannot have any confidence at all that B would turn the other cheek, however rational that might be, in the face of such massive provocation.

A third anxiety for A, which is bound to give him pause, is that he cannot have any certainty about what his first strike would in practice accomplish. As noted earlier, he will never have rehearsed sending even a single missile against the enemy's homeland, much less a barrage of missiles more or less simultaneously. Even in the unlikely event that all went perfectly, the other side would probably retain a significant ability to strike back against military as well as civilian targets. In the more likely event that much went wrong, he might unintentionally blot out large civilian centres in B's country, thus provoking B to a degree he never intended, and B might be left with a far stronger residual nuclear capability than A expected in launching the attack.

Given all these risks and anxieties, it is hard to conceive how any even moderately risk-averse side whose primary concern is to protect his cities could rationally decide on a first, all-out strike against an enemy who possesses a large second-strike capability against cities. The risk to his own cities must, on any rational assessment, be far greater if he strikes first than if he refrains from striking. If he strikes there must be a significant risk (if not more) that his cities will suffer in a retaliatory strike. If he refrains, the other side may well refrain as well, and his cities will not suffer. Alternatively, the other side may strike, and he might then have done better to strike first himself. But at least a first strike by the other side will almost certainly be directed against military targets (for the reasons given earlier) and there will remain a chance of avoiding catastrophic damage to his cities.

If side A's overriding concern is with avoiding catastrophic damage to his cities, therefore, the disincentives to opening the striking will be compelling. But he may have other preoccupations which lessen his risk-aversion. He may be preoccupied with what he perceives to be political or military imperatives. He may be willing to risk paying a huge price in order to obtain military and political dominance over B, or to avoid what he sees as the risk that B will obtain such a position of dominance over him.

A's willingness to take such risks must clearly depend on his assessment of B's likely reactions to a first strike by A. If he believed that B's priority would be to avoid escalation of the conflict at all costs, he might feel that the risks involved in striking first were acceptable. In such circumstances it may be just about conceivable that A might contemplate a 'strike and bargain' strategy. He might calculate that, having delivered a first, counter-force strike against B, he could then deter B from retaliating against his (A's) cities by himself threatening to counter-retaliate against B's cities. He might say to B:

> If you retaliate by destroying my cities, I will destroy yours. And that would be insane. (And remember I am now much stronger than you are.)

In other words, A's aim might be to change the rules of the game and make the system of mutual deterrence work *after*, rather than before, delivery of the first strike.

If A did decide to strike first, there is no question that it would be in his interests to bargain in this way. To that extent the scenario carries conviction. The more difficult question is whether it is credible that A would decide to strike in the first place against an opponent possessing a large second-strike capability, given all the risks and anxieties discussed earlier. Probably the answer which most experts would give in present circumstances, and for the foreseeable future, is – 'Highly unlikely, but not quite incredible'; and this is reassuring, if less than totally so.

FIRST-STRIKER'S ADVANTAGE AND DETERRENCE AGAINST CONVENTIONAL ATTACK

In most of the preceding discussion we have assumed that a would-be aggressor would launch a full-scale nuclear counter-force offensive, designed to reduce as far as possible the enemy's ability to retaliate and to tilt the balance of military power decisively in his own favour. The would-be aggressor would, however, have another serious option: he might attack at the conventional force level in the hope of achieving some cherished objective while keeping the conflict limited and avoiding a nuclear exchange. Such an option would indeed be likely to attract him more than a full-scale counter-force strike, if only because the risks involved, though enormous, would be so much smaller.

The two options of an all-out, incapacitating nuclear counter-force strike and a conventional offensive would appear to dominate all intermediate options for aggression. A limited nuclear counter-force strike, leaving the enemy with ample ability to retaliate in kind, would be as pointless as it would be dangerous: retaliation in the form of a nuclear strike by the other side would be virtually certain; yet the first striker would derive little or no advantage.

The option of aggression at the conventional level raises two issues. First, will the balance of terror deter aggression at this level? Second, how will the existence of first-striker's advantage affect deterrence against aggression at this level (or at any level below an all-out counter-force strike)?

Taking these in turn, there are fortunately solid grounds for supposing that the balance of terror *will* deter aggression at the conventional level. No country will lightly risk making a nuclear country desperate. Any country which launches a conventional attack against a nuclear country runs the appalling risk that the nuclear country will respond, sooner or later, by using his nuclear weapons. The more successful the conventional attack is, moreover, the greater this risk will be. There are no comparable dangers in attacking a non-nuclear country. It is sometimes argued that nuclear retaliation against a conventional attack lacks credibility because it would be potentially suicidal. But a conventional level aggressor could not possibly dismiss the risk that, in the heat and despair of crisis, the nuclear country might retaliate with nuclear weapons sooner than submit, even at the risk of a degree of mutual suicide. Chapters 11 and 12 explore these matters more fully.[31]

As to the second issue, first-striker's advantage seems likely, paradoxically, to *enhance* deterrence against limited aggression, including conventional attack. If the two sides both know that the other possesses a significant advantage in a first strike with strategic nuclear weapons, they are likely to be the more cautious about launching a limited offensive, for example at the conventional level, with the aim of keeping it limited: for they will have all along to reckon with the danger of provoking the enemy to escalate the conflict to the nuclear level so as to exploit his first-striker's advantage. If on the other hand the first striker has no advantage, the initiator of conventional aggression need have no comparable concern about leaving to the other side the option of escalation to the nuclear level.

This line of reasoning suggests the interesting conclusion that, while a really decisive first-striker's advantage would be disastrous in terms of stability because of the incentive it would provide for each side to launch a first, full-scale counter-force strike, a limited degree of first-striker's advantage may actually enhance stability by reducing the attraction to each side of opening hostilities at any lower force level.

VULNERABILITY OF CITIES

As noted earlier in the chapter, a second corollary of the key stability condition that each side must be able to inflict unacceptable damage on the other's cities in a second strike is that neither side should be able to protect his cities against unacceptable damage. Stability under a balance of terror requires that cities be vulnerable. They are the hostages which guarantee good behaviour by both sides.

If one side felt confident that his cities were no longer vulnerable – that his ABM, ACM and air defences could be relied upon to destroy warheads directed against his cities as well as his nuclear forces – there would no longer be a presumption that the risks in war, as he perceived them, would deter him from starting it. The balance of terror would no longer be stable. There would indeed be no balance of terror, only unilateral terror.

If *both* sides felt confident that their cities were no longer vulnerable, there would then be neither a balance of terror nor unilateral terror but a new world order, or a new East/West relationship at least, in which nuclear weapons played no part. Such a world order might possibly have the advantage of ridding the world of the scourge of nuclear weapons, thus fulfilling President Reagan's vision of March 1983 when launching the Strategic Defence Initiative (SDI). It would also have disadvantages, not least the enhanced risk of conventional hostilities: we return to these matters in Chapter 13.

In practice, no country has been able, is able now, or is likely to be able in the foreseeable future, to defend its cities effectively against a determined nuclear strike delivered by ballistic missiles, much less to have confidence that such defences are foolproof. It is this absence of effective defences against ballistic missiles, even slightly old-fashioned missiles, that gives potency and purpose to the independent nuclear capabilities of Britain and France, dwarfed as they are by the strategic arsenals of the superpowers.

If one looks far into the future, one cannot rule out that times may change. The two sides might conceivably at some future date develop foolproof defences against missiles, bombers and other forms of delivery. Nuclear weapons and the balance of terror would then be obsolete, at least until such time as ways were discovered of overcoming the defences.

How likely is such a scenario? On present evidence the answer has to be that it looks *unlikely*. In the Strategic Defence Initiative (SDI) the United States has set itself the task of devising defences against ballistic missiles. The United States Army succeeded in June 1984 in using a ballistic missile to intercept and destroy another ballistic missile in space. One of the problems, however, with this technology is that incoming missiles could be intercepted only in the 'mid-course' or 'terminal' phases of their flight, *after* they had released their multiple warheads and decoys (see figure 7.1), and it would be difficult for the interceptor missiles to distinguish and destroy everything that needed to be destroyed. The SDI programme therefore envisages in addition the possibility of using lasers (chemical or X-ray), whose beams travel at the speed of light, to attack incoming missiles during their boost phase (see figure 7.1 again), *before* they release their warheads and decoys. The idea would be to incapacitate the missiles by burning a hole or causing a small explosion. This would probably require the mounting of a vulnerable laser-platform or mirrors in space. It would certainly require location by satellite of the precise position of the missile within a few seconds of blast-off, development of a laser (or particle beam) many times more powerful than anything currently available, and pointing of the laser for several seconds at the same place on the surface of the travelling missile, the whole operation being directed by a computer system of unprecedented scope and sophistication. The difficulties of bringing this off against a single missile, much more against a barrage of missiles, would be daunting; the opportunities for counter-measures by the attacker, such as a short 'boost' phase, spinning missiles, extra heat shielding, saturation, and attacking the laser system itself, rich. As noted earlier, offence is inherently easier than defence, and the human mind has so far been no less fertile in devising ways of overcoming defensive systems than in devising the defensive systems themselves. There seems a high probability that this will always be so.[32]

Protagonists of the SDI point out that computer chips have transformed the prospects for direction and control of such operations and that it may be possible to target incoming missiles at each successive stage of their flight path, thus raising dramatically the possibilities of successful interception.

Such arguments have weight. It still strains the credulity, however, to suggest that the two sides will succeed in developing ABM systems which are *foolproof*, and will remain so over time, together with similarly foolproof (or near-foolproof) defences against all other possible methods of warhead delivery such as cruise missiles and bombers and furtive deliveries by ships or trucks. This last point is important. Neither side can at present claim to be within sight of foolproof defences against any of these forms of delivery. Yet near-foolproof defences in each and every one of these areas would be needed before nuclear weapons and the balance of terror could safely be considered obsolete.

A more likely scenario for the longer term is that the two sides will develop *partially* effective defensive systems which are *capable* of destroying incoming missiles. Under such a scenario, the balance of terror would not become obsolete but would certainly be affected. Would it be more or less stable?

There are three main considerations which need to be weighed. First, the existence of such defences, even if only partially effective, would *reduce first striker's advantage*. If the two sides possessed such defences, they could be even less confident than at present about their ability to deliver an incapacitating first strike. This could make a major contribution to deterrence in circumstances where first striker's advantage would otherwise be a serious problem. It would not however contribute to deterrence against conventional attack. Second, the two sides might feel obliged to hold *larger arsenals of offensive weapons* than otherwise so as to ensure that they would still have an assured capability to inflict unacceptable damage and hence to deter. That would be an unfortunate consequence, not just in itself but also because of the economic implications. The combination of the defensive systems themselves *and* larger arsenals of even more sophisticated offensive systems would be likely to require vast extra expenditures which could impose formidable burdens on the economies of East and West – burdens which would far better have been avoided. There may accordingly be a case for agreements between the two sides not to deploy the new defensive systems or to limit deployments severely, on the precedent of the 1972 ABM Treaty. Third, a serious *imbalance* in defensive capabilities between the two sides could be a source of anxiety, mistrust, instability. This argues for a certain deliberation in the development of such technologies. Breakneck programmes designed to out-distance potential opponents are unlikely to advance the cause of stability.

To suggest, as we have done, that completely reliable city defences are unlikely to be developed, and would make the balance of terror obsolete if they were, and that partially effective defences could raise serious problems, is not to say that, as a matter of policy, Western countries should close their minds to such defences and eschew research into them. As noted above, there may well be a case for agreements between the two sides not to develop or deploy such defences. To neglect research would, however be a dangerous policy for the West, especially when the Soviets are known to have devoted substantial resources to it. If advancing defensive technology were to prove even partially effective, to forswear such technology would be to opt, potentially at least, for strategic inferiority. If, against expectations, the new technology proved totally effective and reliable, countries which forswore the technology would put themselves at the mercy of those which espoused it (see further chapter 14). The correct response in such circumstances would surely be, not to reject the new technology in the hope of preserving an existing world order, but rather to accept the demise of the balance of terror and to fashion the bravest possible new world.

CONCLUSIONS

In this chapter we have considered what military capabilities are required to make a balance of terror intrinsically stable and how far existing capabilities fulfil these requirements. Our main analytical conclusions have been:

1. The key military requirement for stability is that each side should have, and be seen to have, the capacity to inflict unacceptable damage on the other's cities in a second strike, even after absorbing a first, all-out counter-force strike. Stability will, moreoever, be enhanced if the capabilities of the two sides are evenly matched.

2. A first corollary of this is that neither side should have, or believe himself to have, an overwhelming advantage in a first, all-out counter-force strike: neither side should consider himself capable of incapacitating the other by striking pre-emptively at his nuclear forces. Even a less than overwhelming degree of first-striker's advantage could in times of deep crisis encourage one side or the other to open the striking.

3. Paradoxically, however, a degree of first-striker's advantage may reinforce deterrence against conventional attack by heightening the would-be conventional aggressor's perception of the risk that the other side might respond with a nuclear strike.
4. A second corollary is that cities must be vulnerable. If they are not, there will indeed be no balance of terror.

If we measure existing military capabilities against these desiderata for stability, the outcome is generally reassuring. The key requirements are unquestionably fulfilled. The two sides both have the capacity to inflict unacceptable damage on each other, even after absorbing an all-out counter-force strike: neither side has the ability either to defend his cities or to incapacitate the other in a first strike. On these criteria, the existing balance of terror has a high degree of built-in stability.

Looking ahead, it seems highly improbable that either side will in the foreseeable future develop really effective ways of protecting his cities against ballistic missile strikes. First-striker's advantage against land-based forces is likely to increase on both sides during the 1980s as the combination of target accuracy, warhead yield and MIRVing becomes ever more formidable. Barring unexpected technological breakthroughs, however, this process will not give either side anything remotely approaching an ability to incapacitate the other in a first strike. The degree of first-striker's advantage may be sufficient, on the other hand, to make situations of international political tension perceptibly more dangerous. It is therefore desirable, in the interests of stability, that the two sides should take steps to reduce first-striker's advantage, unnecessary as it may be to eliminate it totally. There seems no realistic prospect of solving the problem by tacit agreement to forswear the development of counter-force capabilities. The practical solution is likely to lie in some combination of more effective protection for nuclear forces and an enhanced counter-force capability in second-strike forces. The two sides may need also to lessen their dependence on land-based forces and rely more heavily instead on the less vulnerable submarine and bomber-based forces.

In considering how the two sides might tackle the problem of first-striker's advantage, we have moved beyond analysis to policy. The next two chapters address some further policy issues which bear on intrinsic stability. Should the two sides aim to deter or to have a warfighting capability? How much do their relative strengths matter, as against their absolute ability to inflict an unacceptable level of damage? What should be the role of civil defence? What should be the role of arms control agreements?

8 War-fighting and Minimum Deterrence

DETERRENCE AND WAR-FIGHTING CAPABILITY

We begin our consideration of related policy issues by asking: should the two sides aim simply to deter each other from attacking? Or should they each aim to have the capability to fight a war successfully? There are kindred issues of whether nuclear war is 'winnable' and whether it is relative strength or absolute ability to inflict damage that matters.

As American defence specialists like to point out, the deterrent effect of a nation's military might is not perfectly correlated with its ability to wage war successfully. To take a simple example, a smaller country may possess a limited arsenal of strategic and tactical nuclear weapons and relatively modest conventional armed forces. Such a country will not be well equipped to fight a war against a hostile superpower with vastly superior resources of weapons and manpower; but since no country, not even a superpower, is able to defend its cities effectively against a nuclear strike, the threat posed by the smaller country's strategic nuclear arsenal may be highly effective in deterring an attack by the hostile superpower provided that a significant part of the smaller country's nuclear force would survive a first counter-force strike by the superpower.

Both France and Britain provide examples of a smaller country with the military credentials described. Recent French governments in particular have recognised that France is too weak to fight a successful war against the Soviet Union. The conclusion they have drawn is that the threat of strategic nuclear retaliation against Soviet cities offers the best available prospect of deterring a Soviet attack on French soil. French theorists have tended in addition to argue against strengthening France's general war-fighting capabilities on the grounds that a more solid conventional capability would weaken the deterrent effect of the French SLBM force by encouraging the Soviet Union to believe that France would meet a limited conventional attack with a conventional response rather than scalate the conflict forthwith to the strategic nuclear level. The underlying strategic concept has been aptly described as that of the 'cornered beast';[1] for the message transmitted to potential aggressors can be glossed, without excessive caricature, as follows:

> Stop! Keep well away! I am dangerous. If you attack or provoke me, I will bite to kill. I am not equipped to do anything less.

Some theorists are inclined to argue against the NATO alliance's strategy of 'flexible response' or 'effective deterrence' on similar grounds. As discussed in chapter 2, this strategy calls for development by the alliance of a range of options for responding to aggression – for strong conventional and theatre nuclear as well as strategic nuclear forces. The theorists argue that it is at best unnecessary, and possibly even a mistake, for NATO, just as it would be for a small nuclear country, to match the Warsaw Pact's conventional and theatre nuclear capabilities since this encourages the Soviet Union to believe that an attack at one level of force would be met by a response at the same level, and in particular that a conventional attack would be met by a conventional response; and this in turn weakens the deterrent effect of the United States' strategic nuclear arsenal.

The 'cornered beast' philosophy is plainly a lineal descendant of the old United States and NATO strategy of 'Massive Retaliation',[2] applied to a new world order in which the potential aggressor as well has a formidable nuclear arsenal. Its persuasive power is considerable. Improvements in general war-fighting capability do weaken in some degree the deterrent effect of a country's strategic nuclear arsenal. The more clearly a country is perceived to have a policy of reliance on, and early recourse to, strategic nuclear weapons, the more anxious the enemy is likely to be about the dangers of sparking a nuclear conflagration if he should attack at the conventional level. Smaller countries with nuclear capabilities, such as France and Britain, do not in any event have the resources to develop on their own a capability to fight wars against a superpower such as the Soviet Union. Hence it is not surprising that 'cornered-beast' philosophies which make a virtue of relative weakness in general war-fighting capability should have some appeal in such countries – and especially in a country such as France which does not participate fully in the wider NATO alliance. So long as the policy works, and the enemy does not attack, everything is for the best.

But suppose that the enemy *does* attack: what will the beast do then? Suppose in particular that the Soviet Union were to launch a limited conventional attack against one of the smaller nuclear countries, perhaps in support of the local communist party or perhaps against some military target which it claimed to be deeply provocative. The question is: would the government of the small nuclear country really be willing to launch strategic nuclear missiles against Soviet cities given the high risk that the Soviets would retaliate massively against its own cities? Would this not be to drink of hemlock or, as Bismarck put it, 'to commit suicide fo fear of death'?[3]   And might a potential aggressor not decide to attack on the assumption that the small nuclear country would be deterred by such considerations from using his nuclear arsenal? As these questions suggest there is a severe problem of ultimate credibility for any country which relies on the deterrent effect of strategic nuclear weapons without the backing of a formidable war-fighting capability. Such a country must be especially vulnerable to having its bluff called.

The same conclusion applies, with even more cogency, to a superpower such as the United States, and to an alliance such as NATO. There can be little doubt that the temptation to the Soviets to call NATO's bluff and launch a conventional attack in Europe would increase markedly if NATO were weak in war-fighting capability. Instead of being deterred by the fear that NATO would respond at once with a strategic nuclear strike the Soviet leadership could well calculate that NATO leaders, and in particular the President of the United States, would be unlikely to respond to a conventional attack by launching strategic nuclear missiles against the Soviet Union, because they would expect the Soviets to retaliate in kind and they would be anxious at all costs to avoid a major nuclear exchange. The Soviet leaders would be further encouraged to attack if they took the view that the West would suffer more than the Soviet Union in a nuclear exchange so that the Soviet Union would emerge in a stronger position than the West.

The alternative policy of possessing a formidable capability to wage war at all levels of force, though disagreeably expensive, provides a far greater assurance that deterrence will be effective. Deterrence and war fighting capability may be imperfectly correlated. But deterrence work by persuading a potential aggressor to imagine what would happen if he chose to start a war. It may be effective if the potential aggressor perceive simply that he might suffer damage out of all proportion to his potential gains. It is more likely to be effective if, in addition, the potential aggressor perceives that (i) he can have no assurance whatever of *achieving* his potential gains and (ii) his opponent possesses *credible* means of inflicting the disproportionate damage. If the Soviets know that they may be beaten at the conventional level, or at least that they cannot count on winning they must plainly be far less inclined to risk aggression at the conventional level. If they further perceive that NATO has credible nuclear options below the ultimate level of strategic nuclear weapons, the game is likely to look even less attractive. They will be less tempted to gamble on NATO's unwillingness to escalate the conflict to the nuclear level. There will no longer be the same bluff to call.

There does remain, however, a grain of truth in the criticisms of NATO's flexible response strategy which some French theorists have made. If the Soviets interpret the strategy to mean that NATO will meet like with like – conventional attack with conventional response, tactical nuclear with tactical nuclear, strategic nuclear with strategic nuclear – that may seriously weaken the deterrent effect of NATO's military effort. To maximise the deterrent effect, and to heighten Soviet perceptions of the risks involved in initiating conflict, it is important that NATO should leave the Soviet leaders in no doubt that the flexible response strategy is concerned with options, not mechanistic responses, and that it cannot be assumed that NATO will in all circumstances meet like with like.

OTHER NEEDS FOR A WAR-FIGHTING CAPABILITY

The case for possessing a formidable war-fighting capability rests on other considerations as well as deterrence. In the first place, the possibility cannot be excluded that deterrence might fail and war break out. In addition, as we saw in chapter 5, relative war-fighting capabilities may be important in political terms, without a shot being fired.

The need for a formidable war-fighting capability in the event of war is perhaps obvious enough. If deterrence should fail and war break out, it would clearly be important not just to stop the war as quickly as possible but also to 'win' – or, at least, not to 'lose'.

The ability to win, or not to lose, always a corner-stone of Soviet thinking, has been somewhat obscured in the West by the familiar paradox that in nuclear war there would be no such thing as victory – no 'winners' or 'losers'. This paradox expresses an important insight. In common with other paradoxes, however, it is not literally true, and it can mislead seriously if wrongly interpreted. The insight which underlies it is that both sides are likely to suffer so appallingly in a major nuclear exchange that neither is likely to have anything to celebrate. In absolute terms, both sides stand to 'lose' a great deal.

As against this, however, there are serious and familiar senses in which one side or the other may indeed 'win' or 'lose' even a nuclear exchange: the aggressor may or may not succeed in imposing his will on the other side; his original purpose may be fulfilled or frustrated; he may end up with more or less territory than when he began hostilities; he may lose more or less of his population, industry and military capabilities than his opponent and thus end up in a relatively stronger or weaker position.

This last point is especially important. If a conflict involving nuclear weapons were to occur, the world (including the United States and the Soviet Union) would almost certainly continue to function afterwards – perhaps in much the same way as before, perhaps in desperately straitened circumstances – and the underlying hostility between East and West would not necessarily be reduced: it might well be increased. It would clearly be in the West's interest to emerge from such a conflict in as good shape as possible. A potential aggressor could anyway only be encouraged by the thought that, grievously as he might suffer himself in a conflict, the other side would suffer even more, so that the balance of power would change in his own favour.

A policy which seeks to deter without the support of a formidable war-fighting capability has grave disadvantages in political as well as military terms, in peace as well as war. As noted in chapter 5, if the United States or the NATO alliance were clearly and markedly inferior to the Warsaw Pact in conventional forces and tactical nuclear weapons – if 'approximate parity' applied only to the ultimate force level of strategic nuclear weapons which both sides would want to avoid using at almost any cost – that would enable the Soviet Union, if it chose, to pursue even more aggressive reaction-testing policies world-wide, both in the political field and possibly with military interventions as well. The effect on Western leaders could be seriously debilitating, and the resulting distrust and tension would itself threaten stability and raise the probability of war.

The conclusion which emerges is that for reasons of deterrence, defence and politics alike, it must be in NATO's interest to possess a formidable capability to fight wars at any force level. Since stability rests on the success of each side in deterring the other, the possession by NATO of such a capability offers the best hope of stability as well. The 'cornered beast' strategy of deterrence through strategic nuclear weapons, without the backing of such a war-fighting capability, may be the only available option for smaller countries with nuclear capabilities acting on their own; but its lack of ultimate credibility in a world where the potential aggressor too has a formidable nuclear arsenal, together with all the other drawbacks discussed above, makes it a second-best policy, not suitable for the alliance as a whole.

SOME ELEMENTS IN A WAR-FIGHTING CAPABILITY

We cannot discuss in detail the components of an effective war-fighting capability. There are, however, three which are so important for stability that they need to be mentioned briefly.

The first is effective and survivable arrangements for command, control, communications and data-processing (the so-called C^3, now raised to C^4 by the advent of data-processing computers). The importance of this can hardly be exaggerated, whatever the level of conflict may be. If a country's leadership (political and/or military) is wiped out in a first or subsequent strike, or is unable to make contact with its strike forces, there would be acute dangers of paralysis or of the situation going totally out of control. Herein must lie one of the greatest threats to stability. Much more is known about the command and control arrangements, contingency planning and rules of engagement of the United States than those of the Soviet Union.[4] The layman can only hope and pray that the governments of all nuclear countries have attended punctiliously to these matters.

The second component is a strong conventional capability, including a capability for continuous operations by day and night and in all weathers, and a capability to continue the conventional battle for a considerable period of time. It was estimated in 1980 that NATO's stocks of ammunition and spares would begin to run out after 11 or 12 days of sustained fighting in Europe: the Reagan administration hopes to raise the number to 60. The ability to sustain defence at the conventional level over a longer period is required, *inter alia*, to raise the nuclear 'threshold' – that is, to postpone the point at which NATO might have to introduce nuclear weapons in order to avoid defeat. Thus, if war were to begin with aggression by the Soviet Union at the conventional level, a critical initial requirement would be to contain the Soviet advance for long enough to let NATO's leaders decide on their response and negotiate with the Soviet Union: this must contribute significantly to stability. If the war continued beyond this initial phase, then the greater NATO's ability to counter the Soviet threat without resort to nuclear weapons, the greater the chances would be of avoiding the massive destruction and unacceptable damage which a nuclear exchange could cause.

A third requirement is for the greatest possible flexibility of weapon systems, including an ability to match or counter the enemy's specific capabilities. The ability to avoid escalation and unnecessary destruction will depend importantly on this flexibility. Thus the danger of escalation to all-out conflict would plainly be increased if NATO had conventional capabilities at one extreme and massive strategic nuclear counter-city capabilities at the other, with no counter-force capability or capability for striking smaller targets in between.[5] Another important aspect of flexibility is that the design of weapon systems should leave decision makers as long as possible to reach decisions in times of crisis.

In practice the NATO alliance does have considerable flexibility of weapons systems (though it is arguably very short on quantities); but there are some areas where suitable counters to Soviet weapons appear to be lacking. One such area, prior to the deployment of Pershing IIs and cruise missiles now beginning, was intermediate-range nuclear forces. Another is chemical warfare (CW). The Soviets are known to have a large arsenal of offensive chemical weapons of various kinds, which could be used flexibly to paralyse key NATO posts and bases for a chosen period of time. NATO, on the other hand, deploys only limited and out-dated offensive chemical warfare capabilities, though the United States has taken major steps to modernise its chemical arsenal. Defences against chemical attack are being developed; but these significantly reduce efficiency and could never, in any case, be totally effective. In the event of advances by Soviet conventional forces helped by use of chemical weapons, therefore, NATO might find itself compelled to choose between accepting substantial military disadvantage and using theatre nuclear weapons, with serious implications for subsequent escalation and stability. The danger might be removed, in principle at least, by an international treaty banning the production and use of chemical weapons. Pending such a treaty, however, the only satisfactory solution – disagreeable as it is – would seem to lie in the deployment of an effective NATO offensive chemical capability, which should deter the Soviets from using their capability and thus enhance stability.[6]

CIVIL DEFENCE AND WAR-FIGHTING CAPABILITY

The issue of deterrence versus war-fighting capability underlies much of the public argument about civil defence. Deterrence theorists of the 'mutual assured destruction' school tend to see little merit, and even positive harm in civil defence expenditure, while advocates of war-fighting capabilities take the contrary view. The matter calls for a brief discussion.

Some critics of civil defence dislike it simply as indicating that govern ments are prepared to contemplate the possibility of nuclear war. Such criticisms in effect reject the whole concept of nuclear deterrence and lie beyond the scope of this chapter.

There are other critics, however, who question civil defence programmes while accepting the general concept of deterrence. They argue that civil defence is destabilising, can readily be negated by the other side and represents poor value for money compared with many other types of military expenditure.

To take these criticisms in turn, the point about stability is based on an argument discussed in the previous chapter. As with ABM and ACM defences for cities, so with civil defence, highly developed and effective civil defence systems could in principle detract from stability by reducing the ability of the two sides to inflict unacceptable damage on each other. If either side possessed a highly effective civil defence system which could be relied on to limit damage sustained in nuclear conflict, and in particular human casualties, to a level which it considered acceptable *in extremis*, the system of mutual deterrence would become unstable.

This argument is sound as far as it goes. But there are two decisive counter-arguments. First, there is no realistic prospect that civil defence could ever provide such effective protection that the scale of damage from nuclear weapons would become acceptable. There is no direct threat to stability on that account. Second, even if civil defence did detract from deterrence in this way, it still would not follow that national governments should eschew it. The policies of national governments are rightly and necessarily informed by other considerations, such as the need to protect their citizens as effectively as possible, as well as by considerations of global stability.

The second criticism is that the other side can easily negate the effects of a large civil defence programme by increasing the numbers or mega-tonnages of the warheads he uses. This argument, again, is right in principle but probably misses the point in practice. It assumes that the other side would have a deliberate objective to kill a particular number of people. Such an objective is not impossible. But it seems at least equally likely (and probably more so) that his objective would be to destroy particular military installations or industrial complexes, not to kill a defined number of people, and that his decisions on the number and yield of weapons used would not be much influenced by the efficiency of the other side's civil defence programme. In that event failure to provide adequately in advance for civil defence could result in large numbers of unnecessary casualties.

Potentially more persuasive is the argument that really effective civil defence is extremely expensive without being cost-effective, and that better value for money is obtained by spending more on strike capabilities or on other types of defensive capability or even on other parts of the defence programme altogether. For reasons touched on below, however, a heavy onus of proof rests on those who reject civil defence expenditure on such grounds. Some aspects of civil defence, such as public education and even construction of suitable shelters in new homes, are relatively inexpensive.

On the other side of the argument there are two powerful considerations which suggest that civil defence *is* important and that under-provision for it may be dangerous and even destabilising.

The first consideration relates to war-fighting capabilities and civilian casualty rates. If the worst came to the worst and deterrence failed, a country underequipped for civil defence could suffer loss of life on a quite unnecessary scale. One of the lessons of Hiroshima and Nagasaki is that survival prospects depend heavily on where people are at the time of the blast and, assuming they are inside, on the type of building and where they are in it.[7] If people are forewarned about an attack, and know what to do when forewarned, casualties should be considerably reduced. In a ground-burst strike, moreover, directed against hard targets, radioactive fall-out would be another widespread hazard, in addition to those encountered at Hiroshima and Nagasaki. The rate of casualties from this fall-out would depend importantly on the degree of public education and other preparations for dealing with it.

The second consideration relates to deterrence. If one side makes only minimal provision for civil defence while the other has a large civil defence programme, the perceived imbalance in the relative abilities of the two sides to hurt each other can only detract from the effectiveness of the underequipped country's deterrence, and hence from stability. Others may doubt the willingness of a nuclear country to use his nuclear strength in any circumstances if he is manifestly underequipped to deal with retaliation in kind. A serious perceived imbalance in civil defence capabilities could also produce a degree of political debilitation in the side whose defences were less developed.

As is well known, the Soviet civil defence programme is far larger than the United States' programme or that of any other Western country. Some observers have even concluded that, in an all-out retaliatory strike by the United States, the Soviet Union would lose less than 10 per cent of its population (and perhaps as little as 2 per cent) and be able to rebuild its economy to previous levels of output per head within two to four years. The United States, on the other hand – so it is argued – would stand to lose 40–50 per cent of its population from a corresponding strike by the Soviet Union and would require ten years or more to 'rebuild its economy'.[8]

If these estimates, and particularly those for the Soviet Union, were accurate, the political implications and the implications for stability would indeed be serious. In fact, it is barely credible that the Soviets' civil defences would be as effective as this, and even less credible that the Soviets would base critical policy decisions on the assumption that they would be so effective. But the relatively small civil defence programmes of Western countries must detract from the West's deterrence and war-fighting capabilities.

MINIMUM DETERRENCE AND 'SUFFICIENCY'

We turn finally to a cluster of issues closely related to war-fighting capabilities – superiority, inferiority, parity, sufficiency and minimum deterrence. The simple theory of mutual deterrence as expounded in chapters 2 and 6 began by emphasising how important was the *absolute* ability of the two sides to inflict damage on each other, as opposed to their relative strengths: we argued that the minimum condition for stability was that each side should perceive the other to have the ability, and perhaps the will, to inflict a totally unacceptable level of damage, even after suffering a first strike. There is a school of thought which goes further than this and argues that possession of this absolute capability is not just a minimum condition for stability but a sufficient condition also. Provided that the home country possesses strategic forces which are sufficiently powerful to inflict unacceptable damage on the enemy's cities after absorbing a first strike, so the argument runs, the enemy will be deterred from attacking and stability will be assured. Any additional military strength, beyond this 'flat of the curve' point of 'sufficiency' or 'minimum deterrence', is seen as being superfluous, and relative strength as being irrelevant.[9]

The 'minimum deterrence' argument has considerable appeal. Such a policy would presumably involve scrapping all nuclear weapons except a limited number of the more invulnerable second-strike systems. It might, therefore, arguably, enhance stability in one respect – by reducing an enemy's incentive for pre-emptive attack. Its acceptance could also open the way for major savings in the defence budget of the country concerned. Thus it was calculated in 1976 that one-quarter of the existing American SLBM force, one-tenth of their land-based ICBM force and one-third of their operational bomber force would probably suffice to destroy the 50 largest Soviet cities even after absorbing the full force of a Soviet counter-force attack.[10] With the rapid and continuing increase in Soviet counter-force capabilities the forces required for 'minimum deterrence' could now be considerably larger; but the scope for economies offered by a 'minimum deterrence' policy remains substantial.

The practical issue is whether it would make good sense for one side or the other – and in practice for the United States, since the Soviet Union would clearly not contemplate such a policy – unilaterally to reduce its nuclear forces to 'minimum deterrence' levels. Sadly the answer to this question has to be no, and this for a number of reasons, both military and political. The arguments closely resemble those for possessing a formidable war-fighting capability.

In the first place there is the problem of credibility. Restricting nuclear capabilities unilaterally to a 'minimum deterrence' level would amount in practice to forswearing counter-force capabilities and relying exclusively on a second-strike, counter-city capability. Such a capability should suffice to deter counter-city strikes, but there is less assurance that it would deter counter-force strikes, since in this case the threat of retaliation against cities would be less credible. As discussed earlier, there is no substitute for flexible weapon systems and the ability to retaliate in kind.

Second, there is the problem of what happens if deterrence fails and the enemy does adopt an aggressive policy. An enemy who retains his counter-force capability would be able, in principle at least, to pick off the home country's 'minimum deterrence' second-strike force, little by little – submarines on their return to harbour, bombers at their bases and so on. The home country would then be confronted with the intolerable dilemma of whether to do nothing in reply or to retaliate against the enemy's cities, in the near-certainty of provoking retaliation against his own cities: a creeping variant of the 'strike and bargain' scenario discussed in chapter 7. One solution to this problem (and the credibility problem) would be for the home country to retain a counter-force capability, which would need to be as invulnerable as possible; but in the counter-force game relative numbers of weapons and exchange rates become critically important and the effect would be to drive a coach and horses through the policy of unilateral minimum deterrence.

A third problem lies in the difficulty of defining a minimum requirement or 'sufficiency', at a time of continuing technological advance. A second-strike force which looks invulnerable today may no longer be invulnerable tomorrow. Suppose that, against all the odds, the Soviets were to develop techniques for locating nuclear submarines on the ocean floor?

Finally there is the political dimension. To adopt unilaterally a policy of minimum deterrence would be to opt deliberately for major strategic inferiority. We have touched several times on the debilitating effect which even a limited amount of inferiority is capable of having on Western leaders and Western interests. 'What in God's name is strategic superiority? What do you do with it?' - asked an impatient Henry Kissinger at one of his celebrated press conferences. The answer, surely, is 'Try inferiority and you will see'.[11]

For all the reasons mentioned, it would be rash for the West to adopt unilaterally a policy of minimum deterrence. On both military and political grounds, superiority would be preferable. But the Soviets too would prefer superiority, and both sides cannot enjoy superiority simultaneously. For each side, the most important requirement is to avoid clear inferiority, and the only way in which this can be achieved is through approximate parity between the two sides. But what is parity and at what level of armaments can it be achieved? These questions lead straight into the subject of arms control.

9   Arms Control

SHARED INTERESTS

One of the most remarkable developments of the post-war years, especially since the Cuban missile crisis of 1962, has been the ebb and flow of negotiations between East and West on arms control and other aspects of international relations.

Since the early 1960s the governments of East and West have been prepared to acknowledge that, for the foreseeable future, general and complete disarmament, or even nuclear disarmament, lies beyond reach. They would almost certainly feel acutely uncomfortable about agreeing to complete disarmament, or nuclear disarmament, even if the option were available.[2] Both sides would be perpetually worried that the other was poised to steal a decisive march by restarting production of nuclear and other weapons. The Soviets would doubt their ability to hold the Soviet bloc together. The West would worry about the increased scope for Soviet subversion world-wide. As suggested in chapter 4, agreement on disarmament, or nuclear disarmament, would require a degree of mutual trust which plainly does not exist. The early post-war quest for general disarmament has been tacitly abandoned, for the time being at least.

The feeling has persisted, nevertheless, that there do exist important areas of shared interest between East and West; that the mutual antagonism though profound, is also 'incomplete'; that the unfettered evolution of unilateral decisions on armaments is likely to produce a grossly excessive general level of armaments; and that there must be scope for agreements which, while falling well short of complete disarmament or complete nuclear disarmament, would benefit everyone. Especially in the West governments have come under pressure from public opinion to search hard for such agreements, and the Soviets have often (but not always) been willing to negotiate provided that they do not start from a position of inferiority.

AGREEMENTS

The agreements which have been reached fall into two main groups – agreements on general relations between East and West, including communications and crisis management, and armaments limitation agreements.

A key objective of the first group of agreements has been to alleivate the dangers of a nuclear world. The earliest such agreement, reached in 1963 and inspired by the perceived need for better mutual communications after the Cuban missile crisis, provided for a 'hot line' between the President of the United States and the top leadership of the Soviet Union. Subsequent agreements have included those of the early 1970s on the general principles of relations, which provided for the two superpowers to resolve differences by peaceful negotiation;[3] the Helsinki accord of 1975, at the end of the first Conference on Security and Co-operation in Europe, which provided (*inter alia*) for confidence-building measures between East and West, including advance mutual notification of major military exercises;[4] and a set of bilateral agreements between the nuclear countries on action in the event of a nuclear accident.[5]

The agreements on limitation of armaments have either banned particular activities or established numerical ceilings on force deployments. An early example in the former category was the Geneva Convention of 1925, which banned the use of chemical or biological weapons save in retaliation. In the post-war period, the abortive 'Rapacki plans' put forward in the period 1957–62, which sought to ban nuclear deployments in central Europe or Europe as a whole, provide an early example of the quest for a limited agreement falling short of general nuclear disarmament.

The most successful decade for such agreements was that which followed the Cuban missile crisis of October 1962. The crisis itself gave impetus to the quest. The governments of the nuclear powers came increasingly to accept that the balance of nuclear terror had become a fact of life; that the ideal of general disarmament was unattainable in the foreseeable future; that what was ideal must not be allowed to frustrate what was practicable; that the best must not be the enemy of the good. The advent in the early 1960s of surveillance by reconnaissance satellites enabled the two sides to verify military deployments much more effectively than would previously have been possible. By the early 1970s, moreover, the Soviets had built up their strategic nuclear arsenal to the point where it was comparable with its American counterpart. For the first time, therefore, they could negotiate about numbers from a position of approximate parity.

The agreements of this propitious decade included the partial test ban treaty (PTBT) of 1963, banning nuclear tests in the atmosphere but not underground;[6] the agreements of 1966-7 and 1970 prohibiting the use of weapons of mass destruction in outer space or on the sea-bed; the nuclear non-proliferation treaty of 1968 (NPT), providing for the transfer of civilian nuclear technology by the nuclear countries to non-nuclear countries in return for renunciation by the latter of nuclear weapons and willingness to place all their nuclear activities under safeguards and international inspection;[7] and the biological weapons convention of 1972, prohibiting the production of biological weapons.[8] Perhaps the crowning achievement of the decade was the SALT 1 accord of June 1972, when the United States and the Soviet Union concluded an ABM treaty, limiting deployments of anti-ballistic missile systems to two by each side (later reduced by agreement to one), and an interim agreement limiting the deployment of missile launchers by each side for the five ensuing years to approximately their existing levels.[9]

Since 1972 agreements have proved more elusive. The most notable achievement has been the signature by Mr Brezhnev and President Carter in June 1979 of the SALT 2 agreement, providing for more comprehensive quantitative limits on strategic launcher systems, with sub-limits on MIRVed launchers.[10] The United States Congress declined to ratify the agreement after the Soviet invasion of Afghanistan in December 1979 and the Reagan administration criticised it severely; but both superpowers have so far nevertheless broadly complied with it. Other negotiations which have failed at the time of writing to produce agreements include the Vienna talks on Mutual and Balanced Force Reductions in Europe (MBFR), which began in 1973,[11] the talks on a comprehensive test ban treaty (CTBT) and the negotiations on a convention banning chemical weapons to match the 1972 convention on biological weapons.[12]

In November 1981 President Reagan took the bold initiative of offering to cancel deployment of new-generation NATO intermediate-range nuclear forces in Europe if the Soviets would dismantle theirs – the so-called 'zero option'. The Soviets rejected this offer. But talks on intermediate-range forces (INF) began in Geneva on 30 November 1981. President Reagan also proposed that a new round of talks on strategic systems should begin in 1982 and said that the American aim would be to negotiate substantial reductions ('deep cuts') in these systems and in conventional forces in Europe. These difficult negotiations proceeded slowly during 1982 and 1983. The Soviets then suspended them unilaterally in November/December 1983 in protest at the first of the new NATO deployments of intermediate-range nuclear forces in Western Europe. After fourteen wasted months, they agreed to return to the negotiating table provided that space weapons were added to the agenda, and a new round of negotiations began in March 1985.

The record on arms control agreements has in practice been even more patchy than the above account may suggest. Probably the most useful agreements have been those on crisis management; the ABM Treaty of 1972, which has made the two sides feel more comfortable about not spending gigantic sums on the deployment of ABM systems; the SALT 1 and 2 offensive arms limitation agreements of 1972 and 1979; the Geneva Convention of 1925 on chemical weapons and the biological weapons convention of 1972; and the nuclear non-proliferation treaty of 1968. But there have been problems even with these. The SALT agreements did not significantly reduce the level of armaments and have not been scrupulously observed. The Geneva Convention on chemical weapons has been honoured in the breach as well as the observance. The biological weapons convention of 1972 has not been signed by France or China, and there are strong suspicions that the Soviet Union has violated it by retaining a biological weapons establishment at Sverdlovsk and by supplying toxins to the Vietnamese for use in Laos. The nuclear non-proliferation treaty remains unsigned by two nuclear countries, France and China, and several potentially nuclear countries.

Impressive as the sheer volume of international negotiation has been, therefore, the results to date are rather disappointing. The greatest disappointment is that arms control negotiations have failed to prevent the nuclear arsenals from reaching their present, gigantic scale. The impression lingers that the potential of arms control negotiations has not been realised: 'much bruit, little fruit'.

OBJECTIVES

We now turn from history to policy. Do the two sides in fact have interests in common which can form a solid basis for arms control agreements? What should the objectives of such agreements be? And what policies should the two sides have towards arms control – in particular the West?

The answer to the first question is that the two sides do have fundamental interests in common. They have the strongest possible common interest in the avoidance of war. They also have strong common interests in reducing as far as possible the dangers associated with nuclear weapons and in containing the growth of military expenditure. There may be, and in fact are, all manner of political and practical problems which make actual agreements difficult to negotiate. But the existence of shared interests is beyond doubt.

As to the second question, the fundamental objective of arms control agreements should be to promote these common interests, and in particular:

(i) to reduce the likelihood of war, by enhancing the stability of the balance of terror and the security of each side; and/or
(ii) to limit the potential damage from war, or preparations for war, including human casualties, damage to cities and damage to the planet; and/or
(iii) to restrain military expenditures by agreement.

In addition to these fundamental objectives, two intermediate objectives are so important in present circumstances that they need separate mention:

(iv) to reduce the level of armaments deployed by each side; and
(v) to avoid the proliferation of nuclear weapons (the acquisition of such weapons by countries which do not now possess them).

As to the third question, it must be a sensible policy for East and West alike to explore thoroughly the scope for agreements dedicated to such self-evidently desirable objectives, without forgetting the attendant problems. We attempt at the end of the chapter to specify the kind of agreement which the West should aim to negotiate for the medium-term. In the meantime we consider in turn the main objectives and problems of arms control agreements.

The first objective – reducing the likelihood of war by enhancing stability and security – is crucially important. From a global point of view formal agreements on arms control are a component of the general system of mutual deterrence. They need to be assessed by the contribution they make to the stability of that system. From the standpoint of individual countries, similarly, what matters most is having an effective policy for deterrence and defence. Arms control agreements must be assessed by the contribution they make within that policy.

Consistently with this a key question for consideration in evaluating any particular agreement should be whether it will enhance stability, both intrinsic and dynamic. Under the former heading, will it, for example, reduce first-striker's advantage and the incentives to each side to open hostilities? Will it lessen political tensions, such as those associated with an all-out arms race or build-up of military personnel? Under the latter heading, will it, for example, improve the chances of solving crises by negotiation rather than force? Will it reduce the danger of war by accident or miscalculation? In general, will it enhance the security of each side, both actual and perceived?

The importance of the second possible objective of arms control agreements – limiting the potential damage from war or preparations for war – needs little elaboration. This is the objective which has always lain behind test-ban treaties and the quest for nuclear non-proliferation. It now needs to become a central purpose of arms limitation negotiations as well. The need to minimise the potential damage to mankind and the planet from nuclear exchanges argues strongly for deep cuts in the arsenals of each side. The more weapons the two sides possess, the more disastrous such exchanges could be.

The conventional wisdom used to be that the damage from nuclear weapons, appalling as it would be, would be heavily concentrated on the vicinity of the exploding warhead, though radioactive fall-out could substantially extend the areas of hazard and damage. Recent research has suggested that a major nuclear exchange could in addition have catastrophic climatic effects throughout the planet – the so-called 'nuclear winter'.[13] At the time of writing such suggestions are still in the nature of tentative hypotheses. Further research may well show the more alarming claims to be exaggerated. But the possibility that a full-scale nuclear exchange could cause damage to mankind and the planet of a nature and on a scale not previously contemplated must reinforce the case for deep cuts in the present arsenals.

The objective of limiting the potential damage from war, and in particular reducing the size of the nuclear arsenals, could in principle conflict with the objective of reducing the risk of war. Reducing the arsenals could in principle make the balance of terror less stable: if the two sides were to destroy (say) two-thirds or three-quarters of their nuclear forces, they might then be more vulnerable to an incapacitating first strike by the other side.

In present circumstances this dilemma is fortunately unlikely to arise. The existing nuclear arsenals are far larger than they need to be for the sake of mutual deterrence. Given the will on both sides, it should in principle be possible to reduce them by agreement to a fraction of their present levels and to do so in ways which would enhance stability and reduce expenditure as well as lessening the risks of catastrophic damage to the planet. We return to this line of thought at the end of the chapter.

As regards the third possible objective of arms control – restraining military expenditures by agreement – there is no presumption that agreements designed to enhance stability will necessarily lead to economies.

Such agreements may lead to a concentration of expenditure on particularly expensive weapon systems (such as SLBMs). Any resources released from one segment of the military budget (for example, strategic nuclear weapons) may need to be transferred to another segment whose importance has been enhanced by the agreement (for example, theatre nuclear weapons). On the other hand it may suit each side to conclude agreements which enable him to limit his military expenditure (or additions to his military expenditure) without thereby putting himself at a disadvantage. Agreements to limit the deployment of expensive new weapon systems (such as ABM systems) may have this property. It is even possible to conceive of agreements to limit military budgets to stated ceilings, formidable though the practical difficulties of definition and enforcement would be.

PROBLEMS

We turn now from the potential prizes of arms control to the problems and dangers on the way – in particular those which affect negotiations on arms limitation such as SALT and MBFR. It is convenient to consider these under five headings – comparability, verification, obsolescence, conflicts with perceived national strategic requirements, and political dimensions.

The problem of comparability has many aspects. When the two sides are as diverse as are the Soviet Union and NATO in terms of territory, alliances, deployments and weapon systems, it is difficult to find a deal which is, and can be seen to be, fair to both sides. To begin with, it may be difficult to agree on defining the starting position and the scope of the negotiations – witness the 'counting' problem in the MBFR talks and the 'forward-based systems' problem in the successive SALT talks. Thereafter the problems of measuring comparative military strength are likely to cause trouble. Should an agreement on nuclear arms limitation relate to launcher vehicles, warheads, total warhead yield or some combination of the three? What account (if any) should be taken of relative target accuracy? Or of geographical differences, such as the proximity of the Soviet Union to Western Europe? Or of the weapon deployments of allied countries? It is unlikely that any agreement will be able to take explicit account of all these factors. But each side will have them very much in mind in deciding whether or not particular forms of measurement and coverage are acceptable. A further problem is whether the two sides should reduce their weapon deployments by equal amounts or to equal levels. Finding a deal which will leave both sides feeling comfortable may be a highly elusive goal.

The problems of verification are likewise extremely troublesome. No country will want to entrust its security to the good faith of a little-trusted opponent, even if that opponent has a political interest in publicly exaggerating his military strength rather than understating it. Hence policing and verification are crucial. The advent in the early 1960s of satellite surveillance has made it possible for each side to acquire considerable amounts of information about the other's activities. But verification can seldom, if ever, be totally foolproof. There are limits on what satellites can verify, and the Soviets have always been exceptionally resistant to on-site inspection. In virtually any arms limitation agreement, therefore, there is likely to be some scope for undetected cheating, and a limited degree of mutual trust must be a pre-requisite for such agreements. That is why it is virtually impossible to conclude useful agreements at times when tension and distrust between the two sides run high.

Difficulties over verification unfortunately limit the areas which arms control agreements can reach. In some areas the risks of detection by satellite surveillance are so high that neither side would be likely to run the risk of cheating and being caught in the act. Fortunately the important areas of major weapon deployments and major nuclear test explosions fall into this category. It is no accident that they have featured prominently in past arms control agreements. In other areas the prospects for cheating without detection are far greater. It would be relatively easy, for example, to escape detection in breaking bans on the production of biological and chemical weapons, or bans on research and development in particular fields, or limitations on particular properties of weapon systems such as explosive yields or accuracy or numbers of independent warheads. Satellite surveillance reveals little about these matters. It cannot reveal whether cruise missiles have nuclear warheads; nor whether stocks of components are waiting to be assembled at speed if an arms control agreement breaks down; nor even whether small-scale nuclear test explosions have been carried out.

Anxieties about possible cheating by the other side are especially troublesome for the West. The Soviet Union, with its authoritarian system of government and close control of information, is exceptionally well placed for concealment. The West's policy must therefore be to negotiate the most stringent possible means of verification. In areas where verification is bound to be less than satisfactory, a judgement needs to be reached on how serious the risk of cheating by the other side is, how serious the consequences of such cheating would be, and whether the advantages of concluding an agreement would be such as to justify taking those risks.

The problem of obsolescence is simply that the significance of an agreement may change with the passage of time and advancing technology. The ABM treaty of 1972, for example, might in principle outlive its usefulness if it became clear that the deployment of ABM and ACM systems offered the best means of protecting missile silos and other nuclear bases.

The problem that arms control requirements may conflict with other requirements of national defence arose at the end of the 1970s in relation to the American MX ICBM. It is clearly important to make a new ICBM as invulnerable as possible. Invulnerability should enhance national security and intrinsic stability by reducing first-striker's advantage. But the means of making missiles relatively invulnerable – for example, concealment and/or mobility – are almost bound to make verification by satellite more difficult and thus to reduce the chances of effective arms control. In such a case, the primary objectives must, as always, be effective deterrence and stability. If the incompatibilities between the requirements of arms control and protection of weapon systems cannot be resolved, the issue has to be: 'which is going to contribute more to national security and global stability – a more invulnerable missile or greater difficulty in verifying arms control agreements?'

A final set of problems is the political dimension. Arms control excites strong and opposing views. Many people, especially in Western Europe, are passionately in favour of arms control agreements – often without fully appreciating how genuine are the attendant problems and dangers. Many others, especially in the United States, are deeply suspicious of agreements with a potential enemy who, in their perception, cannot be trusted at all. The task for national governments must be to steer a pragmatic course between the Scylla of idealism and the Charybdis of scepticism, while respecting the deeply held convictions of the opposing lobbies. The critical judgement to be made is whether the scope exists for agreements which will positively promote national security, global stability and the other interests which the two sides have in common.

In reaching such judgements, national governments need to have in mind the major political benefits which the pursuit and successful conclusion of arms control agreements may bring, such as reduced international tension and an increased sense of security world-wide. In certain circumstances pursuit of such agreements may be crucial in enabling political agreement to be reached domestically on important military expenditures: NATO's 'twin-track' decision of December 1979 to couple intermediate nuclear forces modernisation with negotiations to reduce these forces is a case in point. But there are also real dangers of exaggerated public expectations followed by disappointment and disillusion. If a particular agreement is highly controversial; if a large section of informed opinion, in the countries affected or in allied countries, believes it to be detrimental to national security; if it is widely interpreted as implying acceptance of strategic inferiority by one side or the other; if, finally, the negotiations for an agreement or the agreement itself should break down – in such cases, the disbenefits may all too easily outweigh the benefits.

It is sometimes suggested that tacit understandings on levels of armaments may be preferable to formal agreements. The effects of the 1972 ABM Treaty, for example, might in theory have been achieved by unilateral decisions, possibly based on informal consultations or on unilateral declarations by each side that it would not deploy more than one such system unless the other side did so. But formal agreements have powerful advantages. It is more difficult for either side to break an agreement than to withdraw an earlier, unilateral undertaking. There are also considerable domestic political advantages in a formal agreement which is fully discussed prior to ratification and then settled one way or the other. In the absence of the ABM agreement, each side would probably be considerably more nervous about not deploying ABM systems.[14]

SALT AND MBFR

We conclude this chapter with a brief evaluation of the SALT, START, INF and MBFR negotiations and the possibilities for the future.

To begin with the positive aspects, the historic accords reached in the 1972 SALT 1 talks proved that useful agreements on limiting nuclear arms are possible. Within SALT 1, the ABM treaty has ruled out, for the time being at any rate, a race between East and West in the deployment of ABM systems. This must have contributed to stability, so far at least. It has probably contributed also to the containment of military budgets. The SALT 1 interim agreement was likewise an historic achievement. By placing agreed quantitative limits on offensive-missile launcher systems, albeit at their existing levels, the two sides took a first step towards regulating the size of their nuclear arsenals by agreement.

The 1979 SALT 2 agreement, through not ratified by Congress in the United States was surely another milestone. It broke a great deal of new ground by coming to grips with difficult problems not touched by SALT 1, notably bombers, multiple warheads, deployments of new systems and verification procedures. Its terms required the Soviets to retire about 250 systems before the end of 1981.

Still on the positive side, there can be little doubt that the very existence of the SALT and MBFR talks contributed to stability and détente. Another achievement of the talks was to concentrate public attention in the United States and NATO on the need to strengthen the West's military capabilities. It was not always clear whether the main negotiating process lay between the United States and the Soviet Union or the United States administration and Congress. SALT 1 probably saved the United States administration in the early 1970s from yielding to Congressional pressure to reduce military commitments even further, at a time of deep disenchantment with military expenditure brought on by the Vietnam war. Similarly, the launching of the MBFR negotiations in 1973 probably enabled the administration to overcome Congressional pressure for troop withdrawals from Europe; and domestic discussions in 1979 and 1980 on the unratified SALT 2 agreement probably helped to rekindle public awareness in the United States of the need for a stronger defence strategy.

In spite of all these positive aspects, the SALT agreements and the MBFR negotiations attracted considerable amounts of criticism from both supporters and opponents of the general concept of arms control. The criticisms vary in quality and cogency. But some of them, at least, are persuasive

The Vienna talks on mutual and balanced force reductions in Europe (MBFR), launched in 1973, have still not reached agreement after 11 years. The West, with its smaller force deployments in the European theatre, has negotiated from a position of weakness. Provisional agreement has been reached on a common level to which the forces of each side should be reduced. But there has still been no agreement on how to count the forces or on the number of Warsaw Pact forces currently deployed in Europe. The phasing of troop withdrawals and procedures for verifying compliance have likewise not been agreed. The fundamental difficulty about these talks is that it is not clear that the Soviets share the Western interest in reducing force levels in Europe. Demographic problems could possibly change that in the 1990s. But in that event NATO would not necessarily have any interest in making compensating reductions – at least until the present predominance of Warsaw Pact forces has been eliminated.

Western critics of the SALT agreements argued that:

(i)   the United States negotiated from a position of weakness and the resulting agreements were unfair;

(ii) the agreements gave the impression that the United States had acquiesced in strategic inferiority;

(iii) they were not susceptible of satisfactory verification or enforcement;

(iv) they should not have been confined to so-called 'strategic' systems when intermediate-range systems can likewise hit targets in the Europe and the Soviet Union; and

(v) they failed to provide for any substantial reductions in the grossly excessive arsenals of the superpowers.

The first of these criticisms, though possibly justified in relation to SALT 2, is perhaps the least cogent. The SALT 1 limits did indeed give the Soviets a numerical advantage for five years in missile launcher vehicles. But the United States was able to retain a substantial superiority in bombers (not covered by the agreement) and number of warheads. The SALT 2 limits, while providing for numerical equality in launcher vehicles (including bombers), permitted larger throw-weights and missile sizes to the Soviet Union, in accordance with existing deployments. Here again, however, it is distinctly unlikely that the United States would have wished to avail itself of the option to raise throw-weights even if the SALT 2 agreement had permitted this.

The second criticism is rather more telling. Both the SALT agreements appeared to suggest to the non-expert (a category which includes the leaders of most other countries)[15] that the United States was now content to settle for a measure (no more) of strategic inferiority. This was admittedly not a useful signal to present to the rest of the world.

The third criticism – about verification and enforcement – carries greater conviction in relation to the more complex provisions of the unratified SALT 2 agreement than in relation to SALT 1. Heroically as the SALT 2 agreement grappled with the problem, the advent of multiple warheads has greatly complicated the business of arms control and verification, and SALT 2 probably depended more heavily than SALT 1 on mutual trust. The Soviets have arguably failed to comply with SALT 2 in certain significant respects.[16] On the other hand, the cheating which either side might plausibly risk could hardly be on a scale seriously to endanger national security or a stable balance of terror.

By far the most disappointing features of the SALT 1 and 2 agreements were those criticised in propositions (iv) and (v) above. As discussed earlier, the scale of the superpowers' present nuclear arsenals is manifestly excessive. Substantial reductions should be in the common interest. Yet the SALT 1 and 2 agreements left the way open for still further increases. The terms of the SALT 2 agreement admittedly required the Soviet Union to retire around

250 old systems. But the confinement of the agreements to strategic systems left the way open for the Soviets to deploy massive new forces of SS-20s directed against the European theatre.[17] The Soviets have thus been able to build up a troublesome superiority in intermediate-range theatre nuclear forces.

START, INF AND THE GENEVA NEGOTIATIONS

The Reagan administration, recognising the flaws in the earlier SALT agreements, entered at the end of 1981 and in 1982 the new negotiations with the Soviet Union mentioned earlier in the chapter, one on strategic and the other on intermediate-range nuclear forces (INF). The United States' declared aim in these negotiations was to reach agreement on substantial reductions in deployments of nuclear warheads. The administration re-christened the talks on strategic systems accordingly as reduction, not limitation, talks – START, not SALT.

Shortly before the INF negotiations began President Reagan offered not to deploy the new American intermediate-range forces in Europe if the Soviet Union would dismantle their intermediate-range forces, notably their SS-20s. This was the 'zero option' mentioned earlier in the chapter. The Soviets responded by rejecting the 'zero' option for themselves while insisting on it for NATO. They maintained, and have continued to maintain up to the time of writing, that they could not accept *any* new NATO deployments. The United States later proposed a world-wide limit of 420 INF warheads for each superpower. The Soviets' latest offer, in the autumn of 1983, was to restrict their SS-20s in Europe to 120, with no limit on those in the Far East, in return for zero deployments by NATO.

The American, British and German governments, resisting Soviet and domestic pressures, proceeded at the end of November 1983 to deploy the first batch of NATO's new intermediate-range forces.[18] The Soviets had thus failed in their objective of stopping the deployment of these forces. Bruised by this and by trenchant international criticism of their shooting down of a South Korean airliner in September 1983, they responded by breaking off the INF talks.

In the START talks on strategic forces, the two sides agreed to concentrate on limiting warheads rather than launcher systems (as in the SALT negotiations). The Soviets soon made clear, however, that they were not prepared to make such deep cuts as the Americans wanted. The latest American proposal in the autumn of 1983 was that each side should reduce its strategic missile warheads to 5000 (approximately two-third of existing figures), with accompanying limits to be negotiated on numbers of missiles, heavy missiles, land-based missiles, bombers and throw-weights. The United States also suggested a 'build-down' approach whereby, with limited exceptions, each side would withdraw more than one warhead for each new warhead introduced, warhead totals being reduced by at least 5 per cent a year.

The Soviets broke off the START talks, too, at the end of 1983, in response to the NATO INF deployments. In the course of 1984 they repeatedly expressed concern about President Reagan's decision to launch a major programme of research into the interception of ballistic missiles in space, the 'Strategic Defence Initiative' (popularly known as 'star wars'). They demanded that the United States should halt the programme (a demand which President Reagan categorically rejected) and argued strongly for negotiations on space weapons while firmly refusing to return to the INF and START negotiations. In practice, the Soviets have as strong an interest as the West in having negotiations on offensive systems and making a success of them, especially if they are anxious to limit further NATO INF deployments and to seek a ban on space weapons. It was therefore no surprise that the American and Soviet Foreign Ministers were able to agree in January 1985 on the launching of 'umbrella' talks covering strategic, intermediate-range and space weapons. These talks opened in Geneva in March 1985, shortly after the death of President Chernenko and the succession of Mr Gorbachov.

For all the reasons discussed earlier in the chapter, the two sides will not find it easy to bring these negotiations to a satisfactory conclusion. Any reductions in nuclear weapons which may be agreed are likely to be much smaller than would be desirable. The issue of space weapons will be a serious complication. The Soviets may well feel nervous about 'deep cuts' in offensive systems if they see development of effective defensive systems as a serious possibility. The United States is unlikely to agree to shelve the SDI programme, especially as the Soviets have already poured large amounts of resources into defensive systems. One must hope, however, that the two sides will reach a sensible agreement in spite of all the difficulties – possibly an agreement which combines 'deep cuts' in offensive systems with an extended moratorium on the deployment of new defensive systems. Arms control agreements are not *necessary* for stability: the balance of terror should continue to keep the world at peace without them. But the potential prizes from such agreements – enhanced security and stability, reduced levels of armaments, reduced dangers to the planet and economies in expenditure – are surely as rich and enticing as any prizes in history, for the nuclear powers and the rest of the world alike.

MUTUAL AND STABLE MINIMUM DETERRENCE (MSMD)

We ask finally: what kind of arms control agreements should the West in principle aim to secure? What should the objective be, in the medium term if not the short term?

The answer is, surely, that the West should set its sights on a *stable* balance of terror based on *mutual minimum deterrence*. The aim should be to negotiate agreements with that end in view – agreements under which the two sides would drastically reduce their nuclear arsenals to a 'minimum' level where they were still amply sufficient to deter but not grossly excessive as at present, the necessary reductions being made in a way which ensured that the remaining forces of each side were not vulnerable to counter-force strikes or at least would not give the other side any incentive to strike first.

We argued in chapter 8 that a strategy of *unilateral* minimum deterrence implied opting deliberately for vulnerability and strategic inferiority and would make the balance of terror unstable. It was unattractive on all those counts. A world order based on *mutual and stable* minimum deterrence *by agreement*, on the other hand, would be a different matter. It would offer security instead of vulnerability, parity instead of inferiority, stability instead of instability. Such a world order, if it could be achieved, would be far better than the balance of terror as it is now. The prizes of arms control would be won in spades. In contrast with nuclear disarmament or general and complete disarmament, moreover, a world order based on mutual and stable minimum deterrence does not strain the credulity: the risks which the two sides would take in reducing their nuclear arsenals, though not negligible, ought to be tolerable, especially if the agreement provided for phased reductions. At no point should it be necessary for either side to leave himself at the other's mercy if the other chose to cheat.

The quest for far-reaching agreements of this kind will encounter, often in severe form, all the problems discussed earlier in the chapter. In such agreements, however, lies the best hope for progress in the balance of terror.

10   Dynamic Stability

INTRODUCTION[1]

The prospects for peace between East and West depend not only on the 'intrinsic stability' of the balance of terror – the risk-aversion of each side, the characteristics of weapon systems, the balance of incentives and disincentives to open the striking and so on – but also on the 'dynamic stability' of actual world situations – on social, economic and political tensions, and on the reactions of political leaders, and peoples, to the march of events.

In the nature of things these dynamic factors are less susceptible of formal analysis, but they are none the less important for that. Two aspects are especially deserving of study – possible scenarios of future conflicts, and escalation processes. Such is the terrain which we explore in this and the two succeeding chapters.

FULL-SCALE ATTACK SCENARIO

So long as the balance of terror remains intrinsically stable, it is difficult to construct convincing scenarios in which either side could rationally decide to launch a nuclear conflict or take a serious risk of provoking the other side to launch one. For the reasons discussed in chapter 7, an aggressor is more likely either to launch a full-scale offensive, or to limit his attack to conventional forces, than to choose any intermediate option. Consistently with this there would appear to be two main ways in which a nuclear conflict might begin:

1. a full-scale attack by one side against the other, and
2. escalation from some local provocation, tension or disturbance, or some combination of such disturbances.

These possibilities are not mutually exclusive: a decision by one side or the other to launch a full-scale attack might be precipitated by escalating local provocations, tensions or disturbances.

We discussed the likely strategy and tactics of a full-scale attack, and the accompanying diplomacy, in the 'strike and bargain' scenario section of chapter 7. The risk that either side would open hostilities with a full-scale attack, delivered out of the blue, now seems extremely remote. But it cannot be totally ignored. Still less can one totally ignore the risk, especially in a context of first-striker's advantage, that one side might decide to escalate a limited conflict to a full-scale attack. Soviet strategic thinking lays heavy emphasis on the value of the surprise offensive, and history suggests that the impulse to prevent or pre-empt can be powerful, especially if the first striker enjoys a major advantage. For planning purposes, moreoever, the full-scale surprise offensive is important as being a 'worse possible' case.

TENSION AND PROVOCATION SCENARIOS

At the first East/West Summit Conference of the post-war years, in July 1955, Eisenhower, Dulles, Eden, Khruschev and Bulganin were able to agree informally that neither side had an interest in deliberately starting a thermonuclear war. The main focus of anxiety shifted accordingly from the scenario of a surprise nuclear attack to scenarios of escalation from local disturbances to all-out war. And there it has remained.

Fortunately for the world, events since 1945 suggest that East and West, for all their differences, do have the potential to coexist peacefully and prevent local disturbances from escalating into general war. The history of recent years is rich in examples of local tensions and disturbances, including several with superpower involvement, which have not so escalated. The Korean and Vietnamese wars, the Berlin crises and the Cuban missile crisis were all contained without leading to general war. Most of the multitude of other crises in recent years have never looked as if they might lead in that direction. Some points of tension, on the other hand, are clearly dangerous – especially those where East and West both believe their vital interests to be at stake.

Where in practice, it may be asked, are the vital interests of East and West most liable to clash? Geographically, the answer continues to lie in Europe. As discussed in chapter 5, East and West have for many years now tacitly accepted the status quo in Europe – the division of the continent into a Soviet bloc, a group of countries allied to the United States

nd a handful of neutral countries; a divided Germany with no independent
nuclear capabilities; a divided Berlin. These features of the status quo are
well understood. The division of Germany, in particular, has been well
described as 'nasty but clear'. There remains, however, the possibility that
a country in one or other of the groups will wish to change the status
quo. There is also some danger of disputes over countries such as Yugoslavia
and Finland about whose political status and allegiance there is no complete
understanding between East and West. Some specific examples of potentially
explosive developments in such areas would be:

1. development by West Germany of a nuclear capability, which the
   Soviets took upon themselves to destroy by a missile attack or limited
   invasion;[2]
2. attempts by neutral countries, such as Finland and Austria, to opt
   unequivocally for NATO or the Warsaw Pact;
3. a pro-Soviet communist takeover in one of the countries in NATO's
   southern flank;
4. revolts in East Germany, Poland or other East European countries
   against Moscow, with requests for Western help; and
5. Soviet intervention in Yugoslavia, accompanied by Yugoslav requests
   for Western help.

   None of these scenarios looks particularly probable at the time of
writing. Perhaps the least improbable is a revolt by one or more Soviet
bloc countries against the Soviet Union, as in scenario 4. But this would
seem less likely than the other scenarios to lead to military confrontation between East and West. In the shadow of the Polish crisis which
began in 1980, there may be more public sympathy in the West for the
lot of the East European peoples than at any previous time. But it remains
highly improbable that any Western country would risk intervening
within the Soviet bloc.
   More dangerous would be the other scenarios. In scenario 1, it would
be difficult, perhaps impossible, for NATO to turn a blind eye. In scenario
2, as well, the West could hardly stand idly by if the Soviets decided to
intervene. If NATO decided to intervene in scenario 3, it would be almost
as difficult for the Soviets to intervene militarily as for NATO to intervene
within the Soviet bloc. But the possibility could hardly be ruled out
altogether. Finally, in scenario 5, a United States administration would
be able to justify non-intervention but might decide, depending on circumstances, that the time had come for action.

It is far from inevitable that a military confrontation in any of these scenarios would lead to full-scale military exchanges between East and West. Each side would doubtless go out of its way to make clear to the other side (if there were any possibility of doubt) that his objectives were strictly limited. The incentives to find a negotiated solution would be powerful. Nevertheless, developments in Europe of the kind envisaged would be extremely dangerous, and the risks of escalation considerable.

Another area, often mentioned, where the superpowers might in principle see their vital interests as clashing is the Middle East. It is difficult, however, to see tensions in the Middle East leading the superpowers into direct conflict (still less, into general conflict) *unless* the Soviet Union embarked on an aggressive policy of subjugating or subverting Middle East oil suppliers. If the Soviets followed up their invasion of Afghanistan by invading Iran (with which they likewise share a long border), or by engineering and sustaining an Iranian communist takeover, the United States might well feel bound actively to support the anti-Soviet forces within the country – especially if there were any threat to the passage of oil tankers through the Straits of Hormuz. Similarly with other Middle East oil producer countries, a United States administration would probably not let Soviet intervention or subversion pass unchallenged. There is no obvious reason, however, why the Soviets should need to pursue such policies. They might be tempted by the prospect of controlling some of the Middle East oil fields, especially if their own production were to fall away and they required oil imports on a large scale. But aggressive policies of intervention or active subversion in the area would be so obviously provocative and dangerous that the Soviet Union would probably hesitate long before pursuing them – except perhaps in the context of an all-out war which had started elsewhere.

There are other areas as well where tensions could in principle become serious. One example would be Soviet interference in Latin America. But Latin America is not an area where the Soviets could claim vital interests, and it would be surprising if the Soviets were to press their luck there too far. Another example is Korea, where resumed conflict between North and South cannot be ruled out and the superpowers would probably become involved. In Korea as in Germany, however, the present division of the country is 'nasty but clear', and East and West are probably both well aware that there is no other possible division in which they could both acquiesce: such was the lesson of the Korean War of 1950-3. It seems reasonable to suppose, moreover, that any renewed conflict in Korea could again be contained within that country. And the same con clusion applies to Third World conflicts in general. If the Soviets were to step up their Third World offensives, the United States might feel bound actively to support the anti-Soviet forces in the countries concerned. One side or the other would then win or (more probably) some formula for withdrawal would be found. There is no necessary reason why the arena of conflict should spread beyond the countries concerned.

Wherever the arena of potential conflict may be, probably the greatest threat to peace and stability lies in aggressive or provocative political behaviour by one or other (or both) of the superpowers – behaviour which offends against the tacit codes of practice developed over nearly forty years of armed peace. We noted in chapter 5 that East and West are committed not just to preserving peace but to preserving it on acceptable terms; not just to avoiding military struggle, but to avoiding political defeat. If either superpower were to push too far and persistently his pursuit of political victories and terms unacceptable to the other, the world would become a truly dangerous place. The superpowers have shown themselves capable of swallowing considerable amounts of unfriendly behaviour by each other; but if one of them were to pursue blatantly aggressive, reaction-testing policies world-wide – if, for example, the Soviet Union were to intensify its policy of building up offensive forces, stationing troops and missiles as close as possible to the United States and its allies, providing military intervention or support in a large number of Third World countries, attempting to subvert democratic governments world-wide, and abetting terrorism in these countries – then peace and stability would be truly threatened. Local tensions may provide the theatres of crisis, and bad relations between the two sides may be much intensified by suspicion and misunderstanding. But provocation, especially cumulative provocation, is the ultimate and fundamental enemy of stability.

To recognise these dangers is one thing. To devise policies for dealing with them is another. We return to this in chapter 14. Suffice it here to say that the West would not be likely to increase the probability of world peace and stability by policies of minimum involvement and accommodation of Soviet political offensives. On the contrary, the surest way of encouraging provocative behaviour by a potential enemy is to accept military inferiority, to convey an impression of weakness of will, to offer him the prospect of sitting targets and risk-free gains. The best way of discouraging such behaviour is to make potential enemies see how dangerous it would be. To this end the West needs to combine military strength and vigilance with perceived firmness of purpose, while avoiding any undue impression of belligerence.

PROLIFERATION, ACCIDENT AND MADNESS SCENARIOS

For the time being at least, scenarios where East and West are drawn into conflict as a result of nuclear proliferation, accident or madness seem even more remote than those discussed in the two preceding sections.

To begin with proliferation, there must unfortunately be a distinct possibility that, in the longer term, a considerable number of countries will come to acquire nuclear weapons. If that does happen, the world could be a more dangerous place. The risk that reckless or irresponsible hands would gain control of these weapons would increase. So too would the risk of wars by miscalculation. It does not follow, however, that there need be catastrophic consequences for peace between the major powers. The new nuclear countries would be most likely to use their nuclear weapons, if at all, against each other. There is no evident or necessary reason why such an exchange, tragic as it would be, should lead to a nuclear confrontation between East and West.[3]

War by accident, in the sense of war resulting from a missile being launched in error by someone who misread instructions or misinterpreted warning devices, is fortunately an improbable scenario. Governments which possess nuclear weapons are likely to take the utmost care to establish foolproof launching procedures which make mischievous or accidental release impossible. If, against all the odds, a missile were released by accident, the government concerned would undoubtedly warn the expected victim as soon as possible and explain that an accident had occurred. In such circumstances the danger of escalation to all-out war should be small. As noted in chapter 9, the United States, France and Britain all have agreements with the Soviet Union on procedures in the event of accidental release.

The danger of war by madness, or sudden insanity, of a country's leader likewise seems remote. Fail-safe procedures should ensure that release cannot occur as a result of the madness of any single person below the supreme leader, and these procedures may even extend to the supreme leader himself. In the Soviet Union a decision to release would presumably be taken, not by one man, but by the politburo. In the United States it seems highly unlikely that subordinate officers would carry out a release order if there were any shadow of doubt about the President's sanity.

MISUNDERSTANDING

War by misunderstanding hardly counts as a scenario in itself. But misunderstanding, suspicion and misreading of the other side's intentions are great catalysts of crisis, both at the outset and at the later stages. All too often in history, misunderstanding has played a major role in the outbreak of wars and their subsequent escalation. The issue of mutual misunderstanding will recur repeatedly in this and later chapters.

ESCALATION AND THE BOUNDARIES OF CRISIS

The other major issue within the subject of dynamic stability is escalation. How probable is it that local tensions or disturbances will in fact escalate to major conflict? And what can be done to minimise the probability?

Before trying to answer these questions, we need to make some preliminary observations about the nature of crises and the escalation process, and to introduce some terminology.

The first observation is that all crises are ultimately political, not military. We referred in chapter 5 to Clausewitz's famous insight about the political nature of war:[4]

> We see, therefore, that war is not merely a political act, but also a real political instrument, a continuation of political commerce, a carrying out of the same by other means . . . The political view is the object, war is the means . . .

> In general it is supposed that [political] intercourse is broken off by war, and that a totally different state of things ensues, subject to no laws but its own. We maintain, on the contrary, that war is nothing but a continuation of political intercourse, with a mixture of other means . . . Thus political intercourse does not cease by the war itself . . . but continues to exist, whatever may be the form of the means which it uses.

As with war, so with the crises which concern us here: the nature of the game is that each side tries to make the other side accept his own political solution or, failing that, a solution acceptable to himself which the other side will not contest. In other words, crises are an exercise in political bargaining, which may be tacit or overt and in which the use of force may or may not play a part.

The second observation is that those participating in the political bargaining will have two main preoccupations – not just the outcome of the crisis but also the risks and costs which the achievement of any particular outcome would involve. Especially in the presence of nuclear weapons, they will be concerned about how far the crisis should be allowed to develop and where its boundaries should be drawn.

The third observation is that the boundaries within which a crisis is to be contained are likely to form a crucial element in the bargaining process. The outcome of the crisis may well depend on how far each side is prepared to go, what risks he is prepared to take in support of his desired outcome, and how far he is willing to extend the boundaries of the conflict.

The fourth observation is that escalation of a crisis consists in decisions by one side or the other to cross such boundaries. Extending the boundaries may be a matter of diplomacy, such as intensifying threats and ultimatums or ordering mobilisation. It may be a matter of the force level used, such as increasing the number of combat troops or introducing nuclear weapons. Or it may be a matter of geography, such as broadening the conflict to a new theatre. Crises can escalate in all these ways.

Finally, the 'boundaries' of a crisis, which are sometimes referred to as 'saliencies' or 'firebreaks', may or may not be plain to see. Between verbal threats and actual use of force, for example, there is the clearest possible firebreak. Similarly, the side which escalates from conventional to nuclear force levels clearly crosses a highly significant boundary, or saliency. Is there, however, a firebreak between theatre nuclear weapons and strategic nuclear weapons? We consider this question in chapter 12.

FACTORS AFFECTING ESCALATION

We can now return to our earlier question: how probable is it that local tensions involving East and West will escalate into major conflict?

The short answer is that, while much is bound to depend on surrounding circumstances, there is one powerful restraint on escalation – the shared interest of each side in avoiding war, especially nuclear war; but there are also several possible inducements to escalation – the loser's temptation to escalate; the temptation on both sides to leap-frog; and the dangers of misunderstanding, misinterpretation, miscalculation.

In crises involving East and West, the shared interest of each side in avoiding war, and in particular nuclear war, must act as an exceptionally powerful restraint on escalation. It cannot be relied on, however, to prevent escalation altogether. One side or the other (or both) may attach the highest importance to obtaining a desired political outcome from the crisis and be prepared to take considerable risks, including substantial escalation of the crisis, in order to achieve such an outcome.

Also relevant in this connection is first-striker's advantage. If the first side to strike with nuclear weapons is perceived to have an advantage, that is likely, initially at least, to intensify the restraints on the two sides by making each the more cautious about opening conventional hostilities in case the other should decide to strike first with his nuclear forces. As we have seen in earlier chapters, however, this restraining influence has to be weighed against the dangerous incentive which first-striker's advantage provides for each side to strike first at the nuclear level – and to strike sooner rather than later – if only to deny the advantage to the other side.

Among the factors which tend to encourage escalation, the desire to obtain military or political advantage, and to avoid disadvantage, is especially important – above all the desire to avoid losing. History is rich in examples of professional advice that victory is within grasp if only force levels can be raised or permission be granted for geographical extension of the conflict, such as strikes against bases in enemy territory. Even more important than the desire to win, however, is the desire to avoid losing. The desire not to lose a battle or confrontation, once begun, to avoid the humiliation of defeat or loss of face, can all too easily tempt the potential loser to escalate the crisis – perhaps by raising force levels, perhaps by applying pressures in another theatre. The problem may be aggravated by the fact that each side's perception of the stakes is likely to rise as the crisis escalates: the further each side has committed himself on an issue, the less acceptable it will be to climb down.

A familiar example of defeat-avoiding escalation as a matter of policy may be found in NATO's flexible response doctrine, which keeps open the option of resort to nuclear weapons in the event of a Soviet advance into Western Europe which NATO's conventional forces are unable to contain. We return to this subject in chapters 11 and 12.

A second factor which may induce escalation is the temptation to react explosively or to 'leap-frog'. One side may decide to demonstrate his resolve or to 'warn off' the other side by 'overtrumping' any trump the other has played, rather than simply matching it. The side in question may or may not be fully seized of the escalatory implications. Especially dangerous is the case where one side or the other (or both) tries to force a solution of the crisis quite unacceptable to the other side by deliberately escalating the crisis and thus demonstrating that he is prepared to go further, and take more risks, than the other side. If the other side also feels strongly committed, there may be competition in risk-taking as each side tries to force his own solution.

A third factor which may lead to escalation is misinterpretation and misjudgement. It is all too easy for each side to exaggerate the other's intentions, especially under crisis conditions. Judgements about intentions may, of course, err in the other direction as well. Wishful thinking may persuade political leaders that the enemy's protestations are more trust-worthy, and his aims more limited, than they really are. But at times of crisis, when the strain on political and military leaders is intense and a chorus of advice floods in from loud-mouthed commentators without operational responsibilities, opinion may polarise towards extremes, and the very occurrence of the crisis may strengthen the hawks more than the doves.

Corresponding to these dangers of misinterpretation is the danger that each side will misjudge how its actions will be interpreted by the other side. A step intended to demonstrate strength of feelings or purpose may be interpreted by the other side as a belligerent act, indicating warlike intentions.

One conclusion suggested by this analysis is that dynamic stability is likely to depend importantly on the ability of the protagonists in the drama to perceive the dangers of crisis situations and restrain their actions accordingly. It is likely to depend, in short, on their understanding of certain aspects of crisis management.

CRISIS MANAGEMENT

The art of crisis management is not simply a matter of perceiving the risk in crisis situations and then avoiding them. There are some risks which it may be essential to take. As the exponents of game theory in the 1950s and early 1960s recognised, the art lies rather in seeing how to combine achievement of the best available outcome with the avoidance of un-necessary risk – in judging what the range of available outcomes is, what risks should and should not be taken, how the bargaining should be conducted, how and when the crisis should be escalated or de-escalated. It is this combination of requirements that makes the task of crisis manage-ment difficult – this, and the strains on political leaders in times of crisis which have been well compared to those on a driver in a skid.[5]

To elaborate the point a little, crisis management would be a simple matter if the objective were simply to minimise the dangers in the immediate crisis. The decision rule would be to make all the concessions needed to placate the other side. The reality is different. The way in which the crisis is settled matters as well. The crisis manager may be compared with an entrepreneur. Without risks there will be no profits. Yet he must choose his risks carefully. Wrong choices may bring severe penalties, such as heavy losses or even bankruptcy.

All that being said, it is clearly of the first importance that crisis managers should have the keenest perception of the risks in crisis situations. Security and stability may be seriously endangered if they do not. The prospects for preserving peace will be greater, the more conscious national leaders are of the dangers of escalation; of the need to stop conflicts at the earliest possible stage; of the need to avoid inflated expectations; of the need to save the other side's face too, if necessary; of the need to evaluate his intentions carefully (and likewise the impressions he will receive from the home country's own actions); and of the need for good communications and dialogue.

The importance of a high awareness of the escalation process – how it works and what the dangers are – needs little elaboration. The chances of avoiding wars which neither side wants must be greatly enhanced if each side is conscious of the significance of crossing boundaries, saliencies or firebeaks, in the sense discussed earlier, and if each side is able to look beyond the next, immediate move to later moves.

It is sometimes suggested that the Soviets have a different *Weltanschauung*, based on the advantages of surprise and the necessity for winning, which is incompatible with the notions of escalation, boundaries, saliencies and firebreaks. On this view, the Soviets will never play the game according to rules of this kind. If such a view were correct, the implications for dynamic stability would be serious. But it is surely not correct as it stands. It seems highly improbable that, in any danger scenario where the Soviet leaders are wondering what steps to take next, they would neglect to consider likely responses by the West and the dangers for the Soviet Union if the conflict were extended to higher force levels or different geographical areas.

A tendency to underrate the risks of escalation does appear to run through some European strategic thinking, and in particular the thinking of those who criticise the United States for not committing itself more unequivocally to use its nuclear arsenal in defence of Europe. It is easy for those who would not bear the responsibility to advocate the use of nuclear weapons by others. But the Americans, and likewise others who have the responsibility, must inevitably reserve the right to weigh the balance of risks and potential benefits at the time – not least the risks of escalation and the dangers to the United States itself. It is quite unreasonable to expect the Americans to provide assurances which no responsible possessor of nuclear weapons could possibly give and which, if they were given, would detract perceptibly from dynamic stability.

The risks of escalation, and the tendency for the stakes to rise as conflicts continue, underline the importance of stopping conflicts at the earliest possible stage. The longer they continue, the greater the dangers are likely to become.

It is hardly less important that crisis managers should have the ability to avoid inflated expectations about the outcome of a crisis – to be realistic in their assessment of what outcome can be expected without a major conflagration, and to recognise that there are limits to the extent to which the other side will be prepared to lose face. In the latter connection, there is obvious importance in leaving the other side a tolerable 'way out', if he is making the major concession. A classic example of this is provided by the Cuban missile crisis of 1962 when, in return for Khruschev's agreement to remove the missiles, President Kennedy undertook to lift the American blockade and not to invade Cuba.[6]

The importance of evaluating carefully the other side's objectives likewise needs little elaboration. It is all too easy for each side to exaggerate the other's intentions, or to lose perspective. Hardly less important is the need for each side to evaluate carefully the interpretation which the other side is likely to put on his own actions. Misunderstanding is the enemy of stability.

Lastly, there is the matter of communication. It would be hard to exaggerate the extent to which dynamic stability depends on the willingness and ability of the two sides to open a dialogue with each other at the earliest possible stage and continue the dialogue throughout the crisis. The chances of successful dialogue will be greatly enhanced by established channels of communication with the other side and a habit of negotiation – two aspects which we discussed earlier under the heading of intrinsic stability.[7] Dialogue also depends on time: weapon systems need to be designed, as far as possible, to leave political leaders maximum time for decision, consultation and dialogue. Even with dialogue, the dangers of misunderstanding and miscalculation are considerable. Without dialogue, they must be far greater.

11 Extended Deterrence and First Nuclear Use

INTRODUCTION

We now turn to the crucial issues of escalation from conventional to nuclear force levels and from one nuclear force level to another.

For the NATO alliance, these issues are far more likely to arise in the European theatre than anywhere else, and they are complicated by the fact that one country, the United States, controls most of the alliance's nuclear forces. Hence the question of nuclear use is intimately connected in practice with that of 'extending' the deterrent power of the United States' strategic nuclear forces to protect Western Europe as well as the United States, by means of a close 'linkage' or 'coupling' between the alliance's conventional forces and the United States' strategic nuclear forces – the so-called nuclear 'umbrella'.

EXTENDED DETERRENCE

The deterrence strategies of the NATO alliance rely crucially on the perceived willingness of the United States to use its military strength, nuclear as well as conventional, in the defence of Western Europe. The military forces of the West European countries would, on their own, be no match for those of the Soviet Union. Hence NATO's ability to deter Soviet aggression, or intimidation, against Western Europe depends on persuading the Soviets that the United States stands behind Western Europe. Specifically, it depends on persuading them that, if they were to launch an attack against West European or other NATO countries, even a conventional attack, they must reckon with the certainty of a conventional response by the United States and the possibility of a nuclear response, not excluding a strategic nuclear response if necessary. The 'coupling' of the alliance's conventional forces in Europe to the United States' nuclear arsenal lies at the heart of NATO's strategy. 'Uncoupling' would leave it in ruins. For effective deterrence in Europe, therefore, the United States needs to reinforce and amplify the 'flexible response' message from NATO to the Soviet Union discussed in chapter 2 with a bilateral 'extended deterrence' postscript, on the following lines:

> It would be madness for you to attack Western Europe, or to behave as if Western Europe lay at your mercy. If you did attack, we would regard that as we would regard an attack on the United States itself, and we would fight back alongside our European and NATO allies. Do not imagine, either, that you could count on limiting the war by attacking at the conventional level with your massive conventional forces. We reserve the right – especially if your conventional attack should show any sign of succeeding – to respond by using our nuclear forces, including our strategic nuclear forces if necessary. So you see how appallingly risky the game would be, and how insane it would be for either of us to begin such a game in the first place.

FIRST NUCLEAR USE

As the 'postscript' implies, NATO's strategy for deterrence depends not just on the United States' commitment to Western Europe but also on the willingness of the alliance – in particular, the United States – to use nuclear weapons first if necessary. Compared with earlier philosophies of 'massive retaliation', flexible response may be a strategy of minimum force. But it is also a strategy of *enough* force. It warns any potential aggressor that NATO may be expected to escalate a conventional conflict to the nuclear force level if necessary, and even *in extremis* to the strategic nuclear force level, rather than submit to defeat.

NATO's perceived readiness to escalate the conflict in this way, and use nuclear weapons first if necessary, is perhaps less widely understood than most other aspects of the alliance's strategy. It is, however, a key element in the alliance's deterrence against a conventional Soviet attack.

If NATO were clearly superior to the Warsaw Pact at the conventional level, this aspect of the strategy would be rather less important. In practice however, NATO's conventional capabilities have always been, and remain inferior to those of the Warsaw Pact, in quantitative terms at least (see figures 11.1 and 11.2). That is why it has been a cornerstone of NATO thinking that the alliance might need to use nuclear weapons first, especially if its conventional forces were driven back by a conventional Soviet attack or approached the point where they were unable to continue fighting.

CREDIBILITY

A strategy which depends on the willingness of the United States to use nuclear weapons first, if necessary, for the defence of others is bound to suffer in some degree from credibility problems. The decision to cross the nuclear Rubicon would be one of supreme gravity, possibly the most awesome and momentous decision in history. The risks involved – escalation to general nuclear warfare in Europe or even an all-out nuclear conflict – would be on a scale to dwarf those involved in any previous decision. There must inevitably be a degree of doubt as to the willingness of the President of the United States, when it came to the point, to take such a decision – to carry his commitment to the defence of Europe to the point of authorising first use of nuclear weapons against an enemy possessing an enormous arsenal of such weapons and a capability to retaliate massively against the United States itself. It would be idle to pretend otherwise. As we argued earlier, however, the system of mutual deterrence is fairly robust in this respect. NATO's credibility would have to be extraordinarily low, and the Soviet leadership's willingness to take monumental risks extraordinarily high, before deterrence would be likely to fail. The Soviet leaders might well think it improbable – even highly improbable – that a particular President of the United States would ever escalate a conflict from conventional to nuclear force levels; but they would have to feel all but certain about this judgement – all but certain that, even in the heat of crisis, he would never authorise first use of nuclear weapons – before they could safely decide to open hostilities. In the nature of things such a degree of certainty is highly unlikely.

That said, it has to be a continuing task for the United States and NATO to enhance the credibility of the strategic posture of 'extended deterrence' – to convince the Soviets that the alliance means what it says when it talks of its readiness to escalate if necessary from conventional to nuclear force levels. How can conviction and credibility be enhanced?

In the first place, the general credibility of the posture will be enhanced to the extent that the United States and other NATO powers show, by word and deed, that they are united and have the will to protect their own legitimate interests, and those of their allies, by use of force if necessary. We discussed in chapter 5 the importance of sending the correct signals to potential opponents.

A second, crucial requirement is that NATO should raise the nuclear threshold as high as possible by postponing as long as possible the point at which the alliance might feel obliged to escalate the conflict to the nuclear force level for the avoidance of serious disadvantage or defeat. The higher the nuclear threshold is, the less heavily the alliance's deter-

132

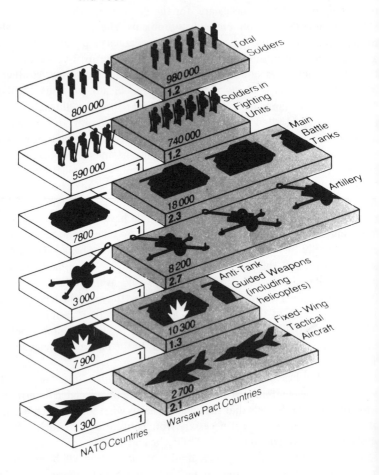

FIGURE 11.1   *Balance of conventional forces on the Central Front, end-1983*

Total Soldiers
980 000
1.2
800 000
1

Soldiers in Fighting Units
740 000
1.2
590 000
1

Main Battle Tanks
18 000
2.3
7800
1

Artillery
8 200
2.7
3 000
1

Anti-Tank Guided Weapons (including helicopters)
10 300
1.3
7 900
1

Fixed-Wing Tactical Aircraft
2 700
2.1
1 300
1

Warsaw Pact Countries

NATO Countries

Source: Statement on the Defence Estimates 1984.

Reproduced by kind permission of the Ministry of Defence, London.

rence will have to depend on the threat of nuclear escalation by the United States, and the more credible that threat will become. A high nuclear threshold depends in turn on the possession of strong capabilities below the nuclear level – in particular, strong conventional capabilities.

FIGURE 11.2 *Balance of ready maritime forces in the Eastern Atlantic, end-1983*

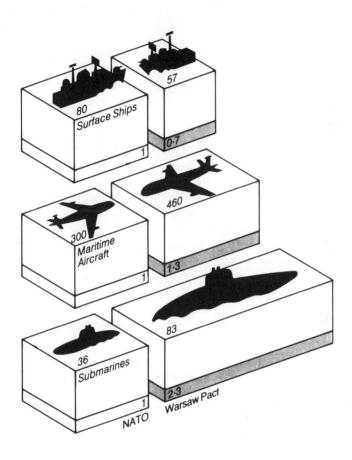

Source: Statement on the Defence Estimates 1984.
Reproduced by kind permission of the Ministry of Defence, London.

Also crucial to the credibility of NATO's posture are the physical presence of American forces in Europe – which means that a Soviet invasion would immediately bring the Soviet Union into direct military conflict with the United States – and the perceived ability of the United

States to send massive reinforcements of men and equipment across the Atlantic to Western Europe in the event of hostilities. NATO's ability to sustain a conventional conflict in Europe depends, and can be seen to depend, on these reinforcements, and hence on the Atlantic 'bridge'. The 'bridge' in turn depends on continuing possession by NATO of superiority at sea in the places which matter.

GLENDOWER : I can call spirits from the vasty deep.

HOTSPUR   : Why, so can I, or so can any man;
                     But will they come when you do call for them?

Lastly, the credibility of NATO's option for first use of nuclear weapons must be enhanced by possession of flexible weapon systems and in particular a range of small and intermediate theatre nuclear weapons. Clearly, a decision to introduce nuclear weapons would never be easy. But equally clearly a decision to introduce nuclear weapons on a basis which was strictly limited, and publicly declared to be so limited, would be significantly easier than a decision to escalate straight to strategic nuclear weapons. It can be assumed that the Soviets are well seized of this point. Hence weapon flexibility is likely to enhance deterrence by making NATO's option for first use of nuclear weapons more credible.

As this implies, theatre nuclear weapons have a key role to play in deterrence strategies which depend on the threat of first nuclear use. It is therefore necessary to consider the role of these weapons in some depth.

ROLE OF THEATRE NUCLEAR WEAPONS

What are 'theatre' nuclear systems and how do they differ from 'strategic' systems? The term 'strategic nuclear weapons' has traditionally been applied to the larger-yield missiles of intercontinental range, and long-range heavy bombers, which can be launched from bases in the homeland of one superpower against military or civilian targets thousands of miles away in the homeland of the other superpower. The terms 'tactical nuclear weapons' or 'theatre nuclear weapons' have traditionally been applied to smaller-yield, shorter-range weapons, located in a particular theatre of war such as Europe and designed for use in that theatre. Over the period of the Strategic Arms Limitation Talks (SALT) between the United States and the Soviet Union, however, the definitions changed somewhat. The term 'strategic' came to be applied to the weapons covered by those talks and the resulting SALT agreements, while the 'theatre' label is now commonly applied to all nuclear weapons other than those covered by those agreements – a recursive as opposed to a functional definition.

Theatre nuclear forces as now defined cover a wide spectrum of weapon systems which vary greatly in size, range and purpose. The spectrum encompasses landmines, artillery shells, short- and intermediate-range missiles, short- and medium-range bombers and depth bombs for use at sea. The warheads carried by these weapons vary in yield from low to high kilotons. The smaller weapons at the lower end of the spectrum are designed specifically for battlefield and tactical use. The intermediate-range missiles at the upper end are functionally akin to strategic systems: NATO's intermediate-range systems can reach targets in the Soviet Union, while the Soviets' intermediate-range systems can reach targets anywhere in Western Europe.

Both the Soviet Union and NATO deploy substantial numbers of theatre nuclear weapons in, or close to, the European theatre. NATO is known to have about 6000 nuclear warheads in the theatre. The role of these theatre systems can be summarised under four main headings:

1. to contribute to deterrence against conventional attack;
2. to deter first use of theatre nuclear weapons by the Soviet Union;
3. to improve the chances of stopping a war once begun, by obliging an aggressor to stop and reconsider; and
4. to enhance the alliance's ability to fight such a war if necessary, and to keep it limited.

THEATRE NUCLEAR WEAPONS AND DETERRENCE AGAINST CONVENTIONAL ATTACK

How can theatre nuclear weapons help to deter the Soviet Union from launching a conventional attack in Europe? The answer is that NATO's deterrence of a conventional Soviet attack depends importantly on its perceived readiness to use nuclear weapons first, especially if the conventional attack shows signs of succeeding, and possession of theatre nuclear weapons makes the option of first use of nuclear weapons more credible. As we argued earlier, a decision to introduce theatre nuclear weapons on a strictly limited basis, appallingly difficult as it would be, would be easier than a decision to escalate directly from conventional to strategic nuclear force levels, and the Soviet Union may be assumed to be well aware of this. Hence deployment by NATO of theatre nuclear forces is likely to heighten the Soviets' perception of the risk that aggression at the conventional level would lead to a nuclear confrontation, and thus to strengthen deterrence.

Also relevant in this connection is the question of temptation. NATO's effective deterrence would be much reduced, and the danger of hostilities in Western Europe correspondingly increased, if the Soviets thought they could snatch a quick victory, or quickly achieve some limited objective, at the conventional level. Local deployment of small 'battlefield' nuclear weapons by NATO must help to increase the perceived risk that NATO would decide quickly to use nuclear weapons in response. Such deployments may also help to reduce the temptation to attack by compelling a potential aggressor to deploy his conventional forces in sub-optimal formations.

How much the deployment of theatre nuclear weapons will strengthen NATO's deterrence against conventional attack depends on a range of further factors, including the relative strengths of the two sides in these weapons, the Soviets' perception of the likelihood that NATO would in fact escalate the conflict to the theatre nuclear level, their perception of the possibility of limiting nuclear war once begun and the degree of first-striker's advantage at both the tactical and strategic nuclear levels. If, for example, the Soviets believed that they themselves enjoyed massive superiority in theatre nuclear weapons and that the principal concern of the United States would be to avoid escalation beyond the theatre nuclear to the strategic nuclear level, the contribution made to deterrence by NATO's possession of theatre nuclear weapons could be small. If, on the other hand, the Soviets felt that the military balance in theatre nuclear weapons was fairly even, and that the Americans would be prepared to use these weapons much sooner than strategic weapons in the event of reverses at the conventional level, then NATO's theatre nuclear weapons should enhance the Soviets' perception of the risks in aggression at the conventional level and thus contribute powerfully to deterrence against such aggression. The Soviets' perception of these risks would be further enhanced if they felt they could not count on the conflict being contained at the theatre nuclear level (and especially if they should perceive the Americans to have a significant first-striker's advantage at the strategic level).

It might be objected that, perversely, deployment of theatre nuclear forces by NATO may actually weaken deterrence against conventional attack by reducing Soviet perceptions of the risk that the United States would use its strategic nuclear forces at an early stage. The increase in the total options available to the United States may, on this view, reduce the perceived probability that the United States would ever decide in practice on the most terrible option of all, thus threatening to 'uncouple' NATO's conventional forces from the ultimate deterrent of the United States' strategic nuclear forces.

This objection recalls the 'cornered beast' philosophy discussed in chapter 8. The comments made there remain pertinent. It is doubtless true that possession by NATO of theatre nuclear capabilities is likely to reduce Soviet perceptions of the risk that the United States would resort early to use of strategic nuclear weapons. In that sense the deterrent effect against conventional attack of the United States's strategic nuclear forces may be diminished. But it makes little sense to talk in this way about the deterrent effects of particular weapons systems in isolation. What matters is the deterrent effect of the alliance's military posture as a whole. This in turn depends ultimately on the credibility of the posture – without credibility, deterrence is nothing – and it is on credibility that the 'cornered beast' posture breaks down. Certainly, such a posture might work. The Soviets might very well be deterred from committing limited conventional aggression against Western Europe by the fear that the United States might respond at the strategic nuclear level. But they might alternatively judge that the Americans would be at least as concerned as themselves to avoid the cataclysmic consequences of a strategic nuclear exchange, and that could encourage them to discount heavily the risk of a strategic nuclear response by the United States. In that event, they might not be deterred from limited aggression at the conventional level, still less from attempting to exercise political muscle, or blackmail, over Western Europe. Hence a 'cornered beast' posture which tried to do without theatre nuclear weapons – like one which tried to make do with weak conventional forces – would leave NATO exposed to the danger of having its bluff called. Deterrence would be weakened.

THEATRE NUCLEAR WEAPONS AND DETERRENCE AGAINST THEATRE NUCLEAR ATTACK

A second role of Nato's theatre nuclear weapons is to deter aggression by the Soviet Union at the theatre nuclear level (as well as the conventional level) and to discourage first use of nuclear weapons at the theatre level by the Soviet Union.

It is easy to overlook this role. For if the Soviets are stronger than NATO at the conventional level – as is generally believed – their interest must evidently lie in limiting any conflict to the conventional level rather than taking the terrible risk of introducing nuclear weapons. But it is possible to conceive of a number of scenarios in which the Soviets' perception of where their interests lie might be different.

In the first place the Soviets might judge that they enjoyed superiority in theatre nuclear weapons and could obtain a decisive military advantage provided that they struck first. The possibility of their using these weapons first in such circumstances cannot be ruled out. Second, they might judge that NATO as well had a major first-striker's advantage in theatre nuclear weapons. In that event, they would have the added incentive of preventing or pre-empting first use by NATO. The danger of first use by the Soviet Union would then be especially acute.[1] Yet another possibility is that in contrast with the scenario most often discussed, the Soviets might find themselves facing defeat by NATO at the conventional level. In such circumstances they might be tempted to avoid defeat by escalating to the theatre nuclear force level – a temptation which would be stronger the greater they believed their superiority over NATO to be in a first strike with theatre nuclear weapons.

In all these cases the Soviets would have a considerable incentive to use theatre nuclear weapons first. That is not to say that they would actually do so. Against the incentives to use such weapons they would have (as would NATO in similar circumstances) to set the dangers of escalation to a full-scale nuclear exchange – dangers which would be enhanced from the Soviet point of view if the United States possessed a substantial first-striker's advantage at the strategic level. Yet the possibility of first use of theatre nuclear weapons by the Soviets cannot be ruled out, and NATO needs a strong theatre nuclear capability so as to make that scenario as remote as possible.

STOPPING A WAR ONCE BEGUN[2]

If deterrence has broken down initially, and an aggressor has launched an attack at the conventional level which is succeeding or shows signs of doing so, NATO's next priority would be to compel him to stop and reconsider.

The United States could in theory launch a strategic nuclear weapon or weapons for this purpose. But any President of the United States would be bound to postpone recourse to the ultimate force level for as long as possible. Even then, the choice of target – real or demonstrative – would be problematic.

Controlled use of small theatre nuclear weapons against the enemy's front line, or a key target or targets behind the front line, would be less dangerous, and probably more effective in terms of the tactical situation. Here, too, the first strike could in principle be purely demonstrative: the warheads could be directed against a target area where minimum damage would be done. But a first strike which also checked the aggressor's advance by destroying a key military target or targets on or behind the aggressor's front line would oblige him to address fresh and dangerous decisions and might more effectively destroy his will to continue.

FIGHTING THE WAR AND KEEPING IT LIMITED

If NATO's first use of nuclear weapons failed to halt the aggressor, it would be a continuing objective to oblige him to stop and reconsider, while fighting and limiting the war as effectively as possible. Other important requirements might be to buy time for negotiation or to match use of theatre nuclear weapons by the aggressor.

In all these contexts, the role of theatre nuclear weapons could be crucial. Without such weapons, and in particular a range of relatively small 'battlefield' weapons, NATO could find itself confronted by an impossible choice between conceding defeat at the conventional level and resort to the ultimate force level of strategic nuclear weapons; and this could only increase the dangers of massive mutual destruction.

None of the above is to suggest that theatre nuclear weapons could readily be used alongside conventional weapons as part of a coherent battle plan. Neither is it to suggest that such weapons could be relied on to turn a losing tactical situation into a winning one, still less to turn defeat into victory by removing an aggressor's physical ability to continue the battle. The difficulties of using theatre nuclear weapons in or around the battlefield, and especially over home territory, are plain to see. So too are the possibilities of chaos. In physical terms, the more realistic aim would be to interrupt an aggressor's career by inflicting a major setback on him. More important still, as implied above, would be the aim of destroying his will to persevere.

FLEXIBILITY

NATO's chances of avoiding defeat and keeping the conflict limited are likely to be much increased if its theatre nuclear weapons are flexible.

The theatre nuclear arsenal needs to include smaller battlefield systems and medium-range systems as well as the intermediate-range systems which are more akin to strategic weapons. A range of systems is needed so that the alliance can keep the nuclear bidding low, avoid unnecessary escalation, attack key targets successfully and minimise the risk of unintended collateral damage.

It is sometimes argued that, on the contrary, there are dangers for stability in having too great a flexibility, too finely graded a spectrum, of nuclear weapon systems. One danger is that the dividing line, or fire-break, between conventional and nuclear weapons might become blurred. It is possible to conceive, for example, of battlefield nuclear shells or missiles with no significant radiation or fall-out – weapons which would be virtually identical in their effects (though not in their technology) to highly effective conventional weapons, or groups of weapons: the so-called 'neutron bomb', whose production President Carter vetoed in 1978 but President Reagan ordered in 1981, comes fairly close to this limiting case.[3] If the nuclear powers possessed such weapons, they might find it easier, and hence more tempting, to cross the nuclear threshold.

After the threshold had been crossed, moreover, there would be a second possible danger. A finely graded spectrum of nuclear weapons, by adding extra rungs to the escalation ladder, could make it easier for the two sides to climb the ladder as well as making it easier for them to climb slowly. The danger of massive escalatory steps might be reduced; but the danger of creeping escalation might be increased, and firebreaks within the spectrum of nuclear weapons might be blurred.

Neither of these dangers can be dismissed lightly. In each case, however, there is a balance of conflicting considerations which needs to be weighed carefully.

As regards the Rubicon which divides conventional from nuclear force levels, there are grounds for thinking that stability may actually be enhanced, rather than impaired, by making the river somewhat easier to cross. First, the political and military situation in which either side would contemplate crossing the river would be so fraught, so altogether desperate, that the side which faced defeat might well feel that he had no option but to go nuclear in one form or another. It may be more important that he should be able to do so in a strictly limited way, thus keeping the bidding low, than that his decision should be made more agonising by an absence of very low-level nuclear weapons.

Second, there is the important point that stability depends ultimately on effective deterrence and perceived war-fighting capabilities, and these will both be enhanced, the easier it is (and can be seen to be) for either side to escalate from conventional to nuclear force levels and to use nuclear weapons over the territory of the home country or an ally without causing intolerable damage. For the West in particular, seeking as it does to compensate for quantitative inferiority at the conventional level by readiness to use nuclear weapons first, it would be somewhat quixotic to pursue a policy of making first use as difficult as possible.

The second danger – that extra rungs will make the escalation ladder easier to climb, as well as easier to climb slowly – raises the whole question of escalation within nuclear conflict and the possibility of limiting nuclear war. We will address this question directly in the next chapter. Suffice it meanwhile to say that, while there can be no assurance of maintaining any firebreaks within a nuclear conflict, a finer gradation of theatre nuclear weapons is in most cases much more likely to help than to hinder. In any situation of high international tension, moreover, time is likely to be of the first importance, and the option of escalating slowly may well be crucial.

CIRCUMSTANCES OF FIRST NUCLEAR USE

We have noted already how appallingly difficult would be the decision to use nuclear weapons first. Well might Julius Caesar pause before deciding to cross the small river which divided cisalpine Gaul from the rest of Italy and thus begin the Roman Civil War:

> When he came to the river Rubicon . . . his thoughts began to work, now he was just entering upon the danger, and he wavered much in his mind when he considered the greatness of the enterprise into which he was throwing himself. He checked his course and ordered a halt, while he revolved with himself, and often changed his opinion one way and the other, without speaking a word. This was when his purposes fluctuated most; presently he also discussed the matter with his friends who were about him . . . , computing how many calamities his passing that river would bring upon mankind, and what a relation of it would be transmitted to posterity. At last, in a sort of passion, casting aside calculation, and abandoning himself to what might come, and using the proverb frequently in their mouths who enter upon dangerous and bold attempts, The die is cast, with these words he took the river. Once over, he used all expedition possible.[4]

If the noblest man that ever lived in the tide of times could experience such turmoil and anguish in 49 BC, how much greater would be the turmoil and anguish of Western leaders in the twentieth century before deciding to cross the nuclear Rubicon – a decision which could lead, if the worst came to the worst, to the devastation of Europe's heartland and full-scale nuclear war between the major powers. The alliance obviously has the strongest possible interest both in avoiding defeat and in avoiding full-scale nuclear war and devastation. It is natural, therefore, that the nature and timing of a hypothetical first release of nuclear weapons should have been discussed extensively over the years, especially in an alliance whose strategy explicitly envisages the possibility of first use if necessary to forestall defeat at the conventional level.

There have been three main schools of thought on this subject within the alliance, led by French, German and American theorists respectively. At one extreme, some French theorists tended to argue, especially in the 1960s and early 1970s, for *early use* of theatre nuclear weapons – a warning shot across the bows of the enemy as soon as he threatens the sanctuary of French territory or sets foot on French soil. Only a small number of weapons would be used (perhaps as few as one of two Pluton missiles) and the purpose would be predominantly symbolic or demonstrative – to convey to the enemy a message on the following lines:

> Stop before it is too late! We are simply not prepared to fight your sort of war. If you persist, there is no alternative to an escalating nuclear conflict, possibly a full-scale nuclear conflict, and we are ready to die if necessary rather than submit.

From the standpoint of deterrence, and especially deterrence against an attack on French territory, there is considerable merit in such a posture. It can be argued that early, small, symbolic use of theatre nuclear weapons is less likely to escalate to general nuclear war than use at a later stage, when the stakes are perceived to be higher and the military significance greater. But in an actual war where deterrence had failed, initially at least, early use of nuclear weapons would still, inevitably, be a high-risk strategy, given the massive strength of the Soviet Union at the theatre nuclear level and the terrible dangers of escalation to a higher level nuclear exchange. For a direct threat against French soil, it might be the best strategy available. For the NATO alliance as a whole, such a strategy seems less attractive.

Early first use by NATO would be intended as a gesture or designed to hold the military position pending negotiation. But the question is: how would the aggressor react? One possibility is that he would pause in his tracks and opt for negotiation when he saw this confirmation of NATO's willingness to escalate the conflict to the nuclear level. This may even be considered a strong possibility. But there could be no assurance in advance that the aggressor would react in this way. He might well choose to retaliate in kind, possibly by over-trumping NATO's trump. He might even prefer a conventional-cum-theatre-nuclear battle to a conventional battle – especially if he believed that this would increase his margin of superiority – and welcome first use of nuclear weapons by NATO as giving him the perfect excuse to use nuclear weapons himself while blaming NATO for crossing the nuclear threshold. The result might be a devastating nuclear-cum-conventional conflict in central Europe. The danger of escalation to the strategic nuclear level would be always present. Far from buying time for negotiation and reinforcement, early escalation to the theatre nuclear force level might speed up the war and the destruction.

For all these reasons, and above all because of the enhanced risk of escalation to an all-out global or European nuclear conflict once the nuclear threshold has been crossed, American theorists and others have tended to favour a strategy of *leaving first nuclear release as late as possible* and using it only to prevent substantial military disadvantage. To support such a strategy NATO needs to raise the nuclear threshold as high as possible – that is, to postpone as long as possible the point at which the alliance would feel obliged to introduce nuclear weapons. This in turn argues for strengthening the alliance's conventional forces to the point where they can fight as long and effectively as is likely to be necessary to frustrate the enemy's intentions, while maintaining at the same time the perceived readiness of the alliance to cross the nuclear threshold *in extremis* – notably if threatened with defeat at the conventional level.

In favour of this strategy of late release, supported by strong conventional capabilities, there are two powerful arguments. One is that, compared with a strategy of early release, it should perceptibly reduce the danger of nuclear war – a danger which must rise enormously as soon as the nuclear threshold has been crossed. The other is that, compared with a policy which tries to make do with inferior conventional capabilities, it reduces the Soviets' scope for gambling on NATO's likely reluctance in practice to use nuclear weapons first, and hence makes it much more difficult for them to call NATO's bluff.

Theorists from the Federal Republic of Germany have tended to take an *intermediate position* between the strategies of first release which we have ascribed above to French and American theorists. For the Federal Republic, the prospect of a nuclear war fought over their territory in central Europe is altogether appalling; but so also is the prospect of devastation and loss of territory in a conventional battle, especially if it should culminate in a Soviet victory. Hence German theorists have tended to argue for use of theatre nuclear weapons by NATO, on a limited basis, *as soon as (but not before) the Warsaw Pact forces have broken through NATO's ranks to any significant extent.*

On both the German and American approaches, the purpose of first nuclear use would be partly military, partly demonstrative. The military purpose would be to halt the enemy's advance, for a time at least, either by targeting the spearhead of the invading forces or by striking a major blow against military targets behind the enemy's front line. Care would be taken to minimise collateral damage which might increase the dangers of further escalation. The demonstrative purpose, as in the French case, would be to persuade the aggressor to stop and reconsider – to warn him that the game will not be played according to his rules, that there may be full-scale nuclear war unless he desists, and that NATO will sooner opt for shared suicide than submit to defeat.

INTERMEDIATE-RANGE THEATRE NUCLEAR FORCES

The weapons most likely to be employed in first nuclear use or an initial nuclear exchange are the smaller battlefield systems at the lower end of the theatre nuclear spectrum. The weapons which have recently attracted most attention, however, are the intermediate range cruise and ballistic missiles at the upper end of the spectrum, which have more in common with strategic systems than with smaller theatre nuclear weapons. The role of these intermediate-range systems calls for specific discussion.

In its now famous 'twin-track' decision of December 1979 NATO decided to modernise its intermediate-range systems while seeking new arms control negotiations. The decision provided for deployment over the period 1983–6 of 572 new American missiles capable of reaching targets in the Soviet Union – 108 Pershing 2 ballistic missiles, with single warheads yielding 50 kilotons or more over a range of 1000 miles, to be stationed on fixed sites in West Germany, and 464 mobile Tomahawk ground-launched cruise missiles (GLCMs), with single 200 kiloton warheads and a range of upwards of 1500 miles, to be stationed in Germany (96), Britain (160), Sicily (112), Belgium (48) and the Netherlands (48). The GLCMs fly slowly (around 400–500 knots) but their small size, low-altitude flight (some 50–150 feet) and evasive routing would make radar detection exceptionally difficult.[5]

The modernisation decision caused heart-searching in several member countries. Belgium and the Netherlands, in particular, were anxious about having the new weapons on their soil and did not commit themselves finally to deployment. Partly to soothe these anxieties NATO coupled the decision with an agreement that the United States should propose the negotiations with the Soviet Union discussed in chapter 9 on limiting intermediate-range nuclear systems in the European theatre.

Like other theatre nuclear systems, intermediate-range weapons contribute to deterrence against aggression at the conventional and theatre nuclear levels. They may also improve the prospects of preventing a nuclear exchange, once begun, from escalating to the strategic level. There are, moreover, certain special reasons for deploying and modernising such weapons.

The special reason most emphasised by Western governments since December 1979 is that NATO needs modern theatre nuclear forces of intermediate range to redress the overall nuclear balance between East and West (see figures 11.3 and 11.4). If an unacceptable degree of overall inferiority is to be avoided, NATO needs to deploy up-to-date missiles, capable of reaching targets in the Soviet Union, to offset the new generation of Soviet intermediate-range nuclear forces, which are capable of reaching targets anywhere in Europe. The willingness of the United States and the Soviet Union to lock themselves into approximate parity at the 'strategic' level has given added importance to non-strategic regional balances of theatre nuclear and conventional forces, and the military balance in Europe has been disturbed by the Soviets' rapid deployment of large numbers of new-generation intermediate-range theatre nuclear forces – notably the SS-20[6] and the Backfire bomber – at a time when NATO's existing intermediate-range theatre nuclear forces are ageing, increasingly vulnerable to attack and less able to penetrate improving Soviet air defences. In the absence of the SALT process, additions to the United States' strategic nuclear arsenal would have been a possible alternative response to the new Soviet intermediate-range theatre nuclear force deployments. But common numerical ceilings on strategic systems or warheads are likely to remain the key ingredient in any new agreement in the SALT or START series. Hence the option of net additions to strategic systems is unlikely to be available.

A less discussed but no less important reason for maintaining effective intermediate-range theatre nuclear forces is that such forces have an important contribution to make to NATO's over-all strategy for deterrence. The feature which distinguishes these forces from other theatre nuclear systems is that they have the capability to reach targets well

146

FIGURE 11.3 *Balance of nuclear forces, end-1983*

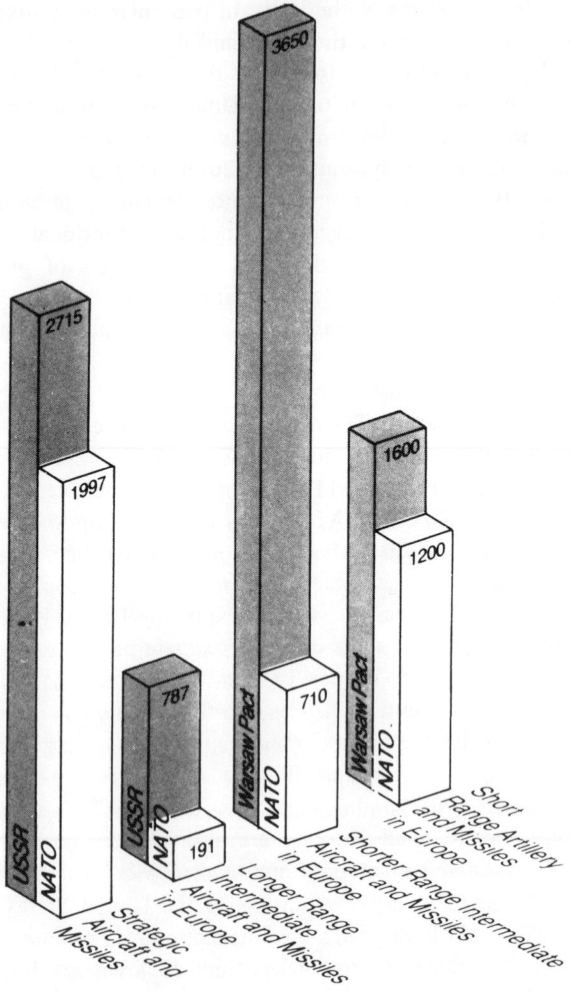

Source: Statement on the Defence Estimates 1984.

Reproduced by kind permission of the Ministry of Defence, London.

inside the Soviet Union, including cities in the Western part of the Soviet Union. NATO's ability to deter the Soviet Union may depend quite significantly on preserving this capability. For the main threat to Western Europe comes from the Soviet Union, not the other East European countries, and it is the Soviet Union rather than these other countries which needs to be deterred from committing aggression against Western

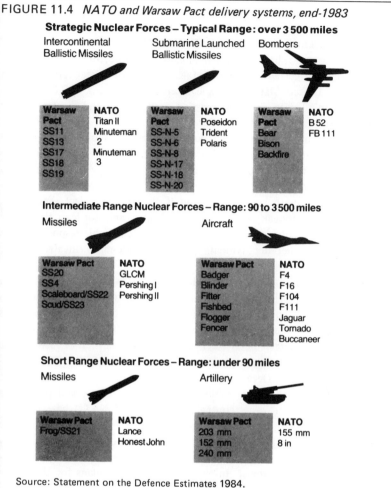

FIGURE 11.4 *NATO and Warsaw Pact delivery systems, end-1983*

Strategic Nuclear Forces – Typical Range: over 3 500 miles

Intercontinental Ballistic Missiles		Submarine Launched Ballistic Missiles		Bombers	
Warsaw Pact	NATO	Warsaw Pact	NATO	Warsaw Pact	NATO
SS11	Titan II	SS-N-5	Poseidon	Bear	B 52
SS13	Minuteman 2	SS-N-6	Trident	Bison	FB 111
SS17	Minuteman 3	SS-N-8	Polaris	Backfire	
SS18		SS-N-17			
SS19		SS-N-18			
		SS-N-20			

Intermediate Range Nuclear Forces – Range: 90 to 3 500 miles

Missiles		Aircraft	
Warsaw Pact	NATO	Warsaw Pact	NATO
SS20	GLCM	Badger	F4
SS4	Pershing I	Blinder	F16
Scaleboard/SS22	Pershing II	Fitter	F104
Scud/SS23		Fishbed	F111
		Flogger	Jaguar
		Fencer	Tornado
			Buccaneer

Short Range Nuclear Forces – Range: under 90 miles

Missiles		Artillery	
Warsaw Pact	NATO	Warsaw Pact	NATO
Frog/SS21	Lance	203 mm	155 mm
	Honest John	152 mm	8 in
		240 mm	

Source: Statement on the Defence Estimates 1984.

Reproduced by kind permission of the Ministry of Defence, London.

Europe. If NATO had no modern weapons below the strategic level which could reach and seriously damage the Soviet Union – no modern weapons to counter the massive threat to all of Western Europe from Soviet theatre nuclear systems – then deterrence could be seriously compromised. True, the Soviets would still have to reckon with the risk that the United States might use its strategic systems in response to aggression against Western Europe; but they might calculate that, when it came to the point, the Americans would shrink from the ultimate step of introducing strategic nuclear weapons, thus putting the territory of the United

States itself more unequivocally at risk; and these calculations might encourage them to pursue aggressive, reaction-testing policies or to attempt political blackmail over Western Europe. Modern weapon systems of intermediate-range, based on the mainland of Europe, must pose an earlier and even more certain threat of retaliation against Soviet territory than would the United States' strategic arsenal on its own - if the Soviets were ever minded to use their massive conventional and theatre nuclear forces against targets in Western Europe.

A third consideration is the political case for deploying up-to-date intermediate-range theatre nuclear forces in Europe. Although many people in Western Europe feel instinctively that they would prefer to have nothing to do with nuclear weapons - Western governments need to deal sensitively with such views even if they finally reject them - it is arguable that European countries in the alliance, and not least the armed forces of those countries, need a visible and identifiable response to the massive new Soviet deployments of intermediate-range theatre nuclear forces targeted on Western Europe.

There are military and economic reasons as well for deployment in Western Europe. The new systems need to be invulnerable and cost-effective. These requirements have pointed to ground-launched missiles in Europe, protected by mobility against enemy attack and not requiring expensive launcher vehicles such as ships, submarines or aeroplanes.

Finally, there were important arms control reasons for NATO's modernisation decision of December 1979. As suggested in chapter 9, the best hope for preserving a reasonable stability of armaments and preventing an arms race lies in arms control agreements. If NATO has firm and adequate plans for maintaining and improving its intermediate-range theatre nuclear capabilities, then the prospects for concluding satisfactory limitation agreements - whether a 'zero option' or something less radical - should be much improved. In the absence of firm plans for these new deployments, NATO would have had to negotiate from weakness. Hence, just as the decision to couple new arms control proposals to the Soviet Union with the decision on theatre nuclear forces modernisation contributed importantly to agreement in NATO on that decision, so the decision to modernise should itself contribute importantly to the success of talks on arms control.

OBJECTIONS TO INTERMEDIATE-RANGE NUCLEAR FORCES MODERNISATION

For reasons easily understood, the Soviets waged a propaganda campaign from 1979 onwards against deployment by NATO of modern intermediate range nuclear forces. Other opponents of the decision, too, have organised substantial campaigns of dissent in West European countries. Their arguments deserve serious consideration.

Some of the dissenters have rested their case on an extreme distaste for nuclear weapons and fears of a continuing, or escalating, arms race. There are probably few people who would not share this distaste and these fears. The contrary argument is that if the first priority is to preserve peace, stability and freedom – as surely it must be – the West cannot afford to drop its guard, to neglect or abandon unilaterally its nuclear weapons, to put itself at the mercy of a country committed to the downfall of most that the West stands for. Chapter 13 discusses these matters further. As to the arms race, we have argued already that the best hope for control lies in arms limitation agreements, and that the best hope for reaching such agreements lies in the ability to negotiate from strength.

Other dissenters are primarily concerned about national safety. They fear that countries which host American nuclear weapons are more likely to be attacked if war breaks out, since the weapons themselves would be prime targets. The validity or otherwise of this concern depends importantly on whether the weapons are vulnerable to attack. Mobile systems such as cruise missiles would be dispersed to different locations in times of crisis, and an aggressor would be unlikely to know where they were. His chances of targeting them successfully would therefore be small. The exchange rate for such an operation would be unlikely to look favourable. He would be more likely to target known military bases and installations.

A more fundamental trouble with the 'national safety' argument is that collective defence of the West requires that countries accept certain risks. It is unreasonable for individual countries to decline any share in the risks of the alliance while continuing to accept the benefits. If all member countries took such an attitude, the enterprise would crumble. We return to these matters in chapter 13.

Another argument maintains that improvements in NATO's intermediate-range nuclear capabilities in Europe would weaken deterrence by 'uncoupling' NATO's European forces from the ultimate deterrent of the United States' strategic nuclear arsenal. Especially if NATO appeared to be aiming at parity of nuclear forces in Europe – so the argument runs – the Soviets might assume that the United States now saw a more important distinction than previously between the defence of Europe and the defence of the United States and would now be less willing to use its strategic systems in support of Europe.

This argument, again, seems unconvincing. The importance of avoiding 'uncoupling' is beyond doubt. For that reason, policy-makers in NATO have been wary of giving currency to Herr Schmidt's concept of a 'Eurostrategic balance' of nuclear weapons. But the argument about 'uncoupling' turns out (as so often) to be the 'cornered beast' argument under another name – the familiar argument that improvement of capabilities below the strategic nuclear level weakens the deterrent effect of the United States's strategic arsenal. We have encountered the argument twice already – in the context of conventional and theatre nuclear forces – and there is no need to rehearse the counter-arguments again. It is simply not convincing to argue that the Soviets would think it safer to commit aggression against Western Europe because NATO has strengthened its nuclear options below the strategic level. True, they may judge that early use of the United States' strategic nuclear forces is now less likely. But the new intermediate-range theatre nuclear forces will be capable of inflicting such damage on the Soviet Union that these forces themselves should provide a deterrent effect comparable to that posed by the strategic forces. Moreoever, the strengthening of this rung in the escalation ladder will probably make, and be seen to make, it easier for the United States to escalate from the battlefield nuclear level to higher levels of nuclear force where the home-land of the Soviet Union itself would be threatened. This should help to enhance deterrence.

THE 'ZERO OPTION'

As discussed in chapter 9, President Reagan surprised the world on 18 November 1981 by combining his call for deep cuts in strategic nuclear systems with a 'zero-option' offer on intermediate-range nuclear forces:

> The United States is prepared to cancel its deployment of Pershing 2 and ground-launch cruise missiles if the Soviets will dismantle their SS-20, SS-4 and SS-5 missiles. This would be an historic step.

The Soviets rejected the President's proposal. But it remains pertinent to consider whether a 'zero-option', even if negotiable, would in fact be advantageous for NATO and good for stability – bearing in mind all the arguments, rehearsed above, in favour of maintaining modern nuclear forces of intermediate range in Western Europe.

Some of the earlier arguments would undoubtedly fall if the Soviets agreed to dismantle their intermediate-range nuclear forces in return for non-deployment by NATO. The contention that new deployments are needed to redress the overall balance of nuclear forces would lose its cogency, as would the argument for establishing a position of greater strength in arms control negotiations.

The other arguments, however, would still stand. In particular, there would remain a cogent argument, even if some form of 'zero option' were known to be negotiable, for NATO to retain the extra deterrent power conferred by a capability to strike the Soviet Union without escalation to the strategic nuclear level – especially given the alliance's quantitative inferiority at the conventional level and consequent reliance on making credible the threat of escalation to the nuclear force level. NATO could retain some such capability in the form of its existing systems, even with a 'zero option' for new deployments. But such a capability would lose credibility with age.

The conclusion which this suggests is that there *is* a rather persuasive case for NATO to retain an up-to-date capability to strike the Soviet Union below the strategic level, even at the cost of retention of a similar capability by the Soviet Union. The scale of the new deployments, on the other hand, would preferably be limited to a small fraction of those now made (by the Soviet Union) or contemplated (by NATO). Certainly the Soviet deployments of SS-20s and other theatre nuclear systems have been grossly excessive and destabilising;[7] and it is arguably only these excesses that can justify NATO in deploying new systems on the scale contemplated in December 1979. The two sides would appear to have a common interest in far smaller deployments.

If, against expectations, the two sides were to reach agreement on a comprehensive 'zero option', under which *all* intermediate-range nuclear weapons were eliminated, NATO would need urgently to increase its conventional capabilities so as to remove its present quantitative inferiority. Such a policy would have merit but would be enormously expensive.

UNITED STATES OR NATO DEPLOYMENTS

We conclude this chapter by mentioning briefly the issue of who should control theatre nuclear weapons located in Western Europe. Should it be NATO collectively or the country which has supplied the warheads? We are concerned here primarily with the American nuclear forces assigned to the European theatre. We consider the independent nuclear deterrents of Britain and France in chapter 13.

Under NATO's rules for nuclear release, the final decision to use nuclear weapons rests with the government of the country which supplied the nuclear warhead – in most cases, the President of the United States. Time and circumstances permitting, however, there would be consultation within the alliance before they were used, and responsibility for their release would thus be shared between the United States and other members of the alliance, particularly the European members. In the special case of American nuclear systems based in the United Kingdom, arrangements for which predate the more general NATO procedures, the launch or firing of a weapon would be a matter for joint decision by the two governments.

On balance, the partial and conditional sharing of responsibility within NATO seems the best available solution to the problem of nuclear control. It reconciles the supplier country's need to retain final and absolute control over release of its nuclear weapons with the right of West European countries to be consulted about a decision which would affect them so profoundly, without the decision-making process being thereby paralysed.

There are many in Western Europe who feel uncomfortable about these arrangements. They fear that the United States might be too willing to resort to using nuclear weapons in Europe. They would prefer individual West European countries to have a more specific power of veto over all theatre nuclear weapons based in Western Europe similar to that for weapons operated under 'dual key' arrangements.

Such anxieties are understandable. It is necessary, however, to register a comment and a contrary consideration.

The comment is that, without in any way doubting the sincerity of the United States' commitment to the defence of Western Europe, the United States is virtually bound to be more reluctant (not less) than West European countries to introduce nuclear weapons into a European war. To be sure, such a war would affect the vital interests of the United States. But it would affect the vital interests of West European countries even more. The more cogent anxiety is surely that the United States would not be willing in Western Europe's hour of need to use nuclear weapons, thus putting its own territory at risk, not that it would use them too soon. It is hard to imagine circumstances in which the President of the United States would decide to use nuclear weapons in Western Europe against the clear wishes of West European countries.

The 'contrary consideration' is that multiplication of controls and rights of veto over nuclear use could all too easily paralyse NATO's nuclear decision-making process in Western Europe's hour of need – especially if national command and control systems had been damaged. The expectation of such paralysis by a potential aggressor could gravely weaken deterrence. It might be thought that NATO's existing consultative procedures must themselves compound the difficulty of using nuclear weapons in practice, and thus weaken their deterrent effect. But such a view would probably be mistaken. Paradoxically, it would probably be easier for the President of the United States to decide on first nuclear use or escalation to higher nuclear force levels after consultation with other members of the alliance, and on the recommendation of the Supreme NATO Commanders, than to reach such decisions entirely on his own responsibility. From the European point of view, too, it is healthy that responsibility should be shared in this way, provided that the sharing is not allowed to frustrate the decision-making process.

A further consideration in favour of shared responsibility within NATO is that a NATO decision to use nuclear weapons would convey an even stronger political signal to the Soviet Union than a decision taken by the United States alone.

12   Limiting Nuclear War

COULD NUCLEAR CONFLICT BE LIMITED?[1]

We now address the momentous question left over from the previous discussion: what are the chances of stopping or limiting a nuclear conflict once begun and preventing escalation to a full-scale nuclear war? As President Reagan found to his cost in the autumn of 1981, leading statesmen are likely to earn more pain than profit from discussing the question publicly. Here truly is an area where, if America sneezes, Europe will catch cold. In the whole field of dynamic stability, however, there is no more critical question. If the answer should be that the chances of stopping or limiting nuclear war are not good, the further question would arise whether there are any circumstances in which it would be rational to initiate the use of nuclear weapons.

On the main question, the first point to be made is that no one knows the answer. War between two nuclear powers is an unexplored country. No one knows whether a nuclear war once begun could be stopped or kept limited, and anyone who believes he knows deceives himself. The one certainty is that certainty is impossible, and the inescapable fact of uncertainty is in itself crucially important. So long as the major powers remain even moderately risk-averse, their uncertainty as to what the outcome of nuclear war would be must contribute powerfully to mutual deterrence at all levels of military force.

In spite of the fundamental and inescapable fact of uncertainty, there are important points which can be made about the possibility of limiting nuclear conflict. There is one, powerful reason for supposing that it might be stopped at an early stage or remain limited, but against this there are several reasons for fearing that it might not.

The one, powerful factor which might stop or limit a nuclear conflict is that the two sides would have the strongest possible shared interest in avoiding a major nuclear war – in stopping short of mutual destruction

154

on the massive scale implied by such a war. The dangers in escalating, or even continuing, the conflict would be as obvious as they would be appalling. In the presence of such dangers, there must be solid grounds for hope that the first nuclear strike, or the initial nuclear exchange, would bring an aggressor to his senses and cause him to stop and reconsider. If that did not happen, there would remain a strong chance that later strikes and counter-strikes would compel a similar reappraisal. The perceived risks of escalation to all-out war would be likely to give pause to any political leader, or group of leaders, contemplating a change from one nuclear force level to another, or continuing strikes at any given force level, as well as to leaders contemplating first or second use. The mounting dangers of proceeding to a stalemate of comprehensive devastation would commend the case for a ceasefire.

An example may help to focus such reasoning. The scenario which, however unlikely in itself, seems more likely than any other to lead to nuclear conflict is one in which the Soviets have launched a conventional attack against a West European or NATO country, which NATO has not been able to contain. In such circumstances NATO would probably feel obliged to introduce theatre nuclear weapons. The object, as discussed in chapter 11, would be, not to embark on a nuclear-cum-conventional war in preference to a conventional one, but to persuade the Soviet leaders to stop, think again, and re-examine the assumptions which had encouraged them to attack in the first place; to bring them to their senses by compelling them to address new and dangerous decisions; to undermine and destroy their will to persevere.[2]

How would the Soviet leaders react? They might, just possibly, have laid their plans on the assumption that NATO would retaliate with nuclear weapons. They might have resolved in advance to proceed nevertheless. More probably, however, they would never have attacked in the first place if they had foreseen a serious risk of nuclear response. More probably they would have been encouraged to proceed by the calculation that NATO would regard the interests at stake as less than vital and would not take the risk of resorting to nuclear weapons. A nuclear reponse by NATO, with accompanying statements about vital interest, would comprehensively shatter such calculations. The fundamental premise of the operation would have been shown to be mistaken. In such circumstances, the Soviet leaders would be virtually bound to reconsider. Even if they had foreseen in advance the likelihood of a nuclear response, the actuality would be quite likely to given them pause. The hope that first nuclear use would compel such a reappraisal is not just wishful thinking.

Even if the Soviets decided to proceed, and to match strike with counter-strike, and even if there were some escalation of hostilities, both sides would remain acutely conscious of the need to keep the conflict limited. Both would be concerned to avoid the ultimate catastrophe, especially if they believed the 'nuclear winter' hypothesis to have substance.[3] The reports of horrendous destruction, the crescendo of appeals for restraint, the mounting sense of impending doom – such developments would be likely to concentrate the minds of both sides on the paramount need for ceasefire, negotiation and survival, as against strike, counter-strike and destruction.

Powerful as the incentive to limit and stop a nuclear conflict would be, however, such limitation could undoubtedly be difficult in practice.

In the first place, the issue over which the war was being fought might seem so vital to both sides that neither side was prepared to lose. In that event the side threatened with defeat would be sorely tempted to escalate. Much would depend, of course, on how vital each side perceived the interests at stake to be, and on their willingness to lose face. If one side had committed the initial aggression as a calculated act, designed to achieve some limited change in the status quo which he desired but did not regard as vital, that side would probably not be willing to take monumental risks in order to achieve his objective. In such circumstances a nuclear strike initiated by the threatened side, or an initial nuclear exchange, might well suffice to bring hostilities to a halt. The aggressor might well decide against further competition in risk-taking and withdraw from the bidding. As implied earlier, there are solid grounds for believing that a Soviet attack against a NATO country would fall into that category: the asymmetry of vital interest would be beyond reasonable doubt. If, on the other hand, the issue which occasioned the war was one about which both sides felt passionately, then it is possible that neither side would be prepared initially to make concessions. The side which faced loss at one force level might well feel impelled to escalate to a higher force level, even though this might result in massive destruction of the home country. Each side might feel obliged to compete in risk-taking and raise the bidding to force levels which must cause massive damage.

Another aspect of the problem of willingness to lose, or lose face, is that the two sides might have different perceptions of the relative degree of damage which they had inflicted on each other. If each side felt that he had suffered more damage himself than he had inflicted on the other, or that a ceasefire based on the military status quo would be unacceptable, they might both feel impelled to continue nuclear exchanges on an increasing scale in mutually frustrating attempts to achieve perceived equality of misery.

A second factor which could work against the limitation of nuclear conflict is the existence of a really powerful first-striker's advantage at the strategic nuclear level – a matter discussed at length in chapter 7 and the algebraic appendix. One danger in such circumstances, which fortunately are unlikely to arise in the foreseeable future,[4] is that each side would want to exploit his own advantage. More serious is the danger that each side would want to prevent the other side from exploiting *his* advantage and would be tempted to launch a preventive or pre-emptive attack to that end. Especially in crisis situations it is possible for the conviction to grow among decision-makers that some development or other – in this case, full-scale nuclear conflict – is bound to occur sooner or later and that the question is when, not whether. The insidious growth of such a conviction might just possibly nourish the temptation to strike preventively or pre-emptively, despite all the risks involved. The leaders of the major powers might come to believe that the risks involved in striking first were now outweighed by those involved in *not* striking first. In the emergence of such beliefs lies a serious potential threat to stability.

A third problem which might possibly bedevil efforts to limit nuclear war is the difficulty of identifying suitable boundaries, limits or 'firebreaks' within which, by tacit agreement, the war would be contained.

FIREBREAK VISIBILITY

It is possible to conceive of a considerable range of potential firebreaks within the nuclear force level, based on general political purpose, the number, size and type of weapons used, the nature and location of targets, the places from which weapons are launched and the identity of those responsible for launching them. Specifically, it is possible to conceive of firebreaks between:-

a) purely demonstrative use of weapons and use for military objectives;

b) use of 'strategic' systems and 'theatre' systems;

c) smaller and larger numbers of weapons and amounts of explosive power;

d) different types of weapons, such as depth bombs, land-mines, shells and missiles;

e) use against specific targets on or close to the battlefield and more general use against military targets;

f) use against military targets and civilian targets;

g) use against targets at sea and on land;

(h)   use against targets in Europe (excluding the Soviet Union) and against targets in the homelands of the superpowers;
(i)   release from the European theatre and from the homelands of the superpowers or the oceans;
(j)   release by West European countries, the NATO alliance and the United States.

The question is whether any of these possible firebreaks would be sufficiently clear or recognisable, either singly or in combination, to serve as a basis for limiting the war.

As we remarked earlier, there is happily no direct empirical evidence on which to base the answer to this question. On *a priori* grounds, however, it seems fair to judge that, while there may be no totally clear and visible firebreak within the spectrum of nuclear weapon systems comparable to that between conventional and nuclear weapons or conventional and chemical weapons, there is nevertheless a considerable wealth of possible limits within which, given the will, nuclear conflict might be contained – for a time at least. The problem of firebreak visibility certainly cannot be dismissed; but neither is it likely to be the main problem in limiting nuclear war.

To begin with the question of clarity, the course of events on the battlefield itself could be much obscured by the chaos and confusion which would be likely to surround a conventional-cum-nuclear engagement, especially if communications were cut off. But many of the possible firebreaks in our list should remain visible even so. Clearest of all, perhaps, would be the geographical firebreaks (h), (i), (j), and also (g), and within this group the most critical would doubtless be that between targets in Europe and targets in the homelands of the superpowers (firebreak (h)) – a matter which we discussed in the preceding chapter. Also relatively clear-cut would be the politico-strategic firebreaks (a) and (b).

Among the functional firebreaks (c–f), the all-important distinction in firebreak (f) between military and civilian targets – counter-force and counter-city – should in principle be reasonably clear, especially at the theatre nuclear force level. For reasons discussed in earlier chapters, a nuclear conflict will almost certainly begin with strikes against military targets. Each side would have a strong interest in avoiding escalation to civilian targets. There must therefore be a good chance that the crucial firebreak between military and civilian targets would be respected. That said, however, there would also be the ever-present danger, mentioned in chapters 7 and 8, that what the striker perceived as a counter-force strike would be perceived by the other side as a counter-city strike, justifying a counter-city response. These contrasting interpretations could arise all too easily as a result of unintended collateral damage in civilian areas, including radioactive fall-out. Strikes against central command and control centres would be especially liable to dangerous differences of interpretation.

The other functional firebreaks (c), (d), and (e) may seem less sustainable. The danger is easy to see that they might crumble as each side stretched its interpretation of them a little further. That is not to say, however, that they could not hold at all. Even allowing for a certain grey area and for the risks of unintended collateral damage, they could well hold for a time at least – especially in conjunction with firebreaks (f) and (h) and especially if the two sides stated publicly what limits they were observing.

Within firebreak (d) there are two weapon types at the lower end of the nuclear spectrum which stand apart from other weapon systems and might possibly, therefore, be used without escalation to other types of nuclear weapon. One is the atomic demolition munition (ADM), or nuclear landmine. There are severe practical problems about making effective use of these weapons.[5] In principle, however, a side which was being driven back at the conventional level might lay them before retreating and warn the enemy that he had done so. In that event, responsibility for first use of nuclear weapons would be shared between the two sides, with the onus of decision being transferred to the enemy. There would seem to be a considerable distinction, and hence firebreak, between an 'avoidable' weapon of this kind and other 'unavoidable' weapons.

A second weapon-type which stands apart is the nuclear depth bomb at sea. It is perhaps unlikely that either side would use these weapons before using nuclear weapons in the land–air battle. Here again, however, there would seem to be a clear distinction, and hence a potential firebreak, between this weapon and other nuclear weapons. The other side might still respond to use of a nuclear depth bomb at sea by introducing nuclear weapons against targets on land; but this would plainly be an escalatory response, tantamount to crossing a second channel of the nuclear Rubicon.

FIREBREAKS BY ANNOUNCEMENT

Perhaps the most important point of all about firebreak visibility is one at which we have hinted already: all firebreaks can be made much more visible if the side which is trying to establish them announces publicly what he is doing and what limits he is observing. Without public announcements or ultimatums it could indeed be difficult, especially in the chaos and confusion of battle, to establish firebreaks based on numbers or types of weapons, amounts of explosive power or proximity to the field of battle (firebreaks (c) and (e) in our list). With the help of such announcements, however, the task of setting up these and other possible firebreaks – even quite artificial ones – should be more feasible.

Some examples may help to illustrate the point. The side which introduced nuclear weapons might announce that he had fired (say) ten warheads but proposed to stop there provided that the other side agreed to a cease-fire (firebreak (c) in our list); or he might warn that he was prepared to use nuclear weapons against any military targets within (say) 50 miles of the battlefield (firebreak (e) in the list). Similarly, a side which opted for purely demonstrative use of nuclear weapons (firebreak (a)) might, and probably would, try to reduce the risks of misinterpretation, escalation and overtrumping by informing the enemy simultaneously:

> This is a gesture, no more. But from it you can see what appalling risks you are taking. If you stop, well and good: we will not fire any more. If you continue, we will fire plenty more, and next time it will be the real thing.

Finally, a side which planned to escalate further a nuclear conflict already begun might announce that he was prepared (say) to use theatre nuclear weapons against any military targets in Europe, thus indirectly conveying the signal that he was not proposing at this stage to use his strategic forces or to attack non-military targets or targets outside Europe. The two sides might, and probably would, bargain in ways such as these over the limits within which the conflict was to be contained.

The question might be asked – is it really probable that, when it came to the point, the two sides would bargain overtly in the way suggested? The answer is surely yes. As suggested in chapter 5, it is rather unlikely that major warfare in the present era would take the form of a simple tournament between silent adversaries. On the contrary, the air would be full of statesmen's voices, of accusations, ultimatums and vindications of actions taken. Leaders of the opposing sides would want to reassure their domestic populations and to justify what they were doing to the rest of the world. Above all, they would want to do their utmost – and be seen to do their utmost – to prevent the ultimate catastrophe of full-scale nuclear war. And this would almost certainly lead them to bargain overtly with each other both about the issues underlying the conflict and about ways of limiting it.

FIREBREAKS AND FLEXIBILITY OF WEAPON SYSTEMS

We have been concerned so far to argue that, fragile as many of the potential firebreaks must be, visibility of firebreaks is unlikely to be the major problem in limiting nuclear conflict. A similar conclusion probably applies to the technical feasibility of holding to particular firebreaks, but this does depend crucially on possession by each side of sufficiently flexible weapon systems.

If we consider the potential firebreaks in our earlier list, it is notable that flexibility of weapon systems must contribute positively and unequivocally – and often crucially – to the technical feasibility of all of them, by enabling the two sides to tune more finely the force levels they use, to escalate more slowly if they feel obliged to escalate, and to match more closely the force levels of the other side rather than be obliged to leapfrog in order to avoid disadvantage. Also of crucial importance is the ability of each side to strike specific targets, and in particular military targets, accurately and with a minimum of collateral damage which could provoke the enemy to escalate the conflict.

We noted earlier that too fine a gradation of weapon systems could in theory encourage creeping escalation[6]; but this really applies only to firebreaks (c) and (d), and not to any of the others. Firebreaks in these areas would probably have in any event, as we have implied already, to be artificial ones, established by public announcement or ultimatum, rather than tacit ones, based on visible differences of kind.

FIREBREAKS AND POLITICAL WILL

We can now proceed to the final step in our argument, which is to suggest that the chances of limiting nuclear conflict are likely to depend more on will than on technique – that the greatest impediment to establishing firebreaks in the forest blaze of nuclear conflict is likely to lie, not in the physical ability, but rather in the willingness of the opposing sides to observe and adhere. This willingness, in turn, is likely to be a function of the factors discussed earlier, notably the degree of abhorrence which the two sides feel towards the risk of major nuclear conflict, the importance they attach to winning, not losing or not losing face, the extent to which they are prepared to raise the competition in risk-taking to that end, and the degree of first-striker's advantage, particularly at the strategic level.

From a Western standpoint, there must be some anxieties as to the willingness of the Soviet Union to observe limits in a nuclear war. The cause for concern most often mentioned is the apparent absence in Soviet military thinking of any dividing line between nuclear and non-nuclear weapons or between one level of nuclear exchange and another. The Soviet Union is believed, however, to exercise tight political control from the centre over major nuclear decisions, and there is little doubt that the Soviet leaders are as aware as Western leaders of the appalling risks in nuclear conflict and would therefore be cautious about escalating the conflict.

More worrying, perhaps, is the vulnerability of command and control systems in conditions of nuclear war, even limited nuclear war.[7] It is one thing to argue that, when it came to the point, the leaders in the Kremlin would be cautious about escalating through the spectrum of theatre nuclear weapons, but quite another to argue that, command and control systems having broken down, Soviet commanders in the field would be similarly inhibited.

GENERAL CONCLUSIONS

The analysis has suggested two important conclusions about the prospects for stopping or limiting nuclear war:

1.   on the one hand, there is no evident reason why the introduction of nuclear weapons into a conflict *must of necessity* result in escalation to a major nuclear war: there are solid grounds for hoping that it would not;
2.   on the other hand, there can equally be *no certainty* that a nuclear conflict once begun could be contained within tolerable limits.

In support of the first conclusion we have argued that the introduction of nuclear weapons could well end the conflict by persuading an aggressor to stop, think again and negotiate. The two sides would anyway have the strongest possible common interest in stopping a nuclear conflict as soon as possible and, failing that, in keeping it limited. We have suggested that, given the will, there should be no insuperable technical problems about keeping a conflict limited, especially if the two sides announced publicly (as they probably would do) what limits they are observing; they might well bargain together, either directly or indirectly, about what the limits were to be. The chances of successful limitation would be greatly enhanced by possession of a flexible range of theatre nuclear weapons.

In support of the second conclusion we have argued that nuclear conflict is an unexplored hinterland, and that the danger of escalation beyond tolerable limits would be especially severe if the issue which provoked the conflict was such that neither side was prepared to lose. Much is likely to depend on surrounding circumstances, on the political will of the national leaders of the day, on their skills in crisis management and on the incidence of unpredictable accidents such as unintended collateral damage. The prospects for containment would be reduced if both sides possessed a major first-striker's advantage, especially at the strategic level.

These conclusions are not just important in themselves. It is no less important that policy makers in the nuclear countries should subscribe to them. If they should reject either conclusion, the implications for dynamic stability would be serious.

Thus, an unduly pessimistic philosophy which rejected our first conclusion and denied the possibility of stopping or limiting nuclear war, once begun, would be terribly dangerous in a situation where nuclear exchange had already begun. It would imply that all hope of avoiding the ultimate catastrophe had vanished with the release of the first nuclear weapon. It would thus encourage the earliest possible use of the strategic arsenals if there existed a significant degree of first-striker's advantage. Such a philosophy would also largely dissolve the credibility of any deterrence posture like that of NATO which envisages first use of nuclear weapons if necessary to counter aggression at the conventional level.

An unduly complacent philosophy, on the other hand, which rejected our second conclusion and heavily discounted the risk of escalation from small nuclear beginnings to a major nuclear conflict, would be at least equally dangerous and probably more so. Such a philosophy could encourage political leaders to cross the nuclear Rubicon too soon – to embark too lightly on a journey whose ending might be a disaster unprecedented in history. It would be far better for the world, far more conducive to stability, that such a journey were never begun. For as soon as the nuclear Rubicon has been crossed, the risk of escalation to a major nuclear conflict cannot but rise enormously.

IMPLICATIONS FOR NATO STRATEGY

What do our conclusions on limiting nuclear war imply for NATO strategy? There are two main points. The first is that these conclusions come close to being prior assumptions of NATO strategy. The second is that the inevitable uncertainty as to whether nuclear war could (or would) be kept limited must strongly reinforce the case for raising the nuclear threshold as high as possible.

Taking these points in order, the NATO strategy of willingness to use nuclear weapons first *in extremis* would manifestly lack credibility if the alliance took the view (and were known to take the view) that nuclear war could not be limited, once begun. A potential aggressor who perceived NATO to take such a view would be encouraged to calculate that the threat of first nuclear use was a piece of empty pageantry, full of sound and fury, signifying nothing, and that, when it came to the point, the alliance would not translate its threats into action. For effective deterrence, therefore, the alliance needs to be perceived as believing that there would be a good chance of limiting nuclear war. For effective deterrence, similarly, the alliance requires a capability to introduce nuclear weapons in a way which is effective yet visibly limited.

This is not to say that the alliance needs to project itself as believing that nuclear war could *certainly* be kept limited. On the contrary, the alliance's willingness to entertain the possibility of escalation to the highest nuclear force levels should enhance deterrence. Neither is it to say that the alliance should commit itself in advance to the observance of any specific firebreaks within nuclear conflict. That could only reduce a potential aggressor's perception of the risks involved in launching aggression at the conventional level.

As to the second point, we already concluded in earlier chapters that the NATO alliance needs strong conventional capabilities and a high nuclear threshold, both for the sake of dynamic stability and to make its deterrence credible. The less the alliance has to rely on first use of nuclear weapons, or the threat of first use, the smaller the risk of major nuclear war will be. The analysis in the present chapter must powerfully support these conclusions. If there can be no certainty about limiting nuclear war, once begun, it must be an objective of the highest importance to postpone as far as possible the point at which the alliance might be obliged to introduce nuclear weapons. The case for a high nuclear threshold is compelling.

13   Policies Towards the Balance of Terror: (1) Rejection and Abdication

INTRODUCTION[1]

The preceding chapters have struggled at length with most of the formidable questions about the balance of terror listed in chapter 1. The two final chapters explore further some of the practical and policy issues for Western countries. We ask in turn:

1.   What are the advantages and disadvantages of a world order based on a balance of terror?
2.   Are there any practical alternatives? Is there scope for rejecting the whole concept of nuclear deterrence and a balance of terror? Or abdicating from it?
3.   If there are no practical alternatives, where do the main threats to stability in the balance of terror lie?
4.   What should the West's policies be? How adequate are existing policies?

NEED FOR A BALANCE OF TERROR

We reached in chapter 4 the sad conclusion that the balance of terror was here to stay – that peace between East and West would continue to depend, in the foreseeable future, on mutual deterrence through a balance of terror. In so concluding, we were keenly aware how tragic it was that the world should have to rely on such a dreadful and dangerous expedient; that such vast sums should be spent on armed forces and armaments; that swords should remain swords and not be turned into ploughshares. But what is the alternative? The only practical alternative to mutual deterrence, we suggested, was mutual trust. With the best will in the world, however, we could not see how the West could possibly trust the Soviet Union when that country is committed, in effect, to the destruction of freedom and democracy throughout the world and debarred by its political system from having normal relations with other countries. We found no evidence to suggest that the Soviet leaders trust the West any more than the West trusts them. Meanwhile, both sides had come to look upon nuclear weapons as their ultimate defence against aggression and the ultimate guarantee of their political independence. Unless relations between East and West were miraculously transformed, therefore, there seemed no realistic prospect that either side would be prepared to take the enormous risk of discarding these weapons even by agreement, much less by unilateral decision.

In the succeeding chapters we have found no evidence to contradict this conclusion. But there exists a significant minority of thoughtful people who argue that, on the contrary, continuation of the balance of terror is not inevitable; that alternative world orders based on rejection of the balance of terror are certainly desirable and possibly attainable; and that, as a minimum, their own countries should abdicate from the balance of terror.

Such arguments deserve respectful and sympathetic examination. No thinking person could dismiss them lightly. We need therefore to weigh scrupulously the advantages, disadvantages and practicability of possible alternatives to the balance of terror and possible alternative policies towards it. And since the assessment of advantages and disadvantages must needs be comparative, we have to begin by considering what are the main advantages and disadvantages of the balance of terror itself.

ADVANTAGES OF A BALANCE OF TERROR

The advantages of the existing balance of terror can be summarised as follows:

1. It has kept the world's strongest powers at peace. It has made the use of force, nuclear or conventional, to change the status quo between East and West incomparably less attractive, and hence far less probable, than in previous eras.
2. It has placed a corresponding restraint on political behaviour.
3. It has enabled the peoples of East and West to feel reasonably secure – possibly more so than ever their ancestors felt.
4. As its existence proves, it is practicable.

5.   For NATO at least it has been economical in the sense that NATO
      has not felt obliged to match in quantitative terms the Soviet Union's
      conventional military strength in Europe.

It is easy to take these advantages for granted. But the presumption of
peace, security and stability is a precious possession.

DISADVANTAGES OF A BALANCE OF TERROR

As the protest movements and marches of 1981 and later reminded us,
there is also plenty to criticise in the existing balance of terror. The
criticisms most often made can be summarised under five headings:

1.   The feeling that nuclear weapons are distasteful and morally re-
      pugnant.
2.   The dangers to human life and the environment, both in individual
      countries and world-wide.
3.   Doubts as to the efficacy of mutual deterrence on the grounds that
      the use of nuclear weapons is now barely credible.
4.   The vicious circle of fear breeding nuclear weapons which in turn
      breed more fear.
5.   The sheer waste of resources.

To these familiar criticisms should be added the anxieties discussed in
earlier chapters as to possible instabilities in the balance of terror - anxieties
to which we return in the next chapter.

Any thinking person is bound to have great sympathy with such criticisms. But there are certain glosses which need to be added.

As regards distaste and moral repugnance, there would doubtless be
general agreement that a world which could manage without nuclear
weapons would be far preferable to the world as it is. Their very existence
is a terrible indictment of human folly. But there are other considerations
as well. A world full of conventional warfare, in which basic liberties
had been suppressed and ordinary people lived in a state of perpetual
intimidation and insecurity, would likewise be morally repugnant - and
arguably more so. That is not to say that the practical choice necessarily
lies between two such worlds. But a moral assessment of any particular
world order needs to weigh in the balance not only the properties of its
weapon systems but other elements as well. We discuss these matters
further below in the context of unilateral nuclear disarmament.

The dangers to human life and the environment are undoubtedly the most disturbing feature of the balance of terror. Estimates of casualties from nuclear strikes vary widely: there is, happily, little practical experience on which to draw, and casualties could vary greatly according to environmental and atmospheric conditions, such as the strength and direction of the wind. In the case of a Soviet strike against American ICBM silos, estimates of American dead range from half a million to 20 million. In the case of a larger strike, a report of April 1979 by the United States Arms Control and Disarmament Agency estimated that a heavy first strike by the Soviet Union against American strategic nuclear forces, military bases and industry, followed by American retaliation in kind, could have effects of the following order in both countries:

(a) 25 to 100 million deaths within 30 days, with many more to follow;
(b) destruction of 65 to 90 per cent of industry; and
(c) destruction of the 200 largest cities.

Other studies have suggested that a full-scale nuclear war which used up between a half and three-quarters of the world's existing megatonnage of nuclear warheads could kill between 300 million and one billion people initially, again with more to follow.

These estimates relate to casualties resulting directly from nuclear exchanges. Another, more recent line of research has suggested that the longer-term, indirect consequences for mankind and the planet of a major nuclear exchange would be even more devastating. According to the 'nuclear winter' hypothesis, a major nuclear exchange which involved the burning of hundreds of cities and industrial and military installations could cover the northern hemisphere at least, and conceivably the southern hemisphere as well, with a pall of smoke and dust which in turn could produce a 'nuclear winter' of darkness and sub-freezing temperatures for several months. If this happened, the effects on plant and animal life throughout the planet could be catastrophic, and many who initially survived the nuclear exchange would starve.[2]

The 'nuclear winter' is clearly a hypothesis of the greatest importance with major implications for nuclear strategy and the balance of terror. Two points in particular need, however, to be noted. The first is that the hypothesis relates to what is (we have suggested) the most improbable form of nuclear conflict, in which very large numbers of cities are burnt. Even the more extreme versions of the hypothesis do not claim that a small-scale nuclear exchange in (say) the European theatre would produce the suggested effects. Second, the hypothesis remains a hypothesis. It i subject, inevitably, to major uncertainties. It rests on necessarily insecure assumptions as to the extent of the fires and the amount of soot which they would create. Other critical assumptions are that large amounts of sooty smoke would reach high altitudes and would not therefore (as would otherwise happen) be dispersed by wind and rain, and that wind patterns at these high altitudes would collect the smoke particles into an unbroken pall.

Whatever view the scientists may later reach on the nuclear winter – and complete certainty is unlikely to be obtainable – the fact that the hypothesis can be entertained at all adds another appalling dimension of uncertainty to the balance of terror. It opens up the possibility, if no more, that use of nuclear weapons on a large scale could in the end inflict almost as much suffering on the user's own country, and on innocent third countries, as on his opponent. It underlines, if any underlining were needed, how unimaginably appalling a major nuclear exchange could be. Small wonder, therefore, that many people feel that the world has gone mad; that a world order based on a balance of nuclear terror is anathema; that total nuclear disarmament is the only solution.

Even here, however, two glosses are needed. First, it is, unhappily, far from clear whether there exists any realistic alternative to a balance of terror in some shape or form. It is difficult to discern either a practical 'way out' or a realistic alternative world order which would bring a comparable presumption of peace and stability. It is the very awfulness of the balance of terror that has made it effective.

Second, it is far from clear whether any alternative which was practicable would also be preferable. There must be a genuine dilemma as to the relative merits of a world order involving a very low probability of monumental devastation and one which involved a much higher probability of repeated devastation on the lesser, but still massive, scale which non-nuclear weapons could inflict. It is well to remember that a heavy exchange with modern conventional and chemical weapons could leave a trail of suffering and destruction far exceeding that of the First and Second World Wars. If nuclear weapons had never been invented, moreover, governments would almost certainly have poured far more resources into the development of conventional explosives, chemical and biological agents. The superpowers might well have built up capabilities to burn as many cities with conventional weapons as they could now destroy with nuclear weapons.

There is some substance in the argument that the balance of terror will become less effective as the use of nuclear weapons becomes less credible. Credibility is a problem which requires constant attention. As argued repeatedly in earlier chapters, however, credibility would have to be far lower than it is now, or ever has been, before nuclear weapons would lose their deterrent power. The mere possession of such weapons is likely to deter. A potential aggressor may think it highly improbable that the other side would ever use them; but he could not afford to ignore the possibility. Nuclear weapons are, in a sense, the *reductio ad absurdum* of warfare. It is precisely for that reason that they have contributed to peace.

As to the argument that the balance of terror is a vicious circle, in which fear breeds weapons and weapons breed more fear, the existence of the nuclear arsenals is undoubtedly a source of international tension as well as a response to it. Sadly, however, it is not uncommon for solutions to one problem to create other problems by the way. The nuclear arsenals have not created the tensions between East and West. Their effect has been largely to remove the possibility of war between East and West at the cost of adding a new and terrible dimension to the relations between them. Consider the analogy with herbicides and pesticides. These undoubtedly create environmental problems. Without them, people would starve.

The serious question is whether the balance of terror is necessarily an explosive, upward-spiralling system, in which tension and armaments are bound to breed and increase over time. The answer, surely, is that it does not have to be so, especially if the nuclear powers can agree on arms control. But the danger is real; the need for vigilance, paramount.

Finally, one cannot but sympathise with the criticism that expenditure on nuclear weapons represents an appalling waste of resources. It is far from clear, however, that rejection of, or abdication from, nuclear weapons would in fact result in economies. Nuclear programmes generally use up a relatively small proportion of national defence budgets. Governments would probably feel it necessary to spend every penny saved from nuclear programmes on larger conventional programmes.

ALTERNATIVE POLICIES

Whatever view one may take about the advantages and disadvantages of a balance of terror, the critical question is whether there exist any realistic alternatives and, if so, whether they would be better or worse. There are several alternatives to, or variations on, the existing balance of terror which it is relevant to consider.

In the first place there are several alternatives which the West as a whole might in theory pursue, some more remote than others, some involving agreements between East and West and others based on unilateral decisions by the West. These include:

(a) general and complete disarmament by agreement;
(b) complete disarmament by the West unilaterally;
(c) nuclear disarmament by agreement;
(d) nuclear disarmament by the West unilaterally;
(e) forswearing aggression in any form, by agreement or unilaterally;
(f) forswearing first nuclear use, by agreement or unilaterally.

There are also several European options including:

(g) a European nuclear-free zone by agreement;
(h) unilateral withdrawal of nuclear forces from West European soil;
(i) abandonment of the nuclear deterrent forces of Britain and France.

GENERAL AND COMPLETE DISARMAMENT BY AGREEMENT

A world order based on general and complete disarmament, conventional as well as nuclear, would clearly have enormous advantages. It would in principle make war impossible – not only nuclear war but conventional war as well, with all the attendant dangers to life and civilisation. It would likewise greatly weaken, if not remove, the political muscle of the larger countries – their ability to influence, intimidate or even dominate smaller countries on the strength of vastly superior military forces. In all these ways, general and complete disarmament would be decisively superior to nuclear disarmament. Not surprisingly, therefore, the most serious advocates of disarmament have tended to argue for general and complete disarmament by agreement between nations, rather than nuclear disarmament.

Sadly, the idea of general and complete disarmament raises problems so intractable that it can hardly be considered realistic. These problems can be considered under the following headings:

(i)   the degree of trust between nations which it presupposes;
(ii)   the need to retain armed forces for the preservation of established governments and law and order;
(iii) the need for international regulation of these forces;
(iv)   the scope for cheating, and the possible consequences;
(v)   the political implications for the superpowers;
(vi)   the problem of transition;
(vii) the problem of reversion; and
(viii) the problem of enforcement.

Taking these headings in turn, the fundamental problem with general and complete disarmament is that it presupposes an unprecedented degree of mutual trust between nations, and between other groupings of people such as religious, tribal and ethnic groups, not just at one moment but over time. Most of the specific difficulties are in effect manifestations of this central problem. It is hard to imagine how even a handful of nations could trust each other to the required extent, much less all 130 of the world's nations, especially when governments change so frequently.

Hardly less difficult is the problem of mutual trust *within* nations. Most countries would think it essential to maintain quite substantial armed forces for the protection of governments, constitutions and vulnerable groups within society against threats from within as well as without, including rival political groups and terrorists. Such forces would also be needed to preserve law and order, both on land and at sea, and to protect persons and property. Their size would be a highly sensitive matter. Individual countries would be likely to perceive the armed forces of other countries as a potential threat to themselves. They would be bound, accordingly, to be concerned about the danger of putting themselves at the mercy of their neighbours and enemies. Finding a stable relativity of armed forces levels, with which the peoples of all countries felt secure and comfortable, would be exceptionally difficult.

In practice the levels of armed forces retained by individual countries would almost certainly have to be the subject of international agreement, regulation and control. It seems inconceivable that 130 countries could move by simultaneous or successive unilateral actions to mutually acceptable levels of armed forces, police forces and armaments which could be described as 'general and complete disarmament'. Both the transition and the 'final' position would need, therefore, to be based on agreement. But the problems involved in the negotiation of a collective agreement by 130 nations would be formidable even in a world of highly developed mutual trust between nations, much more so in the real world.

The reason why agreement would be so difficult lies not just in the difficulty of finding a pattern of residual armed forces levels which would leave all countries feeling secure and comfortable but also in fears about cheating. Such fears would be a constant nightmare. It would be relatively easy for individual countries to cheat – particularly countries with authoritarian regimes. Verification of nuclear disarmament would be difficult enough (see below); verification of total disarmament, much more so. The temptations to cheat could be powerful, especially at times of tension in mutual relations. Such temptations would be reinforced by fears as to the possible consequences of cheating by other countries.

In political terms, general and complete disarmament would be an unattractive option for governments which perceive a need for the political muscle which comes from possession of superior military strength. For the Soviets in particular, this would be likely to pose an acute problem: general and complete disarmament would not be compatible with keeping their present hold on Eastern Europe and other neighbouring countries.

The problems of transition from the existing balance of terror to a world of general and complete disarmament would be formidable – even more so than those of a transition to nuclear disarmament. Each time the various categories of nuclear and conventional weapons were collected and destroyed, governments would be bound to worry deeply about the security of their own peoples. The prospects for successfully carrying through the successive steps on the road to general and complete disarmament in a world full of mutual distrust between nations cannot be considered bright.

The problems of maintaining general and complete disarmament once achieved would be hardly less daunting. In times of tension, individual countries would be sorely tempted to rearm, if only for self-defence. Governments could well perceive such rearmament as being nothing less than their duty towards their own peoples.

Fears about cheating and the perceived rearmament imperative might be reduced if there were some kind of international enforcement authority. But the political direction of such an authority raises an intractable dilemma – a dilemma which bedevilled the early post-war discussions on international control of atomic energy. *Either* the authority would decide to act by some form of majority vote *or* its decisions would be subject to veto by individual member states. In neither case is it likely that individual countries would be prepared to entrust their security to such an authority. Governments would be unlikely to feel that they could rely on fair treatment in all circumstances from an international authority acting by majority vote. An authority whose decisions were subject to veto by individual member states, on the other hand, would more often than not be powerless to act when action was required. A further problem would be the means of enforcement. What forces and weapon systems would the authority have at its command?

With world government, the enforcement problem might be easier. But world government itself lies far beyond the horizon of vision. And even with world government, the same basic problems of mutual tensions and distrust, which cause nations to arm themselves, would tend to reappear in the guise of regional tensions and jealousies. Wars between nations would tend to reappear as civil wars.

It is difficult to avoid the sad conclusion that general and complete disarmament by agreement between nations is unlikely to be attainable in the foreseeable future.

UNILATERAL COMPLETE DISARMAMENT

Complete disarmament by the West unilaterally is, in one sense, a more practical option than general and complete disarmament by agreement: the intractable problems of agreement, verification and enforcement would simply not arise. By adopting such a policy, however, the West would leave itself totally vulnerable to political intimidation, coercion and aggression by other countries, including the Soviet Bloc, in a way which not even neutral countries have generally been willing to do. Not surprisingly, therefore, there are few who have advocated such a policy.

NUCLEAR DISARMAMENT BY AGREEMENT

A world order based on nuclear disarmament would have the huge advantage, compared with the existing balance of terror, that a formidable threat to human life and the environment would be removed. However unlikely a full-scale nuclear exchange may be, removing the possibility of such a catastrophe would be no mean blessing. Removing the possibility of war altogether, through general and complete disarmament, would be an even greater blessing. If general disarmament is thought to lie beyond reach, however, nuclear disarmament can still be seen as a useful second-best provided that it was genuine and permanent.

Sadly, the idea of nuclear disarmament, too, raises problems so difficult that there must be doubts as to how realistic it can be. These overlap with the problems of general and complete disarmament. But there is a new element as well: nuclear disarmament, if genuine and permanent, would tend to remove the restraints on conventional warfare provided by both the balance of terror and general and complete disarmament. A world with nuclear disarmament could be a world full of conventional armaments and conflict. The temptations to resort to force in times of political tension would be much increased; the inhibitions and disincentives restraining would-be aggressors, much reduced. Barring a miraculous improvement therefore, in the relations between nations, ordinary people in East and West could well find themselves living in a state of fear and insecurity which would make the balance of terror seem in retrospect like a golden age. The removal, or temporary removal, of one gigantic, yet remote, danger might seem in retrospect too high a price to pay for a multitude of lesser, but less remote, dangers. If relations between East and West had improved miraculously these concerns might be of small moment. But the prospects of such a miracle do not seem bright.

Conventional forces and conflicts apart, the problems of nuclear disarmament resemble those of general and complete disarmament discussed earlier:

  (i)   the degree of trust which it presupposes;
  (ii)   the scope for cheating, and the possible consequences;
  (iii) the political implications;
  (iv)   the problems of transition, reversion and enforcement.

Some of these problems would be reduced in scale, compared with general and complete disarmament; but they all remain formidable.

The problem of mutual trust between nations would be less serious in two respects with nuclear than with general disarmament. First, the number of countries participating in the agreement could be as small as five instead of 130 or more (though an agreement binding all potential nuclear powers would clearly be preferable). In a statistical sense, five countries would be more likely to reach agreement.

Second, the degree of trust required, and the degree of dependence on international enforcement, would arguably be somewhat less with nuclear disarmament. True, the disarming countries would have to accept the higher risks of conventional warfare. But they would retain substantial conventional forces and might not, therefore, have quite the same fears about leaving themselves naked and defenceless. The risks they would be taking, though great, would arguably be less daunting than with general disarmament.

The hard fact remains, however, that the absolute degree of mutual trust between nations required for agreement on nuclear disarmament would still be unprecedented. As suggested in earlier chapters, there seems no prospect in the foreseeable future that even the five existing nuclear countries could develop such trust in each other that they would be prepared to discard the weapons which they have come to regard as providing the ultimate guarantee of their security and independence.

Similar considerations apply to the problems of cheating and verification. In a comparative sense, it would be easier to police a ban on nuclear weapons by a handful of countries than a ban on *all* weapons (above certain threshold levels) by *all* countries. In an absolute sense, the cheating problem would remain daunting. For cheating would be both relatively easy and potentially of enormous advantage to the offending side.

It may be asked: would cheating really be so easy? The answer has, sadly, to be yes. A world with nuclear disarmament could not be a world in which nuclear weapons were unknown. That possibility was closed for ever by the explosion in the New Mexico desert on 16 July 1945. Especially for the Soviets, with their authoritarian system of government, it would be a relatively simple matter to conceal stockpiles of nuclear weapons and even to continue making small-scale nuclear tests. It would also be relatively easy for each side to maintain a *capability* to produce nuclear weapons and delivery systems which could be activated at short notice.

It may be asked, further: would cheating really be of enormous advantage to the offending side? Once again the answer has, sadly, to be yes. Individual countries could perceive great advantages in cheating. A country which breached the nuclear disarmament agreement by retaining a secret stockpile of weapons and the means of producing more would have a commanding military superiority over countries which had complied faithfully with the agreement and therefore possessed no capability for retaliation in kind. This imbalance of military power would be potentially far more decisive, in both military and political terms, than any imbalance which is likely to develop within the balance of terror.

A further problem is that fears of such cheating by others might well induce 'precautionary cheating' or 'reversion'. Especially in times of international tension, individual countries might be persuaded to start producing nuclear weapons again – either secretly (precautionary cheating) or openly (reversion) – by the calculation that they simply could not afford to take the risk of trusting the other side not to cheat: the penalties for trust misplaced would be too great. It is easy to imagine how such calculations could lead to a hectic race to rearm, fuelled by suspicions and uncertainties as to the other side's progress. In this respect, too, a world with nuclear disarmament could be highly unstable.

Such instabilities might in principle be reduced if there were an effective international enforcement agency, with a nuclear capability of its own. Even assuming that the problems of establishment and political direction could be overcome, however, countries which had forsworn nuclear weapons would not feel secure *unless* they felt able to rely on the agency's willingness to use (or threaten to use) nuclear weapons itself against cheaters. And this strains the credulity.

As to political implications, nuclear disarmament would raise much the same difficulty for the Soviet Union as general and complete disarmament it would loosen the Soviets' hold over Eastern Europe and other satellite countries. As noted in earlier chapters, it is ultimately the Soviet nuclear arsenal that underwrites Soviet hegemony in Eastern Europe. It is because of this nuclear arsenal that the countries of Eastern Europe cannot count on the active Western support which they would need in order successfully to challenge the Soviet Union.

For the NATO alliance, too, nuclear disarmament would raise a political, or politico-economic, problem. The alliance would no longer be able to rely on the threat of first nuclear use to offset its quantitative inferiority of conventional forces in Europe. Conventional force levels would need to be raised. The European countries in the alliance, in particular, would need to spend a great deal more on defence.

The problems of transition from the existing balance of terror to a world of nuclear disarmament, though arguably less formidable than for a transition to general and complete disarmament, would probably be even greater than the problems on arrival. The anxieties and potential insecurity of a world with nuclear disarmament would be foreseen in advance. The anticipation of these problems would give pause to governments and peoples at each stage of the journey. A remarkable degree of mutual trust would be required, and such trust would need to be sustained over the whole period of transition as each weapon or weapons factory was destroyed or transferred to international ownership. Governments of both East and West would be likely to perceive each major step of the transitional period as involving an enormous risk to their own peoples, and the peoples themselves would generally share these perceptions. As noted earlier, governments would probably not feel justified in taking such risks except in the context of a miraculous transformation in relations between East and West.

To summarise, a world with nuclear disarmament by agreement would have the enormous advantage, compared with the existing balance of terror, of removing an appalling threat to life and the environment – at least as long as the agreement endured and was honoured. Nuclear disarmament should be more attainable than general and complete disarmament. Yet a world with nuclear disarmament could not be a world in which nuclear weapons were disinvented or forgotten. Paradoxically, it would be a high-risk and potentially unstable world. The presumption of peace, security and stability brought by the balance of terror would be lost. Instead, there would be greatly increased dangers of conventional conflict, constant fears that the other side might cheat, with devastating consequences, and frequent temptations to rearm with nuclear weapons. Would the peoples of East or West feel secure and comfortable in such a world? It is not obvious that they would. Nuclear disarmament presupposes a degree of trust between the world's strongest nations which seems unrealistic for the foreseeable future.

UNILATERAL NUCLEAR DISARMAMENT

A variant on nuclear disarmament by agreement would be for the West to renounce nuclear weapons unilaterally. As with complete, so with nuclear disarmament, the unilateral option would avoid the practical problems of how to reach agreement, implement, verify and enforce. It would bring relief to all who question the morality of even possessing nuclear weapons. The resulting world order would, however, be so unattractive for most Western governments and peoples that it seems barely conceivable that the West as a whole would ever adopt such an option.

As discussed in earlier chapters, the West has come to rely on its nuclear weapons to provide the ultimate guarantee of its security and political independence. If Western countries as a group were to renounce these weapons unilaterally, they would lay themselves open to military and political domination by the Soviet Union. West European countries, in particular, would be at risk of following the example of Eastern Europe. They could try to resist these pressures by increasing their conventional forces with a view to achieving a decisive local conventional superiority over the Soviet Union. The strategic configuration in Europe would then be the reverse of what it was in the early post-war years, when the Soviets under Stalin were massively superior in conventional forces but had no nuclear weapons. But the costs of such an attempt would be so astronomical that it could hardly be considered realistic except in the context of a gigantic crisis; and in such a context it is even more inconceivable that the West would contemplate renouncing nuclear weapons in the first place. The West's ability to deter aggression in other parts of the world would likewise be severely compromised if Western countries knew that in the last resort they lay at the mercy of the Soviet Union. Most governments and peoples in the West would see unilateral renunciation of nuclear weapons as implying capitulation to the Soviet Union.

Advocates of unilateral disarmament by the West sometimes suggest that the Soviet Union would be likely to follow the West's example and disarm unilaterally herself. If that did happen, most of the above disadvantages would disappear.

In practice, it is far from clear that the Soviets would respond in this way. The experience of the post-war years is not encouraging. Past unilateral actions by the West, like the withdrawal of 1000 tactical nuclear warheads from Europe in 1980-81, have evoked no comparable Soviet response. The West could certainly not *rely* on the Soviets to match a policy of renunciation. More probably their first reaction would be to suspect a trick. Like the Trojan priest before the wooden horse, their instinct would probably be to 'fear the Greeks even when they bear gifts'. They would need to be convinced that the West genuinely was destroying its nuclear weapons before they would even consider dismantling any of their own. And even then they might well decide to retain their own weapons, with the accompanying political benefits.

For all these reasons, the West as a whole is unlikely to renounce nuclear weapons unilaterally in the hope that the Soviets would do likewise. If the objective is nuclear disarmament by each side, the policy of seeking such disarmament by agreement must 'dominate' the policy of seeking it by example.

THE MORAL DIMENSION[3]

Some advocates of unilateral nuclear disarmament rest their case, not on the argument that the resulting world order would be preferable to the existing balance of terror, but simply on the judgement that it is morally indefensible to possess weapons capable of creating so much destruction.

Most thinking people would have considerable sympathy with such a judgement. The moral issue is appallingly difficult and needs to be recognised as such. Realistically, however, it has to be accepted that non-nuclear defences would not be adequate against a nuclear adversary. Hence a decision by Western governments in favour of unilateral renunciation would, as noted above, be a decision to lay the peoples of the West totally at the mercy of the Soviet Union and other potential adversaries, while increasing enormously the risk of conventional conflicts. One is bound to ask: would *this* decision be morally defensible? Whatever judgement one may make as to the likely behaviour of the existing leadership of the Soviet Union or other potential adversaries, can one simply dismiss as a freak the fact that the present century has produced Stalin, Hitler and millions of people who were willing to carry out their orders? If nuclear weapons had been invented 20 years earlier, would it have been right to present these ruthless men with a monopoly of such weapons? Would it be right to take a similar risk in the future? Is there any overriding moral principle which obliges such an act of potential, collective self-sacrifice and prohibits the possession of corresponding weapons for purposes of deterrence? Most of those who have addressed these questions have concluded that, appallingly difficult as they are, the answer to them all must on balance be no.

More troublesome still than the morality of possessing nuclear weapons is the morality of using them. Advocates of unilateral nuclear disarmament sometimes argue that there are no circumstances whatever in which use of a nuclear weapon would be justified and that there is consequently no point in possessing such weapons.

There are, however, two contrary considerations. First, it would in the opinion of many be going too far to say that there are *no* circumstances in which use of a nuclear weapon would be morally justified. If one considers the scenario of a ruthless Soviet advance over Western Europe, one might take the view that, even with such intense provocation, the West would not be morally justified in destroying Soviet cities; it is more difficult to argue that there could be no moral justification for strictly limited use of nuclear weapons against military targets, with a view to halting the advance and forcing the Soviets to think again (as discussed in the previous chapter). If the Soviets had destroyed certain Western cities with nuclear weapons, moreover, and there was evidence that they would destroy more cities if the West showed no will to retaliate, it is hard to argue that there would be no possible moral justification for a measure of retaliation in kind.

The second contrary consideration is that Western governments might still be well advised to retain nuclear weapons even in the unlikely event that they had decided privately that there were no circumstances whatever in which they would use them. Their deterrent power might still be decisive in keeping East and West at peace.

All advocates of unilateral nuclear disarmament emphasise the sheer scale of the destruction and agony which nuclear weapons could cause and the dangers to civilisation from a heavy nuclear exchange. These anxieties are real and daunting. If the solution cannot, for all the reasons discussed, lie in unilateral nuclear disarmament by the West, the search for alternative means of limiting the potential damage to our planet and mankind – through arms control agreements – must be of the highest importance and urgency. We return to this in the final chapter.

FORSWEARING AGGRESSION IN ANY FORM

It is sometimes suggested that, if disarmament in its various forms lies beyond reach, East and West might at least conclude a non-aggression pact, not requiring verification, under which they would both agree not to initiate the use of force against each other.

The trouble with such a pact is that it would not really solve anything. It would not commit the two sides to anything to which they are not already committed by the United Nations Charter.[4] If it were thought to do so, it might lessen the inhibitions on provocative political behaviour. In practice, neither side would trust the other to honour the pact in times of tension. Neither side would be prepared, accordingly, to reduce his military forces. Such a pact would therefore fail to address the key problem of reducing the level of armaments. It would lack credibility.

FORSWEARING FIRST NUCLEAR USE

More promising at first sight is the idea of a pact whereby the nuclear powers would agree not to use nuclear weapons first. The object would be to eliminate nuclear war, if not the nuclear arsenals. Such a pact would permit the use of nuclear weapons only in retaliation, if the other side had used them first. In contrast with a non-aggression pact, it would not purport to prevent war from breaking out but would be intended to limit the level of force used. Like a non-aggression pact, it would not require verification.

The obvious model for a no-first-use agreement would be the Geneva Convention of 1925 prohibiting first use of chemical weapons. The idea of such an agreement teases the intellect in the same way as the Geneva Convention itself. By allowing the production and deployment of nuclear weapons to continue, it would in effect provide for its own failure to be observed. It would implicitly recognise that neither side would trust the other to carry it out.

For all its appeal, the idea of a no-first-use agreement raises major problems. Compared with nuclear or general disarmament, it would have the serious disadvantage that the instruments of nuclear war would remain in being, and hence the possibility of their use. The agreement would add to the political inhibitions on use of nuclear weapons. But it would be no substitute for disarmament.

Compared with the existing balance of terror, the main disadvantages of a no-first-use agreement can be expressed in the form of a dilemma. If, on the one hand, the two sides trusted each other to observe the agreement, the nuclear arsenals would no longer deter them from committing aggression at the conventional force level. A powerful advantage of the existing balance of terror would thus be lost. The effect would be to lessen the fear of war which is mankind's best protection.[5] If on the other hand, as is more probable, the two sides did not trust each other to observe the agreement, it would be worth little and could even serve to enhance mutual suspicion.

For the West, the idea of forswearing first nuclear use raises a further problem, already discussed in relation to nuclear disarmament. It would drive a coach and horses through the strategic postures of NATO and France, which both rely heavily on the threat of first nuclear use to offset a quantitative inferiority at the conventional force level. The effect would be to tell the Warsaw Pact that NATO would let them have whatever prizes their non-nuclear forces might succeed in taking. The NATO alliance could therefore only contemplate acceptance of such an agreement if it had first succeeded in matching or surpassing the Soviets' conventional forces in Europe. This problem is one which also bedevils the European disarmament options discussed in the rest of the chapter.

As with nuclear disarmament, a possible variant would be for the West to forswear first nuclear use unilaterally rather than by agreement. For the reasons already given, however, it is barely conceivable that the West should contemplate such an option. A policy of unilaterally forswearing first nuclear use must anyway be 'dominated', for the West at least, by a policy of seeking agreement on no-first-use.

For the Soviets, with their quantitative conventional superiority and geographical advantages in Europe, forswearing first nuclear use is less problematic than for the West. A no-first-use pact which was honoured would tilt the balance of military advantage in Europe further in their favour. Not surprisingly, therefore, the Soviets have frequently advocated such a pact. In June 1982, at the United Nations' second Special Session on Disarmament, President Brezhnev took the further step of committing the Soviet Union unilaterally not to use nuclear weapons first, while calling on the other nuclear powers to follow suit. A subsequent article by the Soviet Defence Minister in *Pravda* appeared, however, to suggest that the Soviet Union's military options in time of crisis would not in practice be curtailed.

EUROPEAN OPTIONS

The idea of nuclear disarmament in Europe, whether by agreement or example, includes some options which appear rather more practicable than the disarmament options considered so far. Nuclear forces could in principle be withdrawn from Europe without fundamentally altering the present balance of terror between East and West, provided that the United States and the Soviet Union continued to deploy their strategic nuclear forces.

It may be for this reason, in part, that the anti-nuclear protest movements which sprang to life again at the beginning of the 1980s have concentrated their campaign on nuclear deployments in Europe, including the proposed new deployments of American theatre nuclear forces. The Movement for European Nuclear Disarmament, in particular, has sought to revive earlier ideas for a nuclear-free Europe.[6] Many protesters, however, appear also to favour unilateral renunciation of nuclear weapons by all Western countries.

It may seem paradoxical that a renaissance of anti-nuclear protest should have taken place at a time when the enormous build-up of Soviet SS-20 intermediate-range nuclear forces, threatening Western Europe, at last received widespread publicity. The explanation probably lies, in part at least, in the bunching of nuclear issues which hit the headlines in the late 1970s and early 1980s. After more than a decade of comparative dormancy, during which the SALT negotiations were the only substantial item of nuclear business to excite wide public interest, the public was confronted from the latter part of the 1970s by a succession of important nuclear issues – the neutron bomb, the build-up of Soviet SS-20s and Backfire bombers, NATO theatre nuclear forces modernisation, the American MX programme, the non-ratification of SALT 2, the near-disaster at the Three-mile Island nuclear power station in the United States, the French decisions on development of their nuclear forces, the British Chevaline programme and Polaris replacement decisions, and reports of progress towards a nuclear capability in previously non-nuclear countries such as Pakistan, South Africa and Israel. This cluster of new issues was virtually bound to reawaken dormant public concern about nuclear weapons.

For people living in Western Europe, the most immediately significant developments were the Soviet build-up of SS-20s targeted on Western Europe and NATO's decision of December 1979 to modernise its own, obsolescent intermediate-range nuclear forces. Despite the continuing Soviet build-up, some of the protesters continued to oppose NATO's modernisation programme. Fears grew that the superpowers were turning Western Europe into a great armoury of deadly weapons. Such fears were fuelled by the somewhat bellicose posture adopted by the Reagan administration in its early days – not least the public discussion between members of the administration about limited war options in Europe and the decision to develop the neutron bomb. It is perhaps understandable, therefore, that the protesters' instinctive reaction was to recoil. The deadly competition in armaments had to stop.

In practice the three possibilities for nuclear change in Europe most often discussed are:

1.   a European nuclear-free zone by agreement;
2.   unilateral withdrawal of nuclear forces from West European soil; and
3.   unilateral abandonment by France and Britain of their independent nuclear deterrents.

A EUROPEAN NUCLEAR-FREE ZONE

The concept of a nuclear-free zone in Europe, which formed the centre-piece of successive versions of the 'Rapacki Plan' put forward by Soviet Bloc countries between 1957 and 1962, envisages that all the countries concerned would agree not to station nuclear weapons in a defined area of territory – either a limited central area such as the two Germanies, Poland and Hungary, or a wider area such as the whole of Europe from Portugal to Poland, including the Soviet Union's European territory. Such an agreement would not prevent the nuclear powers firing nuclear warheads from outside the zone against targets inside. So the zone, though nuclear-free in peacetime, would not be 'nuclear-safe'.[7] Neither would it necessarily be free of nuclear weapons in wartime.

At first sight the idea of a nuclear-free zone has an undoubted appeal. It would be agreeable in itself to remove the horrendous hardware of nuclear weapons and delivery systems from European soil. Their removal would reduce the number of high-priority targets on European territory in the event of a nuclear exchange and might reduce the degree of devastation correspondingly.

The idea does, however, raise difficulties which in present circumstances look insuperable.

The first and most important is that agreement on a nuclear-free zone would be gravely to NATO's disadvantage. As discussed in chapter 11, NATO relies on the threat of first nuclear use to offset a quantitative inferiority in conventional forces in the European theatre and greater difficulties of reinforcement. Hence any agreement which would shift the theatre nuclear balance in the Soviets' favour or make the introduction of nuclear weapons by NATO more difficult, or less credible, is bound to weaken NATO's defence and deterrence. That, however, is precisely the effect that making Europe a nuclear-free zone would have. Thus most of NATO's existing theatre nuclear weapons would be rendered useless for war in Europe if they could not be deployed on European soil. Nuclear landmines, artillery shells, bombs delivered by land-based aircraft, short-range missiles, ground-launched cruise missiles and Pershing II ballistic missiles would all lose their role. NATO's theatre nuclear forces would be reduced to submarine-launched missiles or nuclear warheads carried by carrier-based aircraft. The Soviets' theatre nuclear forces would not be similarly incapacitated by being stationed (say) east of the Urals. The longer-range systems in particular would still be capable of hitting West European targets.

If it is assumed that the agreement would be disregarded in the event of hostilities, NATO would still be heavily disadvantaged. It would be far easier for the Soviets to wheel back their nuclear forces from the far side of the Urals into the 'nuclear-free' zone than for NATO to transport theirs from the far side of the Atlantic.

Even an agreement whereby the two sides would scrap all their existing land-based theatre nuclear weapons and rely on sea-based weapons would be to NATO's disadvantage. Sea-launched weapons would not have the same flexibility as shorter-range land-based systems. Hence escalation to the nuclear force level would become significantly more difficult for NATO. Since NATO's strategy relies on willingness to escalate in this way, the credibility of NATO's deterrence would fall correspondingly. If NATO did decide to escalate, the starting level of the nuclear exchange would inevitably be higher and more dangerous.

The idea of a nuclear-free zone in Europe raises other difficulties as well, which may be mentioned under the three headings of verification, conventional forces and independent nuclear deterrents. As to verification, the two sides would each be fearful of cheating by the other. There would be no satisfactory way of verifying compliance, even in the unlikely event that the two sides could agree on inspection. And neither side would trust the other to respect the agreement in the event of hostilities. As to implications for conventional forces, NATO would have to be prepared as a minimum to lessen its reliance on the threat of first nuclear use by matching or surpassing the Soviets' conventional strength in Europe. The European countries in NATO have in the past, however, found all manner of excuses for failing to do this. Finally, a nuclear-free zone in Europe as a whole would require France and Britain to abandon their independent deterrents. We return to this matter below.

UNILATERAL WITHDRAWAL OF NUCLEAR FORCES FROM WEST EUROPEAN SOIL

We argued earlier that the option of unilateral nuclear disarmament by the West was 'dominated' by a policy of trying to negotiate an agreement on nuclear disarmament by both sides. In just the same way a policy of unilateral withdrawal of nuclear forces, particularly American forces, from the soil of Western Europe must be 'dominated' by the policy of seeking agreement on withdrawal by both sides. It is unnecessary to repeat the arguments.

There are, however, certain 'European' arguments for withdrawing nuclear weapons from Western Europe unilaterally, if need be, which need to be considered. European unilateralists tend to argue that (1) stationing nuclear weapons in Western Europe increases the likelihood of a nuclear war in Europe – possibly a nuclear war confined to Europe; (2) stationing nuclear weapons in a particular country increases the danger that that country will be attacked, since the weapons would be a prime target in any conflict; and (3) the superpowers might decide to treat Europe as a battleground in which to settle their differences.

The first of these arguments contains more than a grain of truth. A NATO strategy which includes willingness to use nuclear weapons first if necessary, and the stationing of nuclear weapons in Western Europe in support of that strategy, must raise in some degree the risks of nuclear warfare in Europe. The strategy depends on creating just such risks, appalling as they may be. But the alternative of unilaterally removing nuclear weapons would make Western Europe a more attractive target for Soviet aggression or intimidation, especially if NATO did nothing to redress the conventional balance in Europe. The chances of a conventional war in Europe, which itself could be enormously destructive, would be greatly increased. And nuclear forces stationed outside Europe could still be used against European targets.

The cogency or otherwise of the second argument – that individual European countries will be safer in times of crisis if they do not have nuclear weapons on their soil – depends importantly on whether the country concerned has nuclear weapons of its own or merely hosts them, and on how vulnerable the weapons are to attack. Also relevant is the stage which the crisis has reached.

Thus a European country with nuclear weapons of its own is distinctly *less* likely to be attacked in the first place than one without such weapons; for a potential aggressor will have to weigh the risk of nuclear retaliation.

No one will lightly make a nuclear country desperate – not even another nuclear country. A country which only hosts nuclear weapons, on the other hand, and does not control them, may arguably be rather more vulnerable to attack than one which has no nuclear weapons on its soil but benefits from NATO's nuclear umbrella; for an aggressor might, just possibly, try to destroy the weapons pre-emptively, if he thought he could. The case is, however, far from clear-cut. The aggressor would presumably be gambling on the United States being unwilling to retaliate in kind. But a pre-emptive strike against American weapons in a West European country would be an act of such enormous provocation, *vis-à-vis* both the host country and the United States, that an aggressor could hardly place much confidence in an assumption of non-retaliation. If the hosted weapons are mobile, moreover, like NATO's new cruise missiles, an aggressor could not be confident of locating or destroying them. For both these reasons he would not necessarily perceive any particular incentive to attack 'host' countries rather than other countries.

If deterrence should fail and the crisis should escalate into war, the argument about individual safety becomes both more and less cogent. On the one hand, all nuclear weapons would be likely to become prime targets if, as before, an aggressor could locate them. And likewise nuclear bases. In conditions of full-scale war, on the other hand, *all* military bases would become prime targets.

Whatever judgement one may reach on such matters, the basic trouble with any arguments based on risks to individual countries is that they cannot be universalised. If all the European members of NATO calculated that, in the event of hostilities, they might suffer less than other countries in the alliance if they were known not to host nuclear weapons, and refused accordingly to have them, Western Europe would then have no nuclear weapons, and all the individual countries within it would consequently be *more* at risk, not less. The likelihood of hostilities would be increased. It would anyway be unreasonable for West European countries to expect the United States to bear all the risks of hosting nuclear weapons designed for the European theatre.

A rather more respectable variant of the same argument holds that individual countries in Western Europe would do better to imitate the example of the small neutral countries and abdicate from the balance of terror by refusing to admit nuclear weapons on their soil. Once again, however, the argument cannot be universalised. The neutral countries of Western Europe depend more heavily than they usually admit on their proximity to NATO. An important reason why they are able to be neutral is that they know that the Soviet Union would be deterred from invading them by the calculation that such a venture would probably lead to a war with NATO.

The third unilateralist argument carries little conviction. The real danger for Western Europe is, not that the President of the United States might be overly willing to begin a nuclear exchange in Europe, but that he would decline to use nuclear weapons in Western Europe's hour of need for fear of Soviet reprisals against the United States itself. The notion that Europe would somehow be caught up in a nuclear exchange as a result of general tensions between the superpowers, not connected with Europe, likewise strains the credulity. It is hard to see why the superpowers should be persuaded by such tensions to launch unnecessary adventures in the European theatre.

The arguments *against* unilateral withdrawal of nuclear forces from Western Europe cover now familiar territory. Such a policy, which would imply ousting American deployments and possibly abandoning the independent nuclear deterrents of France and Britain, without requiring any matching withdrawals by the Soviet Union, would suffer all the disadvantages of a European nuclear-free zone in an even more serious form. The effect would be to opt for a massive military inferiority in Europe *vis-à-vis* the Soviet Union – especially as the West is quantitatively inferior in Europe at the conventional force level. NATO's deterrence and defence would be emasculated. The ability of the West European countries to resist Soviet political intimidation would be weakened. The people of Western Europe would feel neither secure nor independent.

The strategic nuclear forces of the United States might admittedly continue to provide some kind of nuclear 'umbrella' to protect Western Europe against the Soviet Union. But the credibility of deterrence would be greatly diminished if the Soviets perceived that the West had no options to deploy between conventional warfare and the strategic nuclear arsenal of the United States. They could well gamble on the unwillingness of the United States to use its strategic nuclear forces, thus courting massive destruction of American cities, in response to military or political aggression by the Soviet Union against Western Europe. The American nuclear forces would be perceived as being largely 'uncoupled' from NATO's conventional forces in Western Europe.

If the worst came to the worst, and deterrence failed, there seems little doubt that the United States *would* be more reluctant to use nuclear weapons in support of NATO's forces. The risks perceived by the Soviets in pressing home their offensives, military or political, would be reduced correspondingly. The changes of a major defeat for NATO would be greatly increased.

Some advocates of unilateral nuclear disarmament by West European countries argue that defeat would be preferable to a nuclear exchange and possible annihilation. The argument is sometimes distilled into the slogan: 'Better red than dead'. But the argument and the slogan rest on a false antithesis. There is no simple choice to be made between submission and annihilation. There is also the option of deterrence and defence – an option which is no more likely, and may indeed be less likely, to lead to massive slaughter of civilians than a policy of submission. For a nuclear attack would only occur in the event of war. And war is only likely to begin if one side lets its guard down and the other perceives an opportunity. The trouble with a policy of unilateral nuclear disarmament by West European countries is precisely that it would encourage potential aggressors to perceive such an opportunity. The dangers of war in Europe would be increased, not reduced, if West European countries were to embrace such a policy.

The pacifist will continue to argue even so:

It is morally indefensible to have nuclear weapons and, still more, to use them, whatever the provocation may be. If the other side attacks, let him come. Let us offer no resistance. The avoidance of bloodshed and destruction is all-important.

We discussed earlier the morality of possessing and using nuclear weapons. Suffice it here to note that the extreme pacifist position has the merit of coherence and consistency. It has, however, been a minority view throughout history. And it seems likely to remain so.

INDEPENDENT NUCLEAR DETERRENTS[8]

Whatever attitude the countries of Western Europe may take towards the stationing of American nuclear weapons in their territory, the two nuclear powers of Western Europe, France and Britain, clearly have the option of scrapping their own nuclear forces. In Britain, particularly, there is a significant body of opinion which favours such a course.

Before considering the arguments for and against, we need to note two important preliminary points about the independent deterrents of the smaller nuclear powers. The first is that these forces are of consequence. Dwarfed as they are by the arsenals of the superpowers, the British and French forces are capable nevertheless of inflicting appalling damage on the Soviet Union. In the past this has been especially true of the British forces. What President Carter said about the extraordinary destructive power of 'just one' of the United States' ballistic missile submarines (see chapter 14) applies equally to Britain's Polaris submarines. As noted in chapter 7, the absence of any satisfactory defences against nuclear weapons enables smaller nuclear countries to possess a capability for inflicting massive destruction on the superpowers themselves. In a world where the numbers of strategic systems of the superpowers may be regulated by international agreements, moreoever, the existence of the independent nuclear deterrents may acquire an added significance.

The second preliminary point is to distinguish between two different kinds of independence – independence of operation and independence of procurement. Since the cancellation of Blue Streak in 1960 and the Polaris agreement of December 1962, British governments have contented themselves with the former. Britain has continued to manufacture its own nuclear warheads but has bought American missiles. French governments from de Gaulle onwards have set themselves a more exacting task. They have set their sights on, and achieved, independence of procurement as well as operation.

The arguments in favour of retaining and modernising the independent nuclear deterrents of Britain and France can be summarised under four main headings – strengthening NATO's deterrence through independent nuclear decision centres, insurance for Western Europe against the possibility of inaction or withdrawal by the United States, insurance against bilateral threats from other countries and underwriting of political independence.

Taking these in turn, the possession by West European countries of nuclear forces controlled independently of the United States must strengthen deterrence in the shorter term by discouraging a potential aggressor from gambling on the unwillingness of the United States, when it came to the point, to use its nuclear arsenal in defence of Western Europe. The existence of independent nuclear decision centres must enhance an aggressor's perception of the risk that aggression at the conventional level might provoke a nuclear response. It must reduce any temptation he might feel to discount NATO's declared willingness to use nuclear weapons first. For the aggressor would have to gamble not only on the unwllingness of the American President to put the territory of the United States at risk by using nuclear weapons but also on the French President and British Prime Minister being similarly unwilling. The independent nuclear decision centres must also complicate a potential aggressor's scenario planning for aggression at higher force levels and thus contribute to deterrence against aggression at these levels as well. In all these ways, nuclear forces which are independently controlled (without necessarily being independently procured) must make aggression, or intolerable political behaviour, more dangerous. In the longer term, too, the existence of these forces must help to discourage any hopes which the Soviets may entertain of making Western Europe into a sitting target by 'uncoupling' the United States's nuclear forces from NATO's conventional forces in Western Europe.

In addition to strengthening deterrence, the independent nuclear deterrents provide a useful measure of insurance for Western Europe against American unwillingness to use nuclear weapons in Europe's hour of need or a breakdown in the alliance with the United States. If the United States were ever to decide to accept a defeat in Europe in preference to using nuclear weapons, the existence of the European arsenals would leave Western Europe with another option. And if, against all expectations, the United States were to retreat into isolationism and pull out from its commitments to the defence of Western Europe, then Western Europe would not be left totally naked to its enemies – either militarily or politically. It would not only possess nuclear weapons with which to deter aggression in the shorter term. It would also have, and be seen to have, the potential to maintain and develop its nuclear capabilities. Thoughts such as these may have inspired Mr Heath's description of the British nuclear deterrent as 'held in trust for Europe'. To be fully effective, however, insurance against American withdrawal calls for independence of procurement as well as independence of control.

The argument about insurance against bilateral threats postulates that in the uncertain world of the future there could be other nuclear powers, possibly new and irresponsible, who nurse some bilateral grievance against (say) Britain or France and might be tempted to use their nuclear muscle in circumstances where the United States would studiously avoid involvement. The possession by Britain or France of their own nuclear forces should suffice to deter such potential aggressors.

Finally, the independent nuclear deterrents, by lessening Western Europe's political dependence on the United States, can be seen as the ultimate underwriting of Western Europe's political independence *vis-à-vis* both superpowers. As suggested in an earlier chapter, it is healthy for the alliance that Western Europe should not be totally dependent on the United States in nuclear matters. Yet this would effectively be the case if the United States were alone among Western countries in possessing nuclear weapons. For nuclear weapons are intensely national possessions, and responsibility for using them has to rest ultimately with the national government which possesses them.[9] If only the United States had nuclear weapons, all nuclear decisions in the alliance would ultimately be for the

United States alone. NATO's procedures provide explicitly for consultation before nuclear use if time and circumstances permit. Such consultation is probably helpful to the United States in the sense that it makes nuclear decisions by the President of the United States less difficult than they would otherwise be. But the ultimate decision has to rest with the government which made and owns the nuclear weapons. And it is salutory that more than one government in the alliance should share in this responsibility (see chapter 11).

There are two less respectable arguments, sometimes heard, for maintaining and modernising the independent nuclear deterrents of Western Europe. One is that the independent nuclear deterrents give their owners political influence, sometimes described as 'a seat at the top table'. To argue in this way is to misunderstand the political significance of nuclear weapons. The possession of such weapons does not give the smaller nuclear powers any particular ability to throw their political weight around. What it does do is to give them a degree of defence against aggression or political intimidation which they could not otherwise have (see chapter 5). The grain of sense which lurks beneath the chaff is that possession of nuclear weapons does potentially give Britain and France special responsibilities for the defence of Western Europe as a whole.

The second less respectable argument sees the possession of independent nuclear deterrents as a possible lever for forcing the United States to use nuclear weapons when otherwise they might be unwilling to do so. We noted in chapter 11 that some European observers feel less than fully confident that the United States would be willing, when it came to the point, to use nuclear weapons in the defence of Western Europe. Such observers can sometimes be overheard whispering a more specific argument in favour of the independent deterrents of France and Britain, based on the notion that the European countries might need to 'bounce' the Americans into using nuclear weapons in the European theatre. According to this argument, it might turn out that the only way of persuading the United States to use nuclear weapons in the defence of Europe would be for the European countries themselves to cross the nuclear Rubicon by using their own nuclear weapons first. That momentous step having been taken, so the argument runs, and the Soviets having retaliated in kind the United States would then have no option but to join in.

It is unnecessary to dwell on the dangers in such reasoning. European countries would need to be desperate indeed before they could rationally gamble on drawing the United States into nuclear conflict by such means. If the leaders of the United States had let a war in Europe reach such a desperate pass in preference to using nuclear weapons in the theatre there is no obvious reason why they should be converted by European attempts to 'bounce' them in this way – especially if the Soviets judged their response carefully so as to provoke the United States as little as possible. This 'European bounce' scenario might nevertheless be just credible enough to have deterrent value should the Soviets ever come to discount the willingness of the United States to use nuclear weapons first, if necessary, in the defence of Europe.

The arguments most often heard for abolishing the independent nuclear deterrents of Britain and France are:

(i)   a general distaste for nuclear weapons as being morally repugnant;
(ii) doubts as to whether there are any circumstances in which Britain or France would actually use these weapons independently;
(iii) the increased dangers of involvement in nuclear war for countries which have nuclear weapons on their soil or under their control; and
(iv) the heavy economic burden.

We discussed the first and third arguments earlier in this chapter. The remaining two need to be considered further.

The doubts as to whether Britain or France would ever in fact use their nuclear weapons independently are real in themselves. As discussed in chapter 10, one cannot easily visualise circumstances in which *any* country would introduce nuclear weapons. And the inhibitions must increase when the potential opponent could administer an even more terrible punishment in retaliation.

It does, however, remain possible to imagine circumstances in which independent use of nuclear weapons by West European countries could be a serious option. Suppose, for example, that an isolationist United States administration was no longer prepared to use nuclear weapons for the defence of Western Europe. Suppose, further, that (to adapt examples from earlier in the chapter) the Soviets had launched an initially successful invasion of Western Europe or had used nuclear weapons to demolish West European targets and was known to plan further nuclear strikes *unless* Western Europe showed the will to retaliate in kind. The case for nuclear responses in such circumstances would surely deserve serious consideration.

The case for possessing an independent nuclear deterrent, and its cost effectiveness, cannot, in any event, be measured by likelihood of use. A potential aggressor could never be *sure* that the weapons would not be used against him, any more than the countries possessing the weapons could be sure that they would never use them. The very possession by Britain and France of massive destructive power must make aggression or other provocative behaviour against Western Europe more dangerous in a way which no realistic accumulation of conventional forces could ever do. And effective deterrence consists precisely in making the game too dangerous.

As to economic burden, the cost of maintaining Britain's nuclear forces has been put at 5 to 7 per cent of the defence budget. That is a substantial sum in itself. Yet the increase in conventional forces which could be financed from scrapping the nuclear forces is rather disappointing: one example sometimes given is that scrapping the Trident plan without replacement might enable an extra armoured division to be added to the British Army of the Rhine.

As mentioned earlier there is, in Britain at least, a substantial body of opinion which favours scrapping the independent nuclear deterrent. Such a policy is feasible. It would not have the profound consequences for national security or international stability which would flow from unilateral nuclear disarmament by the West as a whole. But the contribution which the British and French nuclear forces make to the West's deterrence, and the extra insurance which they provide to Western Europe, both military and political, should not be underestimated. Measured against such criteria, the independent deterrents appear surprisingly cost-effective.

There are, finally, several properties which independent nuclear forces should ideally possess if they are to yield in full the advantages discussed earlier:

   (i)   an adequate capability to inflict damage;
  (ii)   flexibility;
 (iii)   invulnerability to pre-emptive attack;
 (iv)   independence of operation; and
  (v)   independence of procurement.

Taking these headings in turn, the independent deterrents will not serve any useful purpose unless they are perceived by potential aggressors to be capable of inflicting an appalling degree of damage. They need not only an impressive megatonnage of explosive power, but also accuracy and an ability to penetrate. Their credibility will be much increased if they are sufficiently accurate for use against 'hard' military targets as well as 'soft' civilian or industrial targets. The D-5 Trident ordered by the Conservative government in the United Kingdom will plainly be far superior to the existing Polaris missiles in this respect. A further important desideratum of the independent deterrents is that they should include a tactical as well as a strategic component, thus providing an option of graded response. A single 'bee-sting' capability must inevitably be less credible.

The small nuclear countries' deterrent forces need also to be as invulnerable as possible. Their deterrent power will be much reduced if a potential aggressor could destroy them in a preventive or pre-emptive strike. In its early days, at least, the French nuclear force suffered from this problem.

As to independence, both French and British forces have effective independence of control. The British forces, though declared to NATO, are available for use by the British government when it considers that supreme national interests are at stake.[10] The French forces have total independence of control.

Independence of procurement, as noted earlier, is another matter. The value of the European nuclear forces in insuring Western Europe against a breakdown in the alliance with the United States will clearly be much diminished in the longer term if the weapon systems depend heavily on American components. This is clearly a major problem with the British nuclear deterrent, which has depended heavily on American missile launchers and will almost certainly continue to do so. The French forces, on the other hand, are totally French-made.

Measured against the above criteria, neither the French nor the British nuclear forces can be considered ideal. And the costs are substantial. But the two forces taken together are probably sufficiently effective, and sufficiently independent, to yield broadly the advantages discussed earlier in this section.

CONCLUSION

We began this chapter by recollecting from an earlier chapter the sad impression that the balance of terror, unattractive as it might be, was here to stay – that peace between East and West would continue to depend in the foreseeable future on mutual deterrence through a balance of nuclear terror. Our exploration of radical alternative world orders, based on general disarmament or nuclear disarmament, universal or unilateral, has served to deepen the impression. All the radical alternatives appeared on close examination to be either unattainable or unattractive or both. It seemed highly improbable that the ordinary people of East and West would feel secure or comfortable under any of them.

None of this is to suggest that everything is for the best in this best of all possible worlds. On the contrary, our world is clearly *not* the best of all possible worlds. It is for that very reason that a balance of terror appears to be needed. Neither is everything for the best with the existing balance of terror. As we have seen in earlier chapters, it raises appalling problems.

The conclusion is rather that, for the foreseeable future at least, the best hope for an imperfect world may lie in accepting a balance of terror, while striving to make it more stable and less potentially devastating.

It is tempting to recall the celebrated quip about democracy – 'a dreadful system, to be sure, but no one has discovered anything better'. The quip appears to fit the balance of terror even more convincingly than democracy. The humour drains away; the jest becomes deadly serious; the cogency of sentiment remains. The balance of terror is surely a dreadful expedient; but in an imperfect world, full of tensions and mutual distrust, where nuclear weapons have been invented and cannot be disinvented, is there any alternative which would be both preferable and attainable? If there is, the world appears not as yet to have discovered it.

14 Policies Towards the Balance of Terror: (2) Acceptance and Improvement

INTRODUCTION

If the balance of terror is indeed here to stay, the practical need is to assess its strengths and weaknesses and the scope for improving it. We need to consider how stable it is – how well it scores under the stability criteria discussed in earlier chapters and where the main threats to stability lie. Then finally we can discuss what might be done to make it more stable, and the West more secure.

REASONS FOR GUARDED OPTIMISM

We noted in chapter 1 that the balance of terror has kept East and West at peace for about two decades, on terms reasonably acceptable to both sides. From subsequent chapters an impression has emerged that, despite all the dangers and subject to some important qualifications, the balance of terror has a very considerable built-in stability and should continue to keep the peace in the future. The impression can be described as one of optimism, but strictly guarded optimism.

The grounds for optimism are several. First, both sides will almost certainly continue to perceive the strongest possible shared interest in avoiding mutual destruction. They will surely continue to regard monumental damage on the scale inflicted by modern weapons of mass destruction as unacceptable. They will probably remain highly averse to even a limited risk of suffering such damage.

Second, the two sides are likely (barring gross mismanagement) to retain, and be seen to retain, an assured capability to inflict such unacceptable damage on each other, even after absorbing a first strike. A potential aggressor might believe that the other side would not in fact use his strength when it came to the point; but it is doubtful whether he could ever be sufficiently confident about such a judgement for aggression to seem attractive.

Third, even if deterrence were to fail initially and one side did commit aggression, there would, so we have suggested, remain a good chance of containing the conflict, even a low-level nuclear conflict, without escalation to a major nuclear exchange.

Finally, the evidence of the post-war years suggests that East and West, for all their mutual distrust and antagonism, can coexist peacefully on the basis of the existing geopolitical status quo. Both sides find the status quo irritating. But both appear to perceive its continued existence as sufficiently respecting their vital interests.

True, stability turned out in our analysis to be a function of a remarkably large number of variables – political tensions, degrees of risk-aversion, thresholds of unacceptable damage, perceptions of the will to retaliate, second-strike capabilities, degrees of first-striker's advantage, relative war-fighting capabilities, intelligence and communications, and dynamic factors. True, many of these variables are themselves functions of other variables too numerous to mention. Despite these complexities, however, the balance of terror turned out to be notably robust. It was hard to find convincing scenarios in which either side would be likely to regard the potential gains from aggression as justifying the risks. As President Carter put it in his State of the Union message on 23 January 1979:

> Just one of our relatively invulnerable Poseidon submarines . . . carries enough warheads to destroy every large and medium-sized city in the Soviet Union. Our deterrent is overwhelming.

This is not, of course, the whole story; but a potential aggressor could not dismiss the point lightly.

MAIN THREATS TO STABILITY

The reason why optimism has to be guarded is that there exist potential threats to stability which cannot be ignored and could become serious, especially in combination. These can be summarised under five headings – a hardening of Soviet policies, political problems in the West, political turbulence world-wide, first-striker's advantage and the hazards of crisis, including escalation and miscalculation. The first three threats are pre-dominantly political in nature. The last two have important military dimensions.

HARDENING OF SOVIET POLICIES

To begin with the Soviet Union, probably the most serious concern is the possibility of a reduced aversion to risk in the Soviet leadership. If the present leaders or their successors were to become willing to take greater risks – to sail even closer to the political wind, to provoke more, to test Western reactions more aggressively, to pursue more dangerously the quest for national advantage or ideological advancement, and possibly even to commit limited aggression – then stability could all too easily totter and crumble. Just as in war the West's aim would be to terminate the conflict on acceptable conditions, so in peace the West's aim must be to preserve stability on acceptable terms. Persistent attempts by the Soviet Union to make the terms unacceptable to the West could seriously rock, or even wreck, the good vessel of international security and stability.

How likely are the Soviets to harden their policies in this way? It is hard to judge. Much will depend on the new generation of Soviet leaders. Much would depend also on the West's reactions.

That said, the catalogue of Soviet actions in recent years gives cause for concern. The Soviet leaders have repeatedly confirmed their willingness not only to foster subversion but also to intervene militarily, both inside and outside the Soviet bloc – witness the interventions in Hungary, Czechoslovakia, Ethiopia, Angola and Afghanistan. In undertaking such missions they are helped by their ability to order their soldiers anywhere, to sacrifice lives, to employ East German and Cuban proxies and thoroughly to entrench régimes favourable to the Soviet Union, all without particular concern for public opinion at home. The Soviets have made no secret of their determination to keep Eastern Europe in subjection (witness the 'Brezhnev doctrine' of 1968) or of their desire to foster 'communist construction' in the West (see chapter 4). They have shown themselves capable of using their political muscle in attempts to intimidate neutral countries on their borders. Finally, their colossal and continuing build-up of armaments in the 1970s and early 1980s has seriously detracted from stability. If the resulting military imbalance, particularly in the European theatre, is not corrected, the resulting tensions could be exceptionally dangerous.

POLITICAL PROBLEMS IN THE WEST

In the West, the main potential threats to effective deterrence, and hence to stability, probably lie in the areas of will, credibility and disunity. In any struggle for political power and influence, democracies are bound to have certain disadvantages, compared with authoritarian countries. The danger is clear to see that a democratic alliance of democracies, such as the West, could be the perfect adversary. The West has been fairly, but not totally, successful since the Second World War in overcoming these handicaps. The NATO alliance must rank among the great achievements of history. Yet there are ever-present dangers in the West of underprovision for defence, under-recruitment of defence personnel, faulty political signalling and disunity.

Taking these in turn, there is probably an endemic bias in democratic countries towards underprovision for defence in peacetime (see table 14.1).[1] Other public spending programmes typically have greater electoral appeal, especially when external threats are out of the limelight. And vocal minorities, with or without Soviet encouragement, often succeed in making defence programmes controversial, especially nuclear programmes such as NATO's intermediate-range nuclear forces modernisation. Western governments are therefore tempted to underprovide, and defence programmes

---

Notes

All military personnel and spending figures need to be interpreted with extreme caution. As discussed in the IISS's 'The military balance, 1984–85', which is the source for the table, every step in the calculation, particularly for the Soviet Union and other communist countries, raises formidable problems – the estimates of defence spending and GNP/GDP in local currencies, the rates of conversion into dollars for comparative purposes (mostly market exchange rates in the table) and the definition of active military personnel. The military personnel figures exclude reservists but include conscripts: C denotes conscription of less than two years; CC, conscription of two or more years. The Soviet figure includes 1.5 million command and general support troops.

Fragile though comparisons must be, NATO would appear to have one and a half times the population of the Warsaw Pact (630 million against 385 million); 15 per cent less military personnel, if the Soviet Union's 1.5 million command and general support troops are included (5.3 million against 6.3 million); about three times the Warsaw Pact GNP; about twice the Warsaw Pact GNP per head; and a somewhat larger total expenditure on defence. The Warsaw Pact probably spends twice as high a proportion of its GNP on defence as NATO.

TABLE 14.1   Defence expenditure and personnel

Population (1984) Millions		Defence expenditure (1982)		Numbers in armed forces (1984)	
		Per head of popu-lation ($)	As per cent of GNP or GDP	Thousands	As per cent of popu-lation
	NATO				
9.9	Belgium	294	3.4	93.6 C	0.9
56.0	Britain	436	5.3	325.9	0.6
25.0	Canada	251	2.1	82.9 C	0.3
5.15	Denmark	274	2.5	31.4 C	0.6
54.6	France	415	4.2	471.4 C	0.9
61.4	FRG (West Germany)	462	4.1	495.0 C	0.8
10.2	Greece	270	7.0	178.0 CC	1.7
58.0	Italy	162	2.6	375.1 C	0.6
0.37	Luxembourg	115	1.2	0.7	0.2
14.4	Netherlands	312	3.3	101.9 C	0.7
4.15	Norway	413	3.0	36.8 C	0.9
10.2	Portugal	80	3.4	63.5 C	0.6
38.8	Spain	119	2.5	330.0 C	0.9
48.6	Turkey	59	5.2	602.0 C	1.2
236.7	United States	846	6.5	2,135.9	0.9
	WARSAW PACT				
9	Bulgaria	141	2.2-2.9	147.3 CC	1.6
15.5	Czechoslovakia	246	2.8-5.2	207.3 CC	1.3
16.86	GDR (East Germany)	434	3.7-6.5	172.0 C	1.0
10.74	Hungary	123	2.4	105.0 CC	1.0
36.9	Poland	172	3.6-4.0	323.0 CC	0.9
23.0	Romania	62	1.4	189.5 C	0.8
274.3	Soviet Union	(1000)	(10-20)	(5,115.0) CC	1.9
	FAR EAST				
1039	China	9	4.2	4,000.0 CC	0.4
180.8	Japan	87	1.0	245.0	0.2
19.6	North Korea	92	10.2	784.5 CC	4.0
41.6	South Korea	110	6.0	622.0 CC	1.5
	MIDDLE EAST				
47.2	Egypt	56	8.6	460.0 CC	1.0
4.2	Israel	1711	35.7	141.0 CC	3.3
10	Saudi Arabia	2796	17.7	51.5 CC	(0.5)

SOURCE and NOTES: *see* facing page.

inevitably suffer – both the conventional component, which accounts for the bulk of military spending, and the nuclear component, which tends to excite the keenest controversy. In some countries, notably the United States, powerful defence procurement lobbies may do something to correct the bias. But such correction tends to be patchy, with a concentation on specific hardware programmes. The fundamental bias against military spending remains. If the underspending proceeds too far, the resulting military weakness may induce a degree of political debilitation in Western leaders. It may also leave gaps in the West's defences which might tempt a potential aggressor by offering the prospect of sitting targets and a quick victory.

The spending problem may be exacerbated by difficulties in recruiting military personnel. Under-recruitment may reflect underspending on defence, demographic constraints or a disinclination among younger people to join the armed services. Whatever the causes, the consequences may be similar to those already described.

Fortunately for the West, underprovision and under-recruitment would have to proceed quite a long way before the threat to stability would become really serious. The present stability has large tolerance margins. There is, moreover, a corrective mechanism which may do something to mitigate the problems of underprovision: perceived increases in the external threat will generally ease the task of raising defence budgets. With the Soviet invasion of Afghanistan at the end of 1979, for example, and the Soviet pressures on Poland from 1980 onwards, it has become easier for Western governments to justify increases in defence spending. The mechanism is rather like a thermostat or heat-alarm system. But its efficiency is low. The incidence of perception-moulding events is uncomfortably random; the delays between brave decisions and enhanced capabilities, uncomfortably long.

A third problem for Western democracies is sending the correct political signals to potential enemies. As discussed in earlier chapters, failure to send the right signals today can all too easily result in crisis tomorrow or the day after and ultimately in war by miscalculation. Yet it is often difficult for Western statesmen, nervous as to domestic political repercussions and the attitudes of their own armed forces, to speak and act as firmly and continuously as the world situation requires. At any one time, moreover, a significant proportion of them may be short on personal experience of defence, deterrence and the idiom of international politics. So rapid is the turnover of political leaders. Once again, the thermostat or heat-alarm system may help to strengthen the native hue of resolution. But here, too, efficiency is low: public perceptions of the threat are so changeable; memories of events, so short-lived.

A further problem for the West, discussed in chapter 11 and elsewhere, is unity – how to convey convincingly to the Soviet Union that Western Europe and the United States are united and will remain so. The leaders of the United States in particular need to signal to potential enemies that they mean business when they say that they stand behind Western Europe, are prepared to take the appalling step of crossing the nuclear Rubicon, if necessary, and do not rule out the use of strategic nuclear weapons in defence of Europe. The leaders of West European countries likewise bear a massive responsibility for preserving unity and conviction. We have suggested that credibility is unlikely to fall so low that the Soviets would find military aggression in Europe attractive (political aggression is another matter); but enhancement of credibility demands constant attention.

POLITICAL TURBULENCE WORLD-WIDE

Another development which could threaten stability would be deepening political turbulence world-wide – not only in areas within the spheres of influence of one of the superpowers (such as Eastern Europe) but also in other sensitive areas, notably those which produce oil and raw materials.

The threat from the latter source has in the past been softened by the near-self-sufficiency of the Soviet Union in fuel and raw materials. If however this were to change – if, for example, the Soviet Union were to become, and the United States to remain, major oil importers from the Middle East – then perceptions might grow of conflicting economic and political imperatives between East and West. Such perceptions could only detract from stability. The tensions would be much increased if the Soviets were to step up pressures on Middle East oil producer countries and threaten the West's main oil supply routes by further building up their military capabilities in the Persian Gulf, the Arabian Sea and the Red Sea.

FIRST-STRIKER'S ADVANTAGE

The potential threat to stability from first-striker's advantage, especially at the strategic nuclear level, has been a *leitmotif* of this study. If one side perceives a major advantage in striking first, he may be tempted to exploit his advantage. If he perceives the other side as well to have a major advantage in striking first, the temptation will be increased; for he will then have the added incentive of preventing the other side from striking first. If in addition he should fall prey to the insidious conviction that a nuclear exchange is bound to come sooner or later, and that the question is when, not whether – a type of thought-corrupting cancer which (we have argued) can all too easily spread among decision-makers in times of stress – then the temptation to open the striking will be strongest of all. A point might be reached where the dangers of striking first appear to be outweighed by the dangers of *not* striking first; and this would bode ill for stability.

There are good reasons for discussing the problem in terms of 'first-striker's advantage' rather than 'vulnerability' or 'counter-force capability'. The first-striker's advantage must obviously depend on his ability to destroy the other side's weapons in a counter-force strike, or (equivalently) on the vulnerability of those weapons to such an attack. When the two sides have similar numbers of weapon launchers, however, the incentive to strike first, and hence the real threat to stability, arises not simply from the ability to destroy the other side's weapons but rather from the ability to destroy *more than one* of his weapons (in practice, at least two or three, on average) with each weapon of his own which the first striker uses up. The potential threat to stability arises, in short, from expectations of favourable counter-force exchange rates in a first strike.

The discussion in earlier chapters concentrated on the *potential* threat to stability from a powerful first-striker's advantage at the strategic level. But how great is the threat in practice?

As suggested in chapter 7, the counter-force exchange rate for a first striker has never so far looked particularly favourable to either side. First-striker's advantage has not, therefore, posed any real threat to stability. With advancing technology, however – in particular the combination of the greatly increased accuracy of modern missiles and the MIRVing which enables one launcher to deliver several independently targeted warheads – the exchange rate for a first strike may now be favourable and is likely to become more so in the years immediately ahead. In the second half of the 1980s both the Soviets and the Americans are expected to have a considerable first-striker's advantage, with the Soviets probably having the edge initially. The two sides may never again have land-based systems as invulnerable as before the days of high accuracy and multiple warheads.

These anxieties need to be taken seriously. On the whole, however, our conclusion has been that concern is more apposite than alarm. A limited degree of first-striker's advantage may even contribute to stability by enhancing deterrence against aggression at the conventional level. The degree of advantage would have in general, so we have argued, to be really decisive before a first, all-out counter-force strike could possibly appear attractive; and there is little prospect that the first-striker would expect anything like a decisive advantage in the foreseeable future. Whether or not current efforts to make land-based systems and aircraft less vulnerable succeed, both sides are likely to retain massive and relatively invulnerable second-strike capabilities in the form of submarine-launched ballistic missiles (SLBMs) and surviving bombers. Even if advancing technology were to increase the chances of discovering and destroying enemy submarines in the oceans, the prospects for destroying them comprehensively in coastal or inland waters are likely to remain elusive. The side contemplating a first, all-out counter-force strike would have, in addition, to recognise the probability of a high failure rate. Neither side has experience of launching even one intercontinental ballistic missile in time of war, much less a simultaneous, all-out attack. The disincentives to launch a major nuclear strike have moreover been further compounded in recent times by the 'nuclear winter' hypothesis.[2] Whatever the conclusions from further research may be, the fact that the hypothesis can be entertained at all is one which neither superpower could afford to ignore.

All in all, therefore, it is hard to visualise either side launching a counter-force strike 'out of the blue' in order to gain military advantage. It is still hard, but somewhat easier, to visualise such a strike in conditions where war has already broken out, especially if one side or the other becomes convinced that escalation to the strategic level is inevitable sooner or later. It is here, surely, that the greater threat to stability lies.

There are some who argue that, unlikely as it may be that the Soviets would attempt a massive counter-force strike 'out of the blue' on the strength of their first-striker's advantage in the second half of the 1980s, their feeling of advantage might encourage them to intensify political pressures against the West – to increase political blackmail and intimidation. This argument is, fortunately, not convincing. For the United States, too, will have a first-striker's advantage in the second half of the 1980s, and this should largely neutralise any extra political muscle which the Soviets might have hoped to obtain from their first-striker's advantage. None of this is to rule out the possibility that the Soviets may toughen their policies. The point is rather that the so-called 'window of opportunity', based on expected first-striker's advantage in the second half of the 1980s, should not of itself provide a foundation for increased political leverage.

HAZARDS OF CRISIS

The balance of terror has made outbreaks of hostilities, and subsequent escalation, incomparably more dangerous than in previous eras, and incomparably less probable. Yet some risk must remain that the heat of crisis may spark limited hostilities which will then escalate out of control. However intrinsically stable the balance of terror may be, the dynamics and other hazards of crisis must add a separate dimension of danger – an extra potential threat to stability.

Provocation, temptation and miscalculation, resulting respectively from political behaviour which is too aggressive, too weak and too equivocal – such are the factors which seem most likely to spark crises and hostilities. Especially dangerous from a dynamic point of view are repeated acts of aggressive behaviour, which may cause a crescendo of provocation, and political actions which, while not military in themselves, blatantly invite the use of force in reply – actions such as the Berlin blockade of 1948-9 or the harassment of ships or aircraft. Hardly less dangerous are policies which tempt a potential aggressor by dangling the prospect of an easy victory or quick attainment of some limited objective. If the Soviet leaders, in particular, were tempted in this way, the threat to stability could be serious: it seems unlikely that they would have themselves strapped to the mainmast, like Odysseus in ancient times, lest they should succumb to the Siren voices of opportunity.

Once hostilities have broken out, even on a limited scale, the dangers of a major conflagration must immediately be multiplied. Both sides will be concerned to prevent the conflict from escalating too far; but they will also be concerned to win, or not to lose, or (at least) not to lose face. The threats to stability are plain to see: the loser's temptation to escalate; the temptation on both sides to leap-frog, or overtrump; the ever-present dangers of misunderstanding, misinterpretation, misjudgement, miscalculation.

Most troublesome of all are the nuclear dimensions of escalation – a subject which has dominated the latter part of this book. NATO relies more heavily than one would wish on the threat of escalation to nuclear weapons to compensate for inferiority at lower force levels, both conventional and chemical: the nuclear threshold is uncomfortably low. We have been more optimistic than many about the scope for limiting nuclear war once begun. But the possibility of heavy nuclear exchange is real, especially in conditions where both sides have first-striker's advantage at the strategic level.

Finally there are the characteristic hazards of crisis: command and communications failures, particularly the destruction of national command centres and top leadership; poor crisis management, including mutual misreading of the other side's intentions; the toll which stress may take of elderly or inexperienced national leaders and their advisers; and poor communications between the two sides. In times of crisis the ability of national leaders to survive, analyse, act sensibly and communicate is likely to be all-important.

COMBINATIONS OF UNSTABLE FACTORS

The potential threats to stability discussed above, political, military and dynamic, need to be seen as different dimensions of a total threat rather than separate threats – dimensions which are likely to reinforce each other powerfully in any actual crisis. All crises are political in origin. But military factors may contribute; and once a crisis has begun both military and dynamic factors are likely to compound the dangers.

As the above implies, the greatest threat to stability probably lies in some combination of political, military and dynamic factors – an outbreak of limited conventional hostilities, provoked by a conflict of perceived political imperatives, miscalculation, intolerable political behaviour or prospects of a quick win, followed by more extensive conventional fighting, followed by first use of nuclear weapons by the losing side, followed by a weightier nuclear response by the other side, followed by a growing conviction that escalation to an all-out nuclear conflict is unavoidable and that it is essential to deny the other side the advantages of a first strike at the strategic level – all this complicated by mutual misreading of the other side's intentions, poor communications between the two sides, a serious breakdown in command and communications on one side, erratic leadership on the other, a tradition of deep distrust between East and West and a background of political turbulence world-wide. It is because the potential threats to stability are so many, so serious, so mutually reinforcing, that optimism about stability in the balance of terror has to be guarded.

POSTSCRIPT ON NUCLEAR PROLIFERATION

Before leaving the subject of threats to stability, we need to consider how stability would be affected if other countries joined the existing nuclear club of the United States, the Soviet Union, Britain, France and China.

As is well known, many other countries could set about developing nuclear weapons if they wished. The requirements are threefold – technical knowledge, access to fissionable materials and willingness to undertake the massive engineering investment required. At the time of writing, more than a dozen non-nuclear countries probably possess the necessary basic knowledge, and more seem likely to follow. Six countries, all non-signatories of the 1968 non-proliferation treaty, are believed to have made significant progress towards production of nuclear weapons – India and Pakistan, Israel, South Africa, Brazil and Argentina. Others are believed to have toes in the water. Despite all the efforts of the United States government and the International Atomic Energy Agency to impose safeguards, moreover, the number of countries with potential access to nuclear materials seems set to rise dramatically with the spread of nuclear power reactors.

In the short to medium term – say between now and the end of the century – there seems no reason to postulate major consequences for stability in the balance of terror between East and West as a result of nuclear proliferation. As we concluded in chapter 10, if a handful of other countries took the momentous step of producing and deploying nuclear weapons, the risk of nuclear weapons falling into reckless hands would increase, and likewise the risk of accidents. The new nuclear countries might conceivably use their weapons against each other. But there is no evident reason why such an exchange, tragic as it would be, should fundamentally affect the existing balance of terror between East and West, still less lead to an East/West nuclear confrontation. There seems likewise no reason why nuclear accidents should have such consequences.

Over the very long term (say, the twenty-first century), the assessment has to be more uncertain. The stability of the balance of terror, and even its relevance, will depend on political change and technological progress. One can conceive of a brave new world in which the major nations will so trust each other that they will feel able to discard their weapons of mass destruction. Perhaps a more likely scenario is that continuing political tensions will persuade more countries to have nuclear forces of their own.

The latter prospect brings no pleasure. The dangers from reckless hands and accidents would increase. There again seems no obvious reason, however, why such developments should upset the stability of the balance of terror between East and West. One can only guess: but it seems more probable that a balance of terror will remain relevant and effective, in some form or other, for as far into the future as the imagination can stretch.

Perhaps the most alarming scenario for the very long term is one in which advancing technology has made the production of nuclear weapons exceptionally cheap and easy, no effective defences have been developed, and at the same time the more extreme variants of the 'nuclear winter' hypothesis have been confirmed. In such a scenario, which fortunately does not seem very probable, the future of the planet could begin to look decidedly precarious.

POSTSCRIPT ON DEFENCES AGAINST NUCLEAR WEAPONS

A quite different scenario for the distant future is that technological progress, in particular the development of effective defences against nuclear weapons, might fundamentally alter, or even nullify, the balance of terror. As discussed in chapter 7 the existing balance of terror depends crucially on the absence of such defences, which leaves cities totally vulnerable. If genuinely comprehensive and foolproof defences could be developed, nuclear weapons would lose their sting. A point might even be reached where they would no longer deter, and governments would have no further use for them. Such was the vision which inspired President Reagan's 'star wars' speech of March 1983 commending a major programme of research into laser-based ABM defences, the 'Strategic Defence Initiative'.[3] If foolproof new defences could be devised against all forms of delivery systems – cruise missiles, bombers, ships and trucks, as well as ballistic missiles – then nuclear and conventional weapons alike might in theory lose their role in international warfare.

In truth, no-one can know what future progress in technology may bring. Remembering all that has happened since the beginning of the industrial revolution, only some two hundred years ago, one is bound to be cautious in surmising what may happen over the next two hundred years.

That said, however, it still seems inherently unlikely that the balance between offensive and defensive capabilities, tilted hitherto so heavily in favour of the former, will shift decisively in favour of the latter. The development of even moderately effective defences against small targets such as ballistic missiles, travelling at great speed along unknown flight-paths through the atmosphere and outer space, will be a formidable task, if indeed it can be accomplished at all; and the task of developing foolproof defences against other forms of delivery – minute, low-flying cruise missiles and furtive deliveries on aircraft, ships or trucks – will be hardly less formidable. Progress in the development of defensive capabilities may well be remarkable. But it is likely to be accompanied by comparable progress in offensive capabilities. As suggested in chapter 7, the human mind is likely to be no less fertile in countering defensive capabilities than in devising such capabilities in the first place – no less fertile in protecting offensive weapons against the new-found defences than in protecting potential targets against the offensive weapons. The chances of devising a defensive shield which combines total reliability with permanent invulnerability to counter-measures look rather remote. The circle of fire with which Wotan surrounded Brünnhilde was apparently impenetrable. Yet Siegfried found a way through.

None of this is to argue against research into ABM and ACM systems and bomber defences. Quite the contrary. As argued in chapter 7, Western countries cannot afford to ignore any area of research whose neglect could endanger their security or leave them at a disadvantage. Least of all can they afford to neglect possible means of defence (or partial defence) against nuclear attack. If the West had no capabilities in these areas, actual or potential, to match those of the Soviet Union, that would be a source of instability in the balance of terror. The Soviets' existing defensive systems are much more highly developed than those of Western countries, and they have deployed an anti-satellite (ASAT) system since the mid-1970s. They are also known, despite their criticisms of the American SDI programme, to have poured substantial resources into the development of laser and particle beam technologies. The West needs to remain at the forefront of technological development, without however threatening stability by setting too hectic a pace.

Our purpose is rather to hazard the thought that, vulnerable as the balance of terror itself may in principle be to the development of effective defensive systems, it still seems unlikely that such systems would be foolproof enough, even in a relatively distant future, to remove the threat posed by nuclear weapons. Subject to all our earlier caveats, technological progress seems more likely to keep the balance of terror in being than to make it wither away.

SOME POLICY IMPLICATIONS

We turn finally to the policy dimension. What can the West do to maximise security and stability? It is convenient to consider this question under the three headings of strategic postures, political signals and military capabilities.

STRATEGIC POSTURES

If the balance of terror is here to stay, the West's strategic posture needs to begin by accepting that reality – reluctantly but with conviction. Reluctantly, because no thinking person can take any pleasure from such a dreadful expedient as a balance of terror. With conviction, because half-hearted acceptance of the balance of terror, steering a middle course between acceptance and rejection, is likely to produce weakness, instability and even disaster.

The West's strategic posture in recent years *has* accepted the reality of the balance of terror, with varying degrees of conviction. The broad strategy has been weighed in the balance in earlier chapters, but not found wanting. The analysis has strongly supported a strategy which aims to combine effective deterrence through flexible response with a continuing and determined search for détente and arms control, circumstances permitting.

If the analysis is accepted, the task for the West in the years ahead must be to pursue *both* facets of the strategy with conviction but without illusions. The strategy must continue to deter. Its success will depend partly on having strong military capabilities and partly on sending the right political signals. Similarly, the search for détente and co-operation needs to continue: it calls for imagination and commitment, tempered by caution and realism.

The West needs in particular to continue with the search for agreements on arms control. We concluded in chapter 13 that complete disarmament, general or nuclear, lay beyond reach and that unilateral renunciation of nuclear weapons was unattractive. But the two superpowers would appear to share, with each other and with the rest of the world, the strongest possible interest in jointly and drastically *reducing* their nuclear arsenals. The scale of the present arsenals far exceeds the requirements of deterrence. The damage which a full-scale nuclear exchange with these arsenals could inflict on mankind and the planet is incalculable. We suggested in chapter 9 that the West should set its sights accordingly on a new and better balance of terror, based on *mutual and stable minimum deterrence* (MSMD), and should work tirelessly for arms control agreements to that end. Such agreements would be likely to involve massive reductions in the nuclear arsenals, perhaps to one-third or one-quarter of their present levels.

As noted in chapter 9, arms control agreements will never be easy.The technical and practical difficulties are legion. The participating governments have to be cautious, realistic, mindful of their awesome responsibilities for national security. But such agreements do appear to offer the best available hope for improving the balance of terror in an imperfect world. The West needs therefore to be patient and to persevere.

POLITICAL SIGNALS AND DÉTENTE

Within the broad strategy of deterrence combined with a readiness for co-operation, a crucial task for the West is to send the right political signals to potential enemies. As we saw in chapter 5, political leaders are transmitting signals to the rest of the world all the time, consciously or unconsciously. Such signals are the stuff of international politics. The prospects for preserving peace and stability on acceptable terms depend importantly on the ability of political leaders, and others, in the West to transmit correct and timely signals.

We have emphasised repeatedly how important it is for Western countries to signal firmness of purpose, even in peacetime – to make crystal clear their determination to protect legitimate Western interests, and their willingness to use force if necessary in the last resort to deal with aggression or intolerable provocation. The 'modest stillness and humility' which Henry V commended as a becoming posture in peacetime are often not a sufficient posture for leading statesmen today. All too often, the paramount need is to disguise fair nature with hard-favoured rage and lend the eye a terrible aspect.

The West's specific aim must be to signal the dangers of aggressive behaviour by making such behaviour not only dangerous, but obviously dangerous – too dangerous, and too obviously dangerous to be attractive. To that end Western leaders need to be scrupulous about condemning aggressive behaviour when it occurs. Depending on circumstances, there may also be a case for limited but significant actions, such as redeploying armed forces, as well as words. The potential enemy may not be deterred immediately; but he may think twice before continuing with such behaviour or embarking on further aggressive ventures. The general principle of making aggressive behaviour dangerous applies, moreoever, to Third World situations as well as threats to Western countries.

Domestic political considerations may tempt Western governments to soften their public postures and turn a blind eye to aggressive behaviour. National leaders may hope by this means to avoid controversy and reassure public opinion. But any impression of weakness or unconcern in the West is likely to convey wrong signals to potential aggressors, and wrong signals can all too easily lead to crisis.

The crises of the post-war period illustrate the point. As noted in chapter 5, several of them would probably not have occurred if only the West had sent more robust signals in advance. Thus the Cuban missile crisis of 1962 ought probably never to have happened. If the United States administration had conveyed the right signals before the crisis began, Khruschev could hardly have proceeded with his extraordinary plan for setting up a missile base in the Caribbean. The same may be true of the decision to build the Berlin Wall in 1961. Recent reports suggest that Khruschev was persuaded to proceed by a conviction, justified in this instance, that the

United States would stand idly by. Even the Korean War of 1950-3 may have been unnecessary. The communist powers appear to have assumed, when launching the war, that the United States would not intervene – an assumption based on public pronouncements of the United States administration.

As with short-term crises, so too over the longer-term, if Western leaders are indecisive in the face of aggressive policies and fail to signal firmness of purpose, the Soviets will only be encouraged to harden their policies, the tensions between East and West are likely to increase, and sooner or later a point may be reached where the risk of military conflict has become serious. Western leaders need to transmit firm signals in good time to prevent such crisis points being reached.

To argue that Western leaders should exhibit firmness of purpose and a resolute political idiom is not to suggest that they should be reckless or bellicose. Neither is it to reject a posture of détente. On the contrary, there is seldom any merit in appearing reckless or bellicose. The aim should be, rather, to convey an impression of toughness without bellicosity – of a capacity for anger without recklessness. Especially when both sides possess a first-striker's advantage at the strategic level, it would be extremely dangerous if either side became convinced that the other side's frame of mind was such that full-scale conflict was unavoidable. Far better for West as well as East, Soviet behaviour permitting, is a posture based on readiness for détente, including agreements on arms control and crisis management.

As the qualification about Soviet behaviour implies, the practical interpretation of détente is all important. Détente is not a policy of friendship. Rather it implies a readiness to maintain whenever possible a reasonable working relationship with a potential adversary, based on common interest – to coexist, communicate and negotiate with him and to avoid an unnecessary degree of overt strain and hostility.

As noted in chapter 4, there are dangers for the West in détente. We quoted there Mr Brezhnev's concept of détente as a cover for peaceful advancement of the communist cause. We mentioned the danger that détente may blur Western perceptions of the threat from the Soviet Union, thus leading to complacency and underprovision for defence. The West needs to be aware of these dangers. Détente must not be allowed to degenerate into policies of weakness or appeasement. Neither must it be allowed to detract from the firmness of the West's political signals to the Soviet Union. Policies based on détente must be flexible. If the Soviet leaders behave intolerably, or show themselves to be untrustworthy, Western leaders need to make their displeasure plain. The Carter administration in the United States took significant steps in that direction in 1980 in response to the Soviet invasion of Afghanistan. They made clear that the Soviets had come close to the brink – that if the Soviets should contemplate similar adventures against Pakistan or the Persian Gulf, the United States would consider vital interests to be at stake. But both the Carter administration and (still more) European governments could arguably have done more than they did. They could, for example, have decided to strengthen their military capabilities specifically in response to that monstrous act. How much more telling the political signal would then have been.

Important as these qualifications are, policies based on a readiness for détente, including far-reaching arms control agreements, seem far better for the West than the earlier cold war postures. A world of détente should be considerably safer for both sides than a belligerent world, especially when first-striker's advantage gives each side an incentive to strike pre-emptively. The less contact the two sides have had, the less developed their habit of negotiation, and the smaller the degree of circumscribed trust they have in each other, the more inclined they will be in times of crisis to suspect each other of a base intent and 'stand like greyhounds in the slips, straining upon the start'.

It is also valuable to maintain the degree of contact with people behind the Iron Curtain which détente has made possible. The West Germans in particular are anxious not to lose spiritual contact with their brothers in the East. The least tolerable aspects of existing communist regimes are more likely to survive in total quarantine than if these countries are exposed in some degree to the outside world.

Finally, there are many responsible people in the West who, while supporting NATO's policies of deterrence and defence, worry deeply about the morality of war and nuclear weapons. This whole section of opinion would be alienated if the West were to replace the policy of flexible détente by policies of mindless belligerence. It would be foolish to risk tearing Western society apart in this way.

MILITARY CAPABILITIES

We ask finally – what level of military capabilities does the West need in order to preserve effective deterrence and stability? How adequate are existing capabilities?

For reasons discussed in earlier chapters, the answer to the first question has to be that the Western alliance really needs strong and flexible capabilities at *all* force levels, conventional, chemical, theatre nuclear and strategic nuclear – capabilities which will make it a match for any potential opponent in any type of war, nuclear or conventional, limited or unlimited, on land or at sea, in Europe or outside.

The conclusion grates upon the ear. It implies such large expenditure on defence; and it can easily sound bellicose, especially when expressed in terms of 'war-fighting' capabilities. We need therefore to recapitulate briefly the reasons which lead to such a conclusion.

The first reason has to do with defence, or 'war-fighting'. If, against expectations, deterrence broke down and war began, the West would need strong and flexible capabilities at all force levels both to minimise the dangers of escalation to higher force levels and to avoid defeat.

At the risk of labouring points discussed extensively in earlier chapters, strong conventional and chemical capabilities are needed so as to maximise the chances that aggression at the conventional force level – the level which an aggressor is almost certain to choose – could be successfully resisted without the need for recourse to nuclear weapons. Weak conventional and chemical capabilities imply a low nuclear threshold – an early choice between accepting defeat and escalating to nuclear force levels which would far better have been avoided.

At the other end of the spectrum, strategic nuclear weapons need a combination of destructive power, accuracy, ability to penetrate, flexibility and invulnerability to attack such that no remotely sane aggressor would want to take any serious risk of letting a conflict escalate to such a level. If this should happen nevertheless, the West's strategic forces need to be (and be seen to be) strong enough to deliver as much damage as those of the aggressor and thus discourage any thought which he might entertain of continuing the conflict in the hope of ending up in a stronger position than the West.

Between the conventional/chemical and strategic nuclear force levels, the West's defences will be enhanced by strong, flexible and invulnerable intermediate- and short-range nuclear systems, particularly in the European threatre – systems which will provide a formidable range of options for responding to aggression which cannot be contained at the conventional level, without escalating to the ultimate force level of the strategic nuclear arsenals themselves. Without theatre nuclear weapons, the President of the United States would have no means, short of the strategic nuclear arsenal itself, for compelling an initially successful aggressor to reappraise his original decision to open hostilities. He could all too easily find himself confronted by an impossible choice between accepting defeat at the conventional level and engaging the American strategic nuclear arsenal.

The weaker the West's conventional forces are, moreover, the more likely it is that NATO might feel obliged to escalate to the theatre nuclear force level. The more important it becomes, correspondingly, that NATO's theatre nuclear forces should be flexible enough to permit a strictly controlled escalation, and strong enough to scotch any hope an aggressor might entertain of coming off better in a tactical nuclear exchange.

There are various schools of thought which seek to reject this whole chain of reasoning on the grounds that there could be no winners in a nuclear war and the concept of nuclear war-fighting is anyway anathema. Any thinking person is likely to have instinctive sympathy for such views. There *is* a sense, and an important sense, in which neither side in a nuclear war would be a 'winner': both would be likely to suffer grievous damage. As noted in chapter 8, however, this is the language of paradox. The proposition that there would be no winners in a nuclear war vividly expresses a particular insight, without being literally true. The world would continue in some shape or form after a nuclear exchange, including the nuclear countries of East and West, and it would be all too possible for one side to end up in better shape than the other. There could be no advantage for the West in having weak capabilities such that at certain force levels it would be likely to end up in far worse shape than potential aggressors. To confront paradox with paradox, there might be no winners in a nuclear exchange; but there could certainly be a loser.

The argument which seeks to make 'nuclear war-fighting' a pejorative term likewise has a strong intuitive appeal. There is a natural instinct to recoil from even thinking about such matters. In time of crisis, however, the question of how to bring nuclear strength to bear could suddenly assume the highest importance. It cannot be right to ignore such issues until they actually arise. On the contrary, Western governments surely have a duty to think through the forms which conflicts might take and to determine their strategic, procurement and deployment programmes accordingly. They need to plan in advance how best to compel an aggressor to reappraise his initial decision to attack (surely the overriding objective of any first nuclear use); how best to control the amount of nuclear force used if used it had to be; how best to reinstate deterrence against further escalation of the crisis if deterrence has failed initially; how best to minimise the dangers of escalation to a full-scale strategic nuclear exchange. There would be all the difference in the world between a limited and a full-scale nuclear exchange. The former would be an appalling, but limited, disaster; the latter, a monumental catastrophe. For all the reasons discussed in this and earlier chapters, keeping a nuclear conflict limited would be likely to depend importantly on having strong, flexible and accurate capabilities at all levels of military force.

The preceding discussion has been concerned primarily with defence and war-fighting. But strong and flexible war-fighting capabilities, including limited war capabilities, are needed no less for reasons of deterrence, political muscle and arms control. Deterrence works precisely by anticipation of the appalling damage which war would inflict. It can indeed be seen as war-fighting in the imagination. If a potential aggressor believes he could win a war, especially without excessive cost to himself, deterrence will be gravely weakened. If the other side can be seen to have weak conventional capabilities, a potential aggressor may be tempted to gamble on his own ability to win at the conventional level and the other side's unwillingness to escalate to nuclear weapons. If the other side can be seen to be inferior in nuclear capabilities as well, the potential aggressor will be even more likely to doubt the other side's willingness to go nuclear, and the perceived risks in aggression will be further reduced.

The analysis applies equally to political muscle. The stronger a country's deterrence and war-fighting capabilities, the better able it will be to resist political intimidation and blackmail.

The proposition that strong military capabilities are needed also for reasons of arms control may at first sight seem surprising. There is, however, much circumstantial evidence that disparities in relative strengths make it more difficult both to launch negotiations and to clinch agreements. The two superpowers have shown an understandable reluctance to enter negotiations at all from positions of weakness. Once negotiations have begun, the more effectively the West's forces match those of the Warsaw Pact countries, the more similar the required reductions in armaments will be and the easier, consequently, it should be to reach agreements.

As noted in earlier chapters, there are several schools of strategic throught which, while accepting the reality of the balance of terror, deny the need for war-fighting capabilities at all force levels or a capability to fight limited wars. Some argue for unilateral 'minimum deterrence', and some for a 'cornered beast' philosophy. Some argue that limited war capabilities only make war itself (or nuclear war) more likely. Some insist that flexible weapon systems make escalation too easy, especially if the distinction between nuclear and conventional weapons becomes blurred.

We have given reasons in earlier chapters for rejecting these philosophies. Unilateral 'minimum deterrence' is a policy of opting deliberately and openly for major inferiority at the strategic level (and possibly at other force levels too) – a policy which would leave the West acutely vulnerable to counter-force strikes, bluff-calling and political blackmail. A 'cornered-beast' policy is one which would preserve parity in strategic nuclear weapons but opt for inferiority at lower force levels – a policy which would leave the West wide open to the risk of having its bluff called by an enemy prepared to gamble on NATO's unwillingness, when it came to the point, to escalate to the strategic nuclear level. The argument that capabilities for fighting limited wars make war itself (or nuclear war) more likely contains a germ of truth; but if war (or nuclear war) looks too unlikely – and especially if the other side possesses a capability to fight limited wars while the home side does not – deterrence against political aggression, and even limited military aggression, can only be weakened, and the dangers of all-out war, if war does occur, multiplied. Much the same considerations apply to the argument that flexible weapon systems make escalation to the nuclear level too easy. It can hardly be in the interests of an alliance such as NATO, whose deterrence relies heavily on the threat of escalation to the nuclear level, to make such escalation incredible or impossibly difficult.

ADEQUACY OF EXISTING CAPABILITIES

How adequate are the West's actual war-fighting capabilities at the various force levels? How well do they score against the criteria discussed above?

To do such questions justice it would be necessary to assess not only the military personnel, hardware and software, of East and West, but also the likely courses and outcomes of the widest possible range of war-fighting scenarios. The latter task in particular calls for a combination of military expertise and judgement far beyond the pretensions of the present author. There are, however, some untutored impressions which have emerged in the course of the preceding chapters.

The main such impression is that the West's military capabilities are rather patchy, or second-best. In many areas, such as command, control and communications, electronic systems, reconnaissance and intelligence, it is virtually impossible for the layman to judge adequacy. But there are several crucial areas where NATO looks to be either clearly inferior to the Warsaw Pact, in quantitative terms, or barely adequate (see figures 11.1, 11.2, 11.3, 11.4). Such areas include land/air conventional forces in Europe, where the Warsaw Pact is significantly superior in personnel deployments and far superior in reserves and most types of equipment; offensive chemical capabilities, where modernisation of NATO's arsenal has been long postponed; air defences and civil defence, where NATO has not attempted to match the Soviet deployments; and research and development, where the Soviet effort is reported substantially to exceed that of the West. In the area of sea/air conventional forces, where the

West badly needs superiority in order to overcome geographical disadvantages, NATO has seen its margin of superiority greatly eroded in recent years.

In the area of nuclear weapons judgement becomes more precarious. On many of the standard measures, such as numbers of launcher systems, throw-weight and explosive power, the Soviets appear to have achieved superiority in 'strategic' systems over recent years, and much of the American hardware is old. The Reagan Administration has, however, acted decisively to correct the imbalance, and it is far from clear that swapping the American strategic arsenal for its Soviet counterpart would be a good bargain. The Soviets have built up a troublesome superiority in intermediate-range nuclear forces, which the West is only now beginning to redress.

Be that as it may, it is difficult to do otherwise than conclude that Western countries collectively have skimped on conventional and chemical forces; that the West's deterrence and defence consequently depend too heavily on the threat of first nuclear use; and that this threat is bound to carry less conviction now that Soviet nuclear deployments appear fully to match Western deployments. An impression lingers that, if deterrence should fail, Western countries could well suffer more than the Soviet Union, with heavy civilian casualties – a perception which, if shared by potential aggressors, is bound to weaken deterrence.

If these conclusions are accepted, there must be a powerful case for strengthening NATO's conventional and chemical capabilities. Such strengthening is needed both to raise the nuclear threshold and to enhance NATO's ability to fight a limited war successfully. There must also be a powerful case for redressing the nuclear balance between East and West as the Reagan Administration has vowed to do – preferably through agreed reductions in deployments but failing that through increased deployments by the West.

There are, of course, a multitude of arguments which can be rehearsed to justify inferiority in specific military capabilities – the advantages conferred in certain areas by more advanced technology; the presumption of defender's advantage in the land/air battle; the use of protective clothing to counter the chemical threat; the ineffectiveness of air defences against ballistic missiles; the limited utility of civil defences in all-out war; the possibility of finding certain statistical measures of nuclear capability which look favourable to the West. Such arguments, however, are cumulatively less than convincing. They bear the hallmarks of special pleading.

The alternative strategic philosophies mentioned earlier – unilateral 'minimum deterrence', the 'cornered beast' and 'non-flexible' nuclear systems – can likewise be prayed in aid of inferiority at particular force levels. Here too, however, the argument has a quality of special pleading, designed to excuse second-best capabilities.

The true explanation for the West's second-best military capabilities surely lies elsewhere – in the habitual temptation among democratic peoples, discussed earlier in the chapter, to underprovide for defence in peacetime and to avoid controversial decisions. The West has accepted the reality of the balance of terror, but with less than total conviction. The strategy may be unexceptionable. Implementation has suffered from rival demands on scarce resources. Concessions have been made to rival strategic philosophies formally rejected. It has proved easier to will the end than the means.

As between Western countries, the record is uneven. Table 14.1 shows the United States as spending 6½ per cent of its national income on defence; Britain over 5 per cent; France and Germany over 4 per cent; most other European members of NATO between 2½ and 3½ per cent; Japan, around 1 per cent. The comparison with authoritarian countries, in particular the communist world, is much more uneven. These countries generally spend much higher proportions of their (generally smaller) national incomes on defence. In the Soviet Union, the proportion may possibly have been of the order of 15 per cent in recent years; but the calculation is notoriously difficult.

To say that the West's military capabilities look second-best from the standpoint of defence and deterrence is not to say that they are necessarily second-best from the standpoint of wider national and international ideals. Crucially important as defence may be, there are many competing claims on national resources, almost all of which are important or desirable in their different ways. Hence a defence policy which is second-best, in the sense that security and stability are under-insured, might still be the best available policy, all things considered, especially in a second-best world.

There are also some genuine supporting arguments. As we have seen in earlier chapters, the balance of terror does appear remarkably stable: even an imperfect balance between the two sides seems likely to keep the world at peace, barring gross mismanagement by either side. The difficulties of closing the gaps between Western and Soviet force deployments should not, moreover, be under-estimated: it cannot be assumed that the Soviets would do nothing as the West expanded and increased its capabilities. The danger of an escalating arms race is real.

The point remains, however, that the West's capabilities do look to be second-best from the standpoint of security and stability. The risks of intimidation, aggression and nuclear conflict, though probably not great, are consequently greater than they need to be, as are the risks of defeat. This explains most of the anxieties which have darkened the preceding pages. It is a point for all thinking people to consider.

Appendix: The Algebra of Mutual Deterrence and Stability

A SIMPLE MODEL

The theory of intrinsic stability set out in chapters 6 and 7 can be summarised in algebraic form. The algebra is no substitute for the fuller discussion presented earlier; but it is concise and helps to concentrate the mind.

The system we are describing is one where we hope that peace will be preserved between two sides, A and B, by means of mutual deterrence through a balance of terror. The question is: what are the necessary conditions, or desiderata, for stability in such a system? How can the probability of peace be maximised?

The first point to be made is that peace and stability must depend importantly on political relations between the two sides and above all on political tensions. For any given degree of political tension, however, peace and stability are likely to depend primarily on the continuing effectiveness of each side in deterring the other, an even balance of war-fighting capabilities and good arrangements for mutual communication and negotiation. Hence we may begin by writing:

$$S = f_1 (\overset{(+)}{Dt_A}, \overset{(+)}{Dt_B}, \overset{(-)}{WF_{|A-B|}}, \overset{(+)}{CC} : PT) \qquad (1)$$

where S stands for intrinsic stability,

Dt_A for A's effectiveness in deterring B,

Dt_B for B's effectiveness in deterring A,

$WF_{|A-B|}$ for any imbalance of war-fighting capabilities between the two sides,

CC for effective channels of mutual communication and consultation, and

PT for mutual political tensions.

222

The signs written in brackets over the arguments of the function indicate the signs of the first partial derivatives. For any given degree of mutual political tensions, therefore, stability is seen as an *increasing* function of (i) each side's effectiveness in deterring the other and (ii) effective communications and consultations, and a *decreasing* function of any major disparities in war-fighting capabilities:

$$\frac{\partial S}{\partial Dt_A} \geqslant 0$$

$$\frac{\partial S}{\partial Dt_B} \geqslant 0$$

$$\frac{\partial S}{\partial WF_{|A-B|}} \leqslant 0$$

$$\frac{\partial S}{\partial CC} \geqslant 0$$

It is arguable that, beyond some critical levels of effective deterrence, each side should be able to count on deterring the other side, provided he is rational, from attacking or pressing his unilateral advantage too far. Hence we might consider writing as stability conditions for the system:

$$Dt_A \geqslant Dt_A^* \tag{2}$$

and

$$Dt_B \geqslant Dt_B^* \tag{3}$$

where Dt_A^* is the critical level of effective deterrence achieved by A and Dt_B^* the critical level achieved by B.

In the real world, however, stability can never be absolutely guaranteed; hence influences which tend to enhance stability, such as an even balance of war-fighting capabilities between the two sides and good communication and consultation, are likely to be important as well as the necessary conditions at (2) and (3). In other words, the problem can alternatively, and probably better, be seen as one of maximising the function at (1) above, subject to the constraints of economic and political feasibility.

The effective deterrence achieved by each side is a function of all the variables discussed in chapters 6 and 7 and reflects the balance of risk, as seen by the other side, between attacking and not attacking. So far as the deterrence achieved by A against a first all-out nuclear strike by B is concerned, this function can be written as follows:

$$Dt_A = f_2 \overset{(+)}{(RA_B,} \overset{(-)}{H_B,} \overset{(+)}{W_A,} \overset{(\pm)}{I_B,} \overset{(+)}{S2_A,} \overset{(+)}{WF_{A:B},} \overset{(-)}{FSA_A)} \tag{4}$$

where

$$S2_A = f_3 \overset{(-)}{(FO_B,} \overset{(-)}{El_B,} \overset{(+)}{FD_A;} \overset{(+)}{FO2_A,} \overset{(+)}{E2_A,} \overset{(-)}{FD2_B;} \overset{(+)}{CO_A,} \overset{(-)}{CD_B)} \tag{5}$$

$$FSA_A = f_4 \overset{(+)}{(S1_A,} \overset{(-)}{S2_B)} \tag{6}$$

and

$$Sl_A = f_5 \overset{(+)}{(FO_A,} \overset{(+)}{El_A;} \overset{(-)}{FO_B,} \overset{(-)}{FD_B)} \tag{7}$$

For side B, symmetrically, we have:

$$Dt_B = f_6 \overset{(+)}{(RA_A,} \overset{(-)}{H_A,} \overset{(+)}{W_B,} \overset{(\pm)}{I_A,} \overset{(+)}{S2_B,} \overset{(+)}{WF_{B:A},} \overset{(-)}{FSA_B)} \tag{8}$$

where

$$S2_B = f_7 \overset{(-)}{(FO_A,} \overset{(-)}{El_A,} \overset{(+)}{FD_B;} \overset{(+)}{FO2_B,} \overset{(+)}{E2_B,} \overset{(-)}{FD2_A;} \overset{(+)}{CO_B,} \overset{(-)}{CD_A)} \tag{9}$$

$$FSA_B = f_8 \overset{(+)}{(Sl_B,} \overset{(-)}{S2_A)}, \tag{10}$$

and

$$S2_A = f_9 \overset{(+)}{(FO_B,} \overset{(+)}{El_B;} \overset{(-)}{FO_A,} \overset{(-)}{FD_A)} \tag{11}$$

As before, the suffixes A and B indicate the side possessing the capabilities or qualities denoted by the explanatory variables, and the signs of the first partial derivatives are shown in brackets above the variables. A dot subscript beneath a variable indicates that the other side's perception of it is crucial: for example, W_A means that B's perception of A's will is no less important for deterrence than A's will itself. Thus the effective deterrence achieved by A (Dt_A) against a first, all-out strike by B is seen (expression (4)) as

(i) an increasing function of B's aversion to risk (RA_B);

(ii) a decreasing function of the level of hurt or damage which B is willing to suffer, or risk suffering (H_B);

(iii) an increasing function of A's will and firmness of purpose as perceived by B, including his willingness to use the strength he possesses (W_A);

(iv) in general, but not necessarily always, an increasing function of B's intelligence and knowledge about A, including his perceptions of A's will and capabilities (I_B);

(v) an increasing function of A's second-strike capability as B perceives it, or of A's total remaining ability to strike back and inflict damage, both counter-force and counter-city, after he has absorbed a first strike from B ($S2_A$);

(vi) in general (but not necessarily always: see below) an increasing function of A's general war-fighting capability relative to B's, as perceived by B ($WF_{A:B}$); and

(vii) a decreasing function of B's perception of A's advantage in a first strike (FSA_A): the greater B perceives this advantage to be, the more risky inaction on his part will appear and the more tempted he will be to launch a pre-emptive strike himself.

A's second-strike capability ($S2_A$) is seen in turn (expression (5)) as

(viii) a decreasing function of the damage he would suffer from a first, counter-force strike by B, which would reflect:

    (a) the size of B's counter-force offensive strike force (FO_B) and

    (b) the counter-force exchange rate in B's favour for a first strike by B (El_B), which in turn will be a decreasing function of

    (c) A's ability to defend his own forces against attack (FD_A);

(ix) an increasing function of his capability for counter-force retaliation, which will reflect not only the damage he has sustained but also:

(a)   the size of his surviving counter-force offensive strike force
       ($FO2_A$), which in turn will clearly reflect the size of his
       original force and the damage he has sustained;

(b)   the counter-force exchange rate in A's favour after he has
       sustained the first strike ($E2_A$), which in turn will be a
       decreasing function of

(c) B's ability to defend his remaining forces ($FD2_B$); and

(x)   an increasing function of his capability for counter-city retaliation,
       which likewise will reflect not only the damage he has suffered in
       the first strike but will also be

(a)   an increasing function of his original offensive counter-city
       capabilities (CO_A) and

(b)   a decreasing function of B's capability for defending his
       cities and minimising civic and industrial damage (CD_B).

A's first-striker's advantage is seen (expression (6)) as an increasing
function of his first-strike capabilities ($S1_A$) and a decreasing function of
B's second-strike capabilities ($S2_B$) (expression (9)). A's first-strike capabilities are seen in turn (expression (7)) as an increasing function of the
size of A's counter-force offensive forces (FO_A) and of the counter-force
exchange rate in A's favour for a first strike by A (El_A); and a decreasing
function of the size of B's offensive forces (FO_B) and B's ability to defend
his own forces against attack (FD_B).

The effective deterrence achieved by B against a first, all-out strike
by A can be analysed in exactly the same way, the only changes being to
substitute A for B and B for A throughout (see expressions (8)–(11)).

Of the remaining arguments in the stability function at (1), CC is
concerned with effective communications and consultation between the
two sides and requires no elaboration. WF_{1A-B1} is concerned with the
relative war-fighting capabilities of the two sides. Any imbalance between
these can be measured as the absolute value ($\| \ldots \|$) of the difference
between them:

$$WF_{1A-B1} = \| WF_A - WF_B \| \tag{12}$$

In the algebra thus far we have been concerned with effective mutual
deterrence against a first, all-out nuclear counter-force strike by the other
side. The requirements for effective deterrence against conventional
attack are somewhat different. Relative war-fighting capabilities (WF)
become even more important. In addition, deterrence against conventional
attack is an *increasing* function of first-striker's advantage and of general

first-strike capabilities, counter-force as well as counter-city; for a potential aggressor is more likely to be deterred from attacking the home country at the conventional level, the greater he perceives the home country's advantage to be if the home country decides to escalate the conflict to the nuclear level. For this form of deterrence, therefore, the partial derivative of the perceived first-striker's advantage variables (FSA) in expressions (4) and (8) becomes positive rather than negative. If the partial derivative signs on the FSA variables are left ambiguous, we obtain the following more general expressions for total effective deterrence (Dtt) against nuclear and conventional attack:

$$
\overset{(+)}{\text{Dtt}_A = f_6 } \left(\overset{(+)}{\text{RA}_B}, \overset{(-)}{\text{H}_B}, \overset{(+)}{\text{W}_A}, \overset{(\pm)}{\text{I}_B}, \overset{(+)}{\text{S2}_A}, \overset{(+)}{\text{WF}_{A:B}}, \overset{(\pm)}{\text{FSA}_A} \right) \tag{13}
$$

$$
\overset{(+)}{\text{Dtt}_B = f_7 } \left(\overset{(+)}{\text{RA}_A}, \overset{(-)}{\text{H}_A}, \overset{(+)}{\text{W}_B}, \overset{(\pm)}{\text{I}_A}, \overset{(+)}{\text{S2}_B}, \overset{(+)}{\text{WF}_{B:A}}, \overset{(\pm)}{\text{FSA}_B} \right) \tag{14}
$$

FUNCTIONAL FORMS

One point highlighted by the algebraic analysis is that the system of mutual deterrence is rather more complex than might appear at first sight. In the first place, the number of variables is large: no less than three dozen are included in expressions (1) to (14), and several of these – for example, war-fighting capability (WF) – are themselves compounds of a considerable number of other variables, not specifically shown. Moreover, the signs of the first partial derivatives of some of the explanatory variables are ambiguous, and in any event the behaviour of the system is not adequately reflected in the signs of the first partial derivatives: the other properties of the functional forms are also important, and the variables interreact with each other in important ways. Thus, to take a simple example, side A's perceived will (W_A) is likely to be a function of his military capabilities relative to B's.

Despite some complexities, however, the system depends crucially on a few simple relationships – in particular the assessments made by each side of the risks involved in (a) attacking or (b) not attacking the other side. As implied earlier, this is another way of summarising the arguments of the deterrence functions (4) and (6): the deterrence achieved by A can be seen as the obverse of the balance of risks as seen by B. B's assessment of the risks involved in attacking A, and hence the effectiveness of A's deterrence, will depend in turn on the arguments in A's deterrence functions

(4) and (9). In particular it will depend on (i) B's own aversion to risk and the magnitude of damage he is willing to contemplate (RA_B and H_B), (ii) his assessment of A's capabilities, especially his second-strike capability ($S2_A$) and his war-fighting capability ($WF_{A:B}$), and (iii) his assessment of A's will to use the strength he possesses (W_A).

The remainder of this appendix discusses briefly what the functional forms of these relationships might be.

RISK-AVERSION AND THE WILL TO RETALIATE

If we make the (realistic) assumption that B perceives A to be capable of inflicting intolerable damage in a second, retaliatory strike, we can then illustrate in diagrammatic form (figure A1) how the effectiveness of A's deterrence against a first, nuclear strike by B is likely to be affected by B's risk-aversion and his perception of A's will to retaliate.

The vertical axis shows the effectiveness of the deterrence achieved by A, which can be conceived as a scale indicating the probability that B will deliver a first nuclear strike, and the dotted ray yy' indicates the point at which A's deterrence is maximised, in the sense that whatever else he may do in the matter of perceived will he cannot make his deter-

Figure A1 *Risk-aversion and perception of opponent's will*

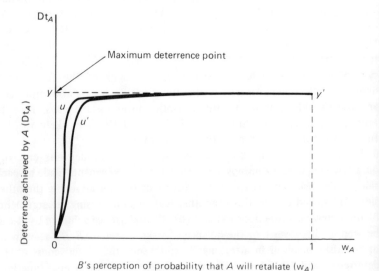

B's perception of probability that A will retaliate (w_A)

rence any more effective than it is already. The horizontal axis shows *B*'s perception of *A*'s willingness to retaliate, measured as a probability scale between zero and one. The degree of *B*'s risk aversion is reflected in the slopes of the schedules, *u* and *u'*.

At zero perceived probability of retaliation, *B* sees no risk in attacking and *A* achieves no effective deterrence. Hence both schedules begin from the origin. But if *B* is highly averse to the risk of suffering a nuclear holocaust (as all governments are likely to be), the schedule will rise very sharply as soon as there is perceived to be any significant risk that *A* would retaliate: it will then quickly approach very closely to the maximum deterrence level, *yy'*, and will finally reach it at a perceived retaliation probability of 1. Two illustrative schedules are shown: if *B* becomes less risk-averse, the schedule might move, as shown, from *u* to *u'*.

The rapid rise of the *u* schedules to a point close to maximum deterrence is of the utmost importance for stability. Provided that both sides have an extreme aversion to the risk of nuclear holocaust, they should be deterred from attacking, or provoking the other side too far, even if they think it highly improbable that the other side would in fact retaliate by using his capability to inflict intolerable damage. It is the likelihood that both sides will have the highest degree of aversion to the risk of nuclear holocaust that makes the system fairly robust and provides a considerable presumption of stability in the balance of terror.

ABILITY TO INFLICT UNACCEPTABLE DAMAGE

In the diagram at figure A1 we made the crucial assumption that *B* perceives *A* to be capable of inflicting intolerable damage in a second, retaliatory strike. If this assumption cannot be made, the balance of terror reduces into a balance of power, and the presumption of stability withers away. This point is illustrated in figure A2, which is drawn on the assumption that *B*'s perception of *A*'s will to retaliate is given and is significantly greater than zero.

On the vertical axis we again measure the deterrence achieved by *A*, and the ray *yy'* again indicates the maximum deterrence level defined as the level at which, whatever else *A* might add to his second-strike capability, he could not make his deterrence more effective than it is already. On the horizontal axis we measure *A*'s second, retaliatory strike capability, as perceived by *B*. The schedule (*v*) is drawn as a logistic curve, beginning from the origin and becoming almost horizontal (approaching asymptoti-

Figure A2 *Perception of opponent's capacity to retaliate*

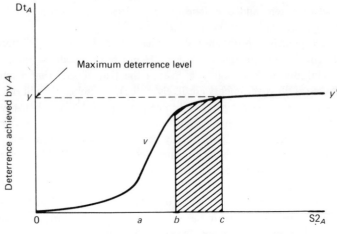

B's perception of *A*'s second strike capability ($S2_A$)

cally to the maximum deterrence level) beyond a certain level of perceived second-strike capability ($0c$).

If *A* is perceived to have *no* second-strike capability, *B* will perceive no risk in attacking, and the deterrence achieved by *A* will be nil. Hence the *v* schedule begins from the origin. If *A* has a certain, but relatively limited, ability to inflict damage in a second strike, *B* is still unlikely to be deterred. Hence the *v* schedule rises slowly at first. But as soon as *A* acquires any ability to strike with nuclear warheads against *B*'s territory, the risks as perceived by *B*, and therefore *A*'s effective deterrence and the *v* schedule, will begin to rise sharply (point *a* in the diagram). The point will soon be reached where *B* begins to regard the level of damage he is liable to suffer as probably intolerable, whatever the other issues at stake (point *b*), and then a further point will be reached where the potential level of damage is definitely intolerable (point *c* and the *v* schedule will be very close to the maximum deterrence level, *yy'*. Beyond this point, additions to *A*'s perceived retaliatory capability will not of themselves add significantly to effective deterrence. Hence the *v* schedule flattens out and approaches asymptotically to the *yy'* maximum deterrence ray. The hatched zone above *bc* can be seen as indicating the border area between damage which *B* might find acceptable, *in extremis*, and damage which he would find unacceptable whatever the issues at stake. Once again the slope of the schedule reflects *B*'s risk-aversion.

The diagram is intended to illustrate the point that the perceived capability of each side to inflict an intolerable level of damage on the other after absorbing a first strike is vital for stability. It can also be read historically. The section of the schedule above Oa illustrates the old 'balance of power', before the advent of nuclear weapons. In the pre-nuclear era, the perceived ability of the opponent to inflict damage in retaliation was simply not on a scale, or of a speed, to provide adequate deterrence or to assure stability. Today, on the other hand, the second-strike capabilities of the United States and the Soviet Union are probably well to the right of point c; and the nuclear capabilities of France and Britain probably put them somewhere between b and c. China is probably in the process of progressing from a point between a and b to a point between b and c.

WAR-FIGHTING CAPABILITY

Also important for B's assessment of the risks involved in attacking, and hence for A's effective deterrence, is B's perception of A's general war-fighting capability. We argued strongly in chapters 8 and 14 that the best assurance of achieving effective deterrence must lie in the possession of a formidable overall war-fighting capability, though it is sometimes argued that a small nuclear country might weaken its deterrence by giving the impression that it would respond to aggression at the conventional level with conventional rather than nuclear forces.

The w schedule at figure A3 gives a possible interpretation of the relationship between effective deterrence and overall war-fighting capability. On the vertical axis we again measure the effective deterrence achieved by A, and the ray yy' again denotes the maximum deterrence level, defined as before. On the horizontal axis we measure B's perception of A's general war-fighting capability relative to his own.

If A's general war-fighting capability has to be strictly limited relative to B's (for example, because A is a small country) two interpretations are possible (see left-hand side of figure A3). One is that an increase in this capability might weaken A's deterrence by encouraging B to believe that A would respond conventionally to a conventional attack and thus reducing B's perception of the risk that A would retaliate with his strategic nuclear forces. This is reflected in the downward slope of the continuous w schedule above point a on the horizontal axis. The other possiblity is that B would simply not believe that A would use his nuclear weapons in response to aggression at the conventional level. In that case, A's deterrence

Figure A3 *Deterrence and war-fighting capability*

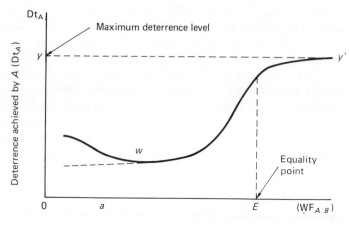

B's perception of A's war-fighting capability relative to his own (WF$_{A:B}$)

would be strengthened, even at this level, by stronger general war-fighting capabilities, as in the dashed variant of the schedule.

As *A*'s general war-fighting capability grows substantial, it will begin to pose a genuine threat to *B*, and there is then no question that the schedule will begin to slope upwards. When *B* perceives *A*'s war-fighting capability to approach his own, the risks which he perceives in attacking at any level of force will begin to look formidable, and the upward slope will become pronounced. *A* will not achieve maximum deterrence until *B* perceives him to be unequivocally and decisively superior in war-fighting capability – well to the right of the point of perceived equality, *E*. But given the horrendous destructive power of modern weapons a high degree of effective deterrence is likely to be achieved as long as the war-fighting capabilities of the two sides are perceived to be fairly close to equality, and this is another factor which contributes to a presumption of successful deterrence and stability.

FIRST-STRIKER'S ADVANTAGE

We concluded in chapters 6 and 7 that one of the greatest threats to stability lies in the possibility of circumstances in which the risks involved in *not* attacking seem to one side or the other even greater than those involved in attacking. An explosive situation of this kind is most likely to arise if there is a tense political crisis between the two sides and one or both sides believe the other to enjoy a decisive first-striker's advantage which he is likely to exploit unless they themselves strike first to forestall him – an advantage which, if exploited, would leave them at his mercy. If this is B's perception of the risks from A, the balance of terror will become highly unstable and could even break down.

A further illustrative diagram (figure A4) may help to stimulate thought about the likely functional form of the relationship between first-striker's advantage on the one hand and deterrence and stability on the other. We are concerned in this figure, and also in figure A5, only with deterrence against a first nuclear strike by the opponent, and not with deterrence against a conventional attack.

As before, the vertical axis and yy' ray show the effective deterrence achieved by A and the maximum deterrence level: they can also be interpreted as measuring the stability of the system. The horizontal axis measures B's perception of A's first-striker's advantage (FSA_A): this is largely a function of the perceived counter-force exchange rate in A's favour for a first strike ($E1_A$) but reflects also A's second-strike counter-force capability and the relative sizes of the two sides' nuclear forces.

If B perceives A to have no first-striker's advantage, he will have no incentive to strike pre-emptively, and there will be nothing to detract from

Figure A4   *Stability and first-striker's advantage*

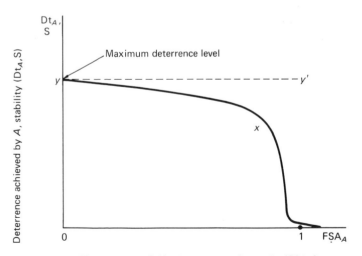

B's perception of A's advantage in a first strike (FSA_A)

A's effective deterrence. Hence the schedule (x) begins from the point on the vertical axis which indicates the maximum deterrence level (y).

Thereafter, the schedule is drawn as sloping downwards very gently over most of its course. The reason for the downward slope is that, in general, the greater B believes A's first-striker's advantage to be, the more tempted he will be to deny him that advantage by a pre-emptive strike. The reason why the downward slope is so gentle is that, until a point is reached where A's first-striker's advantage is absolutely overwhelming, B's second-strike capability will be sufficient to inflict massive damage on A, and this is very likely to deter A from striking first (unless he is willing to run enormous risks and attempt a 'strike and bargain' strategy). What is more, B will know this and will therefore probably regard a first strike by A as unlikely. And this in turn will probably dissuade B from launching a pre-emptive strike so long as the advantage which he perceives A to have in a first strike seems to him less than decisive. It would be irrational for B to be more concerned about a low probability of suffering a first strike (probably counter-force) than about a high probability of suffering a second strike (possibly counter-city as well) in response to a first strike delivered by himself.

B's perception of the balance of risks will be different if he believes that, without using up the whole of his own nuclear arsenal, A could destroy the *whole* of his (B's) nuclear strike force in a first strike and thus leave B totally incapacitated, totally unable to retaliate effectively and totally at A's mercy. By that point, B might possibly regard the risks involved in leaving A the option of first strike as being so great that he would prefer to deliver a first, pre-emptive strike himself, despite the heavy responsibility and all the risks which that involves. In such circumstances A's effective deterrence will have dwindled to almost nothing (point 1 in the diagram). That is not to say that B will necessarily decide to strike: he may still be deterred by moral scruples, domestic political considerations or a reluctance to go down in history alongside Hitler and Stalin. The point is rather that in such circumstances it will not be the system of mutual deterrence that prevents him from striking.

If B believes that *virtually* all his nuclear strike force would be destroyed by A in a first strike and that A will not be deterred from striking by his perception of B's residual capability to inflict damage, he may still decide to strike pre-emptively: hence the schedule remains close to the horizontal axis for a short distance to the left of 1. In the borderline region where B is uncertain whether a first strike by A would be decisive, the schedule is shown as plunging steeply, though in practice it may not be well defined in this area.

BALANCE OF RISK BETWEEN STRIKING AND NOT STRIKING

The crucial balance of risk between striking and not striking is illustrated in figure A5. On the vertical axis we measure B's expectation of suffering intolerable damage. This can be conceived either as B's assessment of the probability that A will strike, multiplied by the level of damage he would expect to suffer, or (perhaps better) as the level of damage which B would be prepared to suffer *for certain* in return for an absolute assurance of no strike by A. On the horizontal axis, we show B's perception of the probability of a first strike by A, measured as an index between 0 and 1.

In making his choice between striking and not striking, B will probably calculate that, if he himself strikes first, A is virtually bound to retaliate with his second-strike force. For simplicity we assume that B regards this retaliation as virtually certain, and B's expectation of suffering damage from A's second strike is shown as the point $S2_A$, directly above 1 on the horizontal axis. If B is less than certain about whether A will retaliate, his expectation of damage will lie somewhere on a ray between $S2_A$ and the origin.

B will also calculate that, if he does not strike first himself, he faces the risk that A will strike first, inflicting a level of damage indicated by the point $S1_A$ on the dotted vertical line above 1 on the horizontal axis. The overall risk, as B perceives it, will depend on the probability which he attaches to A's deciding to strike first, and is indicated by the ray from

Figure A5 *To strike or not to strike?*

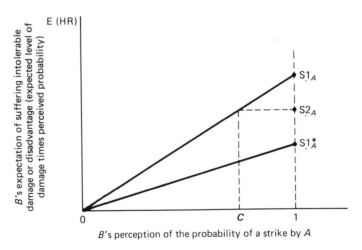

the origin (0) to the point $S1_A$. If B believes this probability to exceed C on the horizontal axis, he will perceive the balance of risk to favour a pre-emptive strike, and the system of mutual deterrence will be in danger of breaking down.

The $S1_A$ ray and the $S2_A$ point are drawn on the assumption that B will expect the damage or disadvantage he would suffer from a first strike by A to be greater than the damage he would suffer from a second strike if he himself had opened the striking. B may, however take a different view of the relative amounts of damage he is liable to suffer. In particular, he may calculate that a first strike by A would be designed to give A a military advantage and would be limited to military targets, whereas a second strike would include city targets as well. If his overwhelming priority is to protect his cities, therefore, he may be more concerned about the damage he would suffer from a second than a first strike. In that event he might compare the $S2_A$ point with a lower ray such as $S1_A^*$ and conclude firmly against a pre-emptive strike, however probable he perceives a first strike by A to be.

In practice, first-striker's advantage is well short of decisive in the present state of technology (well to the left in figure A4), and each side is likely to be dissuaded from striking first by a combination of moral and political considerations and the high probability of retaliation against his own cities.

DETERRENCE AGAINST CONVENTIONAL ATTACK

There remains the important complication and qualification that deterrence against *conventional* attack is an increasing, not a decreasing, function of first (nuclear) striker's advantage. For a side which attacks at the conventional level leaves the other side the option of striking first at the nuclear level and is therefore likely to be the more reluctant to open conventional hostilities, the more decisive he perceives the other side's advantage in a first nuclear strike to be.

We illustrate the point in a final diagram (figure A6), which reproduces figure A4 but superimposes a further schedule, xc, on the earlier schedule, xn. As before, the xn schedule shows how A's effective deterrence against an all-out first nuclear strike by B diminishes sharply as soon as B perceives A to have a decisive first-striker's advantage, since this gives B a strong incentive to strike pre-emptively. The new xc schedule shows how, at the same time, A's effective deterrence against conventional attack by B increases as B perceives A's advantage in a first nuclear strike to increase.

Figure A6   *Stability and first-striker's advantage revisited*

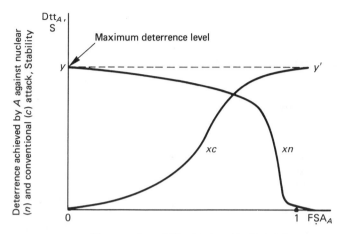

B's perception of A's advantage in a first strike

The reason for drawing the *xc* schedule as a logistic curve is as follows. If *B* perceives *A* to have little or no first-striker's advantage, *A* obviously will not achieve any effective deterrence against conventional attack by this means. Hence the curve begins from the origin and rises slowly at first. At the other extreme, if *B* perceives *A* to have the ability to incapacitate him totally in a first nuclear strike (point 1 in the diagram), or to come close to incapacitating him, he is bound to be extremely wary about provoking *A* with a conventional attack which leaves *A* the option of first nuclear strike. Hence the curve reaches the maximum deterrence level (*yy'*) at point 1, and remains close to this level to the left of 1. Assuming that the function is continuous, this dictates the logistic shape.

If the shapes of these functions correctly reflect the real world, a limited degree of first-striker's advantage may actually enhance total stability by reinforcing deterrence against conventional attack. But the qualification 'a limited degree' is crucial. For it is clearly even more important that the system of mutual deterrence should prevent nuclear strikes than that it should prevent conventional attacks. The latter should in most circumstances be deterred simply by the potential aggressor's perception of the danger that a conventional beginning could escalate into a nuclear ending which would benefit no one.

Notes and References

1 THE BALANCE OF TERROR

1. B.H. Liddell Hart, *History of the Second World War* (Pan Books, 1973) p.727.
2. B.H. Liddell Hart's *History of the First World War* (Cassell, 1970) and *History of the Second World War* contain much detailed information on casualties. The estimate of 50 million deaths in the Second World War includes some 20 million Soviet citizens and an estimated six million Jews and two to three million others killed in Nazi concentration camps. The estimate of ten million deaths in wars since 1945 is in common use at the United Nations and elsewhere.
3. The earliest occurrence of the phrase 'balance of terror' of which the author is aware is in a speech by Lester Pearson at San Francisco on 24 June 1955. Mr Pearson said then that 'The balance of terror has succeeded the balance of power'. Churchill had earlier predicted that peace would become 'the sturdy child of terror'.
4. See chapter 8, second section.

2 BASIC THEORY AND THE EVOLUTION OF STRATEGIC POSTURES

1. See especially Albert Wohlstetter, 'The delicate balance of terror', *Foreign Affairs* (January 1959); Oskar Morgenstern, *The Question of National Defence,* (New York: Random House, 1959); Bernard Brodie, *Strategy in the Missile Age* (Princton University Press, 1959); Thomas C. Schelling, *The Strategy of Conflict* (Harvard University Press, 1960); and Herman Kahn, *On Thermonuclear War* (Princeton University Press, 1960).
2. For an excellent account of the evolution of strategic theory see Lawrence Freedman, *The Evolution of Nuclear Strategy* (Macmillan, 1981). Also Michael Howard, *Studies in Peace and War* (London: Temple Smith, 1970) chapter 10. The author recalls with gratitude distinguished lectures on the subject by both men at the Royal College of Defence Studies in 1979.
3. John Foster Dulles, *The Evolution of Foreign Policy* (Department of State Bulletin 30, no. 761, 25 January 1954) p.108.

4. The unpublished NATO document embodying the 'massive retaliation' strategy is known by its serial number MC 14/2.
5. The term 'assured destruction' was first used in 1964.
6. The unpublished NATO document of December 1967 embodying the 'flexible response' strategy is known by its serial number MC 14/3.
7. Secretary McNamara publicly discussed in 1962 the idea of targeting military installations in a retaliatory response. By 1964 the idea had been dropped.
8. John Newhouse, *Cold Dawn, the Story of SALT* (Holt, Rinehart & Winston, 1973) p.18. See also Alain C. Enthoven and K. Wayne Smith, *How Much is Enough?* (New York: Harper & Row, 1971) p.208.
9. NATO Handbook, March 1978, p.17.
10. Ibid.
11. President Nixon's question is quoted in James R. Schlesinger, *Annual Defense Report for Financial Year 1975* (US Department of Defence, 1974) p.35.
12. Ibid. President Nixon's own answer is quoted in chapter 7, note 17.
13. Robert S. McNamara, 'The military role of nuclear weapons, perceptions and misperceptions' (*Foreign Affairs*, Fall 1983) pp.65–6.

3 HOW IT CAME TO BE

1. An invaluable documentary account of the early development of nuclear weapons in the United States is in Richard G. Hewlett and Oscar E. Anderson, *A History of the United States Atomic Energy Commission*, vols I and II (Pennsylvania State University Press, 1962, 1969). The British programme is documented in Margaret Gowing, *Britain and Atomic Energy, 1939–45* (Macmillan, 1964) and *Independence and Deterrence: Britain and Atomic Energy, 1945–52* (Macmillan, 1974). See also Ronald W. Clark, *The Greatest Power on Earth: the Story of Nuclear Fission* (Sidgwick & Jackson, 1980).
2. The weapon-material of the Alamogordo test bomb was plutonium and the explosive power (yield) was equivalent to some 15 to 20 thousand tons (kilotons) of conventional TNT (trinitrotoluene).
3. These figures are taken from Samuel Glasstone and Philip J. Dolan, *The Effects of Nuclear Weapons*, 3rd edn (US Departments of Defense and Energy, 1979), the *locus classicus* for the effects of nuclear weapons. Also in circulation are higher figures which attribute many deaths in later years to the bombs.

The 68 000 people killed at Hiroshima and the 38 000 at Nagasaki represented about 27 per cent and about 22 per cent, respectively, of the local population. The conventional air attacks of the Second World War killed some 50 000 people in Hamburg (24 July to 3 August 1944), some 130 000 in Dresden (13-14 February 1945) and some 83 000 in Tokyo (9-10 March 1945). See Norman Polmar's book referred to in note 8.
4. See figure 3.1.

5. The Hiroshima uranium bomb and the Nagasaki plutonium bomb (see figures 3.2 and 3.3) were delivered by B-29 bombers based at Tinian island in the Pacific and detonated at heights of 1670 feet and 1640 feet respectively. The yields, very small by the standards of modern 'strategic' weapons, were equivalent to about 12.5 kilotons of TNT at Hiroshima and about 22 kilotons at Nagasaki. The combinations of yield and height of burst were such that no craters were formed and there were no injuries due to fall-out.

6. A convenient survey of political developments since 1945 is Peter Calvocoressi, *World Politics since 1945* (Longman, 3rd edn, 1977). The author had the benefit of hearing an inspiring lecture on the subject by Richard Lowenthal at the Royal College of Defence Studies in 1979.

7. The North Atlantic Treaty, signed on 4 April 1949, unites the countries of Western Europe and the United States in a commitment to collective self-defence against external aggression. The original signatories of the treaty, 12 in all, comprised the two North American countries – Canada and the United States – seven countries from the central area of Western Europe – Belgium, Britain, Denmark, France, Italy, Luxembourg and the Netherlands – and three countries from the flanks of Europe – Iceland, Norway and Portugal. Greece and Turkey joined in 1952, West Germany in 1955 (following the Paris agreement of 1954) and Spain in 1982, thus bringing the total membership to 16. The treaty is of indefinite duration. Since 1969, however, member countries can withdraw on one year's notice. In practice, no country has withdrawn from the treaty as such, though France and Greece have withdrawn from the integrated military structure of the North Atlantic Treaty Organisation.

   The crux of the treaty is the commitment of each member state under article 5 to consider 'an armed attack against one or more of them an attack against them all' and to assist the member country or countries attacked 'by taking forthwith, individually and in concert with other Parties, such action as it deems necessary, including the use of armed force, to restore and maintain the security of the North Atlantic area'. The North Atlantic area is defined as including the Mediterranean and the North Atlantic area north of the Tropic of Cancer.

   As the wording of article 5 shows, the treaty formally commits member countries only to giving such help as they deem necessary for the security of the North Atlantic Treaty area. This apparently qualified commitment reflects the status of the North Atlantic alliance as an association of independent states, not a supra-national organisation. The Central European members of the alliance are committed more unequivocally by the Brussels treaty of the preceding year (1948) to give each other 'all the military and other aid and assistance in their power' if one or more of them is subjected to 'armed aggression in Europe'.

   When West Germany joined the North Atlantic Treaty in 1955, despite strong Soviet opposition, the Soviet Union responded by setting up the Warsaw Pact – a military alliance of the Soviet Union and East European satellite countries, established by the Warsaw Treaty of Friendship, Mutual Assistance and Co-operation of 14 May 1955. The treaty provides for the defence of the European territories of member states. The signatories included East Germany as well as the Soviet Union, Albania, Bulgaria, Czechoslovakia, Hungary, Poland and Romania. Albania left the pact in September 1968, after the Soviet invasion of Czechoslovakia.

The Soviet Union also has bilateral treaties of friendship and mutual assistance with all the present members of the pact, and other members have similar bilateral treaties with each other. Hence the Warsaw Treaty is effectively replicated in a network of other treaties – a factor which needs to be borne in mind when assessing Soviet offers to disband the Warsaw Pact in return for a disbandment of NATO.

The Soviet Union deploys troops in the countries of Warsaw Pact members under agreements concluded with Poland, East Germany, Hungary and Romania in December 1956 to May 1957 and with Czechoslovakia in October 1968 in the aftermath of the Soviet invasion. Soviet troops left Romania after the agreement with Romania lapsed in June 1958.

8. Useful sources for the post-war development of the nuclear arsenals are Norman Polmar, *Strategic Weapons: an Introduction* (Churchill Press, 1975, and Macdonald & Jane's 1976); and Herbert F. York, *The Advisors, Oppenheimer, Teller and the Superbomb* (San Francisco: W. H. Freeman, 1976).

9. By February 1946 American forces in Europe had been reduced from two and a half million to half a million. Soviet forces were reduced from eleven and a half million to three million by March 1947, but then increased again to some five and a half million in the early 1950s, giving rise to Western fears of a Soviet offensive against Western Europe.

10. See chapter 9, note 7. For a full history see the Hewlett and Anderson study in note 1 to this chapter (vol. I, chapters 3-16).

11. See figure 3.4.

12. In the United States, the idea of a bomb combining hydrogen fusion reactions with fission reactions was the brainchild of the Italian scientist Fermi and the American Edward Teller, both of whom worked on the wartime Manhattan project at Los Alamos. The key technological breakthrough was made by Ulam and Teller in the Spring of 1947 (the so-called 'Teller/Ulam configuration').

13. In the Soviet Union, the development of the hydrogen bomb is associated particularly with the physicist Andrei Sakharov, who became known (like Teller in the United States) as father of the hydrogen bomb. The Soviets' early thermonuclear tests were relatively small scale. Much larger tests followed in 1961, after they broke the test moratorium of 1958–61. One of the bombs tested then is believed to have yielded the equivalent of no less than 58 million

14. tons (megatons) of TNT. This compares with about 15 megatons for the American 'Bravo' test of March 1954.
14. For the properties of ballistic and cruise missiles see figures 7.1 and 7.2. Their ranges are conventionally defined as follows:

> Intercontinental (ICBM): 3000 to 8000 nautical miles
> Intermediate-range (IRBM): 1500 to 3000 nautical miles
> Medium-range (MRBM): 600 to 1500 nautical miles

Both the American and the Soviet missile programmes benefited from the help of German staff who had worked at the Peenemunde missile development site. More than 100 German rocket specialists, including Wernher von Braun, surrendered to the United States. The Soviets captured many of the technicians who worked at Peenemunde.

15. The Soviets tested their first intercontinental ballistic missile (the SS-6) over a range of several thousand miles in August 1957, 16 months before the American Atlas ICBM was tested over its full range. They tested an experimental submarine-launched ballistic missile (SLBM) as well, several years ahead of the Americans. But the Soviet programmes ran into technical troubles. The early ICBMs did not achieve their intended range, and 300 people, including the head of the Soviet rocket forces, were killed at a test-launch in October 1960. By that time the Americans had established a substantial lead in both ICBMs and SLBMs.

The most dramatic indication of advancing Soviet technology occurred in October 1957, two months after their first ICBM test, when an SS-6 booster missile put the first artificial satellite, Sputnik I, into orbit three months ahead of the first American satellite. In 1960 both the Soviets and the Americans launched their first reconnaissance satellites, thus preparing the way for the era of mutual surveillance from space.

16. See chapter 2.
17. The International Institute for Strategic Studies (IISS) in London publishes each year in *The Military Balance* an invaluable summary of the nuclear and conventional weapon deployments of the superpowers and other countries.
18. Chapter 7 discusses these developments in more detail (see also chapter 9, note 9).
19. See chapter 7, note 19.
20. See chapter 7, note 26.
21. See chapters 9 and 13.
22. The Stockholm International Peace Research Institute (SIPRI) and the IISS monitor the development of world expenditure on defence (see table 14.1).

4 IS IT NECESSARY?

1. This chapter owes much to distinguished lecturers and colleagues at the Royal College of Defence Studies in 1979, including Lord Brimelow, Sir Terence Garvey, John Wilberforce and Michael Llewellyn Smith.
2. Quoted in Bernard Brodie, *Escalation and the Nuclear Option* (Princeton University Press, 1960) p.44.
3. Reproduced in the IISS's *Survival*, May/June 1976, p.126.

5 NUCLEAR WEAPONS AND WORLD POLITICS

1. This chapter draws heavily on Thomas C. Schelling, *Arms and Influence* (Yale University Press, 1966) and on Edward N. Luttwak, *Strategic Power: Military Capabilities and Political Utility*, Washington papers, vol. II (Centre for Strategic and International Studies, Georgetown University, 1976).
2. A possible exception is Khruschev's threat to use Soviet rockets against Britain and France in the Suez crisis of 1956.
3. General Carl von Clausewitz, *On War*, published posthumously in 1832, translated by Colonel J.J. Graham and revised by Colonel F. Maude (London: Kegan Paul, Trench, Trubner & Co. Ltd 1911) vol. III, chapter 6, p.121.
4. See chapter 4.
5. Bernard Brodie, *Escalation and the Nuclear Option* (Princeton University Press, 1966) pp.48-9.
6. This section draws on Klaus Knorr, *On the Uses of Military Power in the Nuclear Age* (Princeton University Press, 1966).
7. The author wrote this section before seeing the interesting discussion of 'The David and Goliath Act' in Klaus Knorr, ibid. pp.74-9.
8. German zones of occupation and new frontiers for Poland were broadly agreed by Stalin, Roosevelt and Churchill at the Yalta Conference of February 1945.
9. Jeremy R. Azrael, Richard Lowenthal and Tohru Nakagawa, *An Overview of East-West Relations* (New York, Tokyo and Paris: The Trilateral Commission 1978).
10. Clausewitz (see note 3 to this chapter) Vol. III, chapter 6, pp. 124-5.

6 INTRINSIC STABILITY

1. See chapter 2.
2. As noted in chapter 2, the United States administration in the 1960s judged that the Soviets could safely be assumed to regard the loss of 25 per cent of their population and 45 per cent of their industry as an unacceptable level of damage. This was seen as requiring deployment of the equivalent of some 400 one-megaton 'second-

strike' weapons. In 1974 the administration estimated that 'even after a more brilliantly executed and devastating attack than we believe our potential adversaries could deliver, the United States would retain the capability to kill more than 30 per cent of the Soviet population and destroy more than 75 per cent of Soviet industry' (see James R. Schlesinger, *Annual Defense Report for Financial Year 1975* (US Department of Defense, 1974) p.35).

3. See chapter 9.

7 MILITARY CAPABILITIES

1. The author is indebted to General Robert H. Baxter, US Air Force, for invaluable advice and guidance on the subjects discussed in chapters 7 to 9 and the algebraic appendix.

2. 'Strategic' weapons were originally defined in a functional sense as long-range systems capable of striking targets in the homelands of the superpowers. They have come subsequently to be defined recursively as systems covered by the talks between the United States and the Soviet Union on strategic arms limitation and reduction (SALT and START) – ICBMs, SLBMs and (after SALT 1) long-range nuclear capable bombers.

3. The 'yield', or explosive power, of a nuclear warhead is usually measured in terms of the quantity of conventional TNT explosive that would be needed to generate the same amount of energy. Thus a one-kiloton nuclear weapon is one which produces the same amount of energy as 1000 tons of TNT; and a one-megaton weapon has the energy equivalent of one million tons of TNT.

4. 'Overpressure' is defined as the excess over normal atmospheric pressure of 14.7 pounds per square inch.

5. It has been estimated that the silos which house the American Minuteman ICBMs can withstand 'overpressures' of up to around 2000 pounds per square inch. To destroy such a silo a half-megaton weapon such as those carried by the most accurate Soviet MIRVs would need to be detonated within roughly 300 metres of the silo: see Matthew Bunn and Kosta Tsipis, 'The uncertainties of a pre-emptive nuclear attack', *Scientific American*, November 1983, pp. 32–41.

6. The range (ie radius) of blast effects varies directly with the one-third power (cube root) of the weapon yield; and the area of destruction, consequently, with the two-thirds power. If one detonation is N times as powerful as another, therefore, it may be expected to create the same peak overpressure at $N^{\frac{1}{3}}$ times the distance from ground zero (below the point of detonation). An eight-megaton detonation, for example, may be expected to create a radius of destruction only twice as great as a one-megaton weapon, and an area of destruction only four times as great: the area around ground zero would be 'over-destroyed'. Similarly, the duration of the shock wave at any given degree of peak overpressure is increased

by a factor of $N^{\frac{1}{3}}$ for a weapon N times as powerful as another. See Samuel Glasstone and Philip J. Dolan, *'The Effects of Nuclear Weapons'*, 3rd edn (US Department of Defense and Energy, 1979); Home Office and Scottish Home and Health Department, *Nuclear Weapons* (London: HMSO, 1974); see also figure 2.1.

7. Submarine-launched ballistic missiles (SLBMs) are deployed in nuclear-powered submarines (SSBNs). Such submarines typically carry 16 or 24 SLBMs (or 'tubes'), each with between 3 and 14 separate warheads capable of being launched from underwater. Despite advances in anti-submarine warfare (ASW) based on sonar technology and other techniques for active and passive detection of a variety of emissions from submarines, the difficulties of tracking submarines accurately over the vast areas and depths of the oceans remain formidable. It is for this reason that submarines at sea, and hence the SLBM force, remain relatively invulnerable, provided that they only receive communications and do not transmit them. Submarines at base – always a significant proportion of the force – are much more vulnerable.

SLBMs have not in the past been sufficiently accurate for counter-force use (except possibly against large targets such as airfields): essential guidance data on the starting position, true North and the direction of the centre of the earth cannot be as accurate as in a land-based system, and movement of the submarine may introduce further errors. The warheads on American SLBMs have also been too small for counter-force use. At the end of the 1970s the American force of 656 SLBMs in 41 submarines comprised 160 Polaris SLBMs dating from the 1960s, each with three 200 KT warheads (not independently targeted), carried in 10 submarines, and 496 Poseidon SLBMs, each with 10 to 14 separate MIRV warheads, carried in 31 submarines. The separate Poseidon warheads are reported to have a yield of only some 50 kilotons. The range of both missiles is 2500 nautical miles.

A major modernisation programme was agreed in 1972 when the joint Chiefs of Staff accepted the principle of SALT 1. The United States has already developed a new Trident C4 missile with 8 MIRV warheads of 100 kilotons each, a range of 4000 nautical miles and a greatly improved circular error probable of 1500 feet, which is being fitted into 12 of the existing Poseidon submarines. Also being produced are new, 24-tube Trident submarines, and a second-generation SLBM (the Trident II or D-5) is under development; this new missile is expected to carry up to 14 MIRV warheads with a yield variously reported as 150 or 350 kilotons and a range of 6000 nautical miles. It is reported that very high accuracy may be obtainable with the help of star-sighting mid-course corrections, thus giving the prospect of a considerable counter-force capability.

The Soviets built up an effective SLBM force with great speed in the late 1960s and 1970s. By the end of the 1970s they were deploying 950 SLBMs in 64 submarines classified in SALT 2 as 'strategic' and a further 78 in older submarines. The 950 'strategic'

SLBMs comprised 420 SS-N-8s, with a range of 4800 nautical miles, and 144 SS-N-18s, each with 3 MIRV warheads and a range of 5000 nautical miles.

The increased ranges of the new classes of SLBMs now under development or production will contribute to continuing invulnerability by increasing the areas of sea in which submarines carrying SLBMs can be deployed.

8. The United States deployed its first SLBMs at the end of 1960, the Soviet Union in 1968, Britain in 1969 and France in 1972. At the time of writing China appears to be on the point of introducing its first SLBMs.

9. See chapter 2.

10. Ibid.

11. For a fuller discussion of this scenario, see chapter 12.

12. See the algebraic appendix.

13. See next section and note 7 to this chapter.

14. The concentration on 'heavy' ICBMs has been a key feature of the Soviet nuclear arsenal. In contrast with the small, cost-effective American Minuteman, with warhead yield initially of one megaton and specifically designed for the counter-city role, the Soviet SS-9s, first deployed in 1967, were capable of delivering a huge 25-megaton warhead over a range of 6000 miles. In 1968 the Soviets began testing an MRV version of the SS-9 with three warheads of 5 megatons each. The more recent SS-19 (Mark III) and SS-18 (Mark IV) have 6 and 10 MIRVed warheads respectively, each with a yield of some 550 kilotons (see Norman Polmar, *Strategic Weapons: an Introduction* (Macdonald & Jane's, 1976)). See further page 78.

15. In the autumn of 1962, at the time of the Cuban missile crisis, the Soviets had only some 35 land-based ICBMs and no SLBMs. The Americans had 284 land-based ICBMs and 112 SLBMs, deployed in 7 Polaris submarines. By 1970 the Soviets had achieved numerical superiority over the Americans in land-based ICBMs, with deployments of some 1100 (including more than 275 SS-9s) as against the stabilised American figure of 1054. By 1975, they had one and a half times as many ICBMs as the Americans, with a megatonnage six times that of the American force (see reference in note 14 of this chapter).

16. The Johnson administration decided by 1964 to stabilise strategic delivery systems at the following levels, which were to remain throughout the 1970s and early 1980s:

1000 Minuteman ICBMs
54 Titan II ICBMs
656 SLBMs in 41 submarines, and about
450 Strategic bombers, mainly B52s

Secretary McNamara publicly discussed in 1962 the idea of targeting military installations in a retaliatory response. But by 1964 the idea had been dropped. The United States deliberately eschewed the objective of building up a counter-force capability, mainly on the grounds that this would be destabilising from a global point of view. It was hoped that the Soviets would follow the American example. The second generation American missiles – Minuteman and Poseidon – were equipped accordingly with small, economic warheads, optimised for counter-city use and not large enough for the counter-force role. In contrast with the older Titan IIs, which could deliver a 10-megaton warhead, the original Minuteman could deliver only a one-megaton warhead against targets 6300 miles away. In the early 1970s, 500 of the original warheads were replaced with 3 MIRVed warheads, each with a yield of 170-200 kilotons and a nominal range of 8000 miles (see note 23 of this chapter). Similarly, the Poseidon SLBMs, which were introduced to replace some of the Polaris missiles from 1970, mostly carried 10 independently-targeted warheads of about 50 kilotons, each with a reported range of some 2500 nautical miles.

17. James R. Schlesinger's *Annual Defense Report for Financial Year 1975* (US Department of Defense, 1974) p.35, quotes President Nixon as having raised in 1970 the question:

> Should a President, in the event of a nuclear attack, be left with the single option of ordering the mass destruction of enemy civilians, in the face of the certainty that it would be followed by the mass slaughter of Americans?

The answer which President Nixon himself gave (quoted in Polmar (see note 13 of this chapter), p.110) was that:

> No President should be left with only one strategic course of action, particularly that of ordering the mass destruction of enemy civilians and facilities. Given the range of possible political -military situations which could conceivably confront us . . . we must be able to respond at levels appropriate to the situation.

18. Polaris A-3 multiple (MRV) warheads, with three re-entry vehicles (RV) all aimed at the same target, were introduced from 1964. Their purpose was partly to overwhelm ABM defences by increasing the number of vehicles which such defences had to intercept and partly to increase warhead efficiency in terms of the expected area of destruction for any given warhead yield (see note 6 to this chapter).

19. The United States announced in 1967 the successful development of multiple independently-targeted warheads (MIRVs). MIRVed Minuteman and Poseidon warheads were introduced from 1970 onwards and were imitated subsequently by the Soviets. With MIRV systems, each of the smaller re-entry vehicles and warheads can be aimed at a different target. The re-entry vehicles are carried in the final stage of the missile, which is known as a 'bus'. When the rocket boosters have burned out and fallen away, the 'bus' continues towards the target area under a single guidance and propulsion system. It darts around and zig-zags, releasing real warheads, chaff and other decoys in accordance with a pre-set programme which alters the

speed and orientation of the 'bus' after each release. The necessarily limited area of some 30 by 100 miles over which the separate re-entry vehicles can be aimed is known as the 'footprint'. See further figure 7.1.

20. President Carter decided in 1979, after long deliberation, that work should proceed on 200 MX ICBMs, each carrying 10 MIRVed half-megaton warheads, for delivery by 1987. Vulnerability was to be reduced by shuttling the new missiles around 4600 launching sites in Utah and Nevada by means of a specially constructed 10 000 miles of roads system. The Reagan administration rejected this proposal and has proposed instead to deploy 100 MX or 'Peacekeeper' missiles by the end of the decade, at least 50 of them in Minuteman silos, vulnerable though these would be. See further page 77.

21. See note 7 to this chapter.

22. See James Meacham, survey article on 'Nuclear Weapons' in *The Economist*, 1 September 1984: an invaluable survey of recent weapon developments.

23. The 170 kiloton warheads in 300 of the Minuteman 3-MIRV missiles mentioned in note 16 of this chapter have been replaced with new Mark 12A warheads with an estimated yield of some 350 kilotons.

24. Matthew Bunn and Kosta Tsipis, 'The uncertainties of a pre-emptive nuclear attack', *Scientific American*, November 1983, pp.32–41.

25. John Newhouse, *Cold Dawn: The Story of SALT* (Holt, Rinehart & Winston, 1973) pp.151–7. Apart from the intrinsic difficulties of intercepting incoming missiles travelling at 4 miles per second, the critical computer nerve-centre of an ABM system would have been highly vulnerable to attack.

26. See in particular the penultimate section of this chapter and the further discussion in chapter 14.

27. See note 20 to this chapter.

28. See James Meacham (note 22 of this chapter) pp.17–18.

29. The United States began deployment of ALCMs in 1982 and had deployed about 200 by July 1983. Their range, circular error probable and warhead yield are reported to be some 1500 miles, 100 metres and 200 kilotons respectively. They are expected to be superseded by smaller, faster, more accurate 'advanced cruise missiles', with autonomous terminal homing.

30. See references in Jan M. Lodal, 'SALT II and American Security' *Foreign Affairs* (Winter 1978/79) p.256. Bunn and Tsipis (note 24 of this chapter), p.41, suggest that an all-out counter-force attack involving more than 2000 near-ground explosions of megaton-range nuclear weapons would cause between 20 and 40 million civilian casualties.

31. Robert S. McNamara has argued the contrary case in 'The military role of nuclear weapons: perceptions and misperceptions', *Foreign Affairs* (Fall 1983). Having stated on pages 73–4 the reasons for supposing that (tactical) nuclear weapons strengthen NATO's deterrence against any form of aggression, he rather surprisingly

concludes on page 79 that nuclear weapons 'are totally useless –
except only to deter one's opponent from using them'.

32. For a fuller discussion, see James Meacham (note 22 of this chapter)
and *The Economist* for 13-19 April 1985, pp.89–92.

8 WAR-FIGHTING AND MINIMUM DETERRENCE

1. By General Sir David Fraser, in an unpublished lecture at the Royal
College of Defence Studies, 1979.
2. See chapter 2.
3. Quoted in Michael Howard (note 2 to chapter 2).
4. The United States' contingency planning provides for airborne
command posts and emergency communications systems, the
assumption being that the Soviets might well target in their first
strike the underground command and control posts at the Pentagon,
Fort Ritchie, Omaha and Cheyenne Mountain, Colorado. The North
American Aerospace Defence Command at Cheyenne Mountain,
Colorado (NORAD) would receive early warning of the launch of
Soviet missiles from its geostationary early warning satellites, which
employ infra-red and other sensors to detect heat from the exhaust
of ballistic missile rocket launchers. Radar scanners in Alaska,
Greenland, Fylingdales and the American coast would track their
flight paths. NORAD would alert the other command centres, and
the bomber force would take off minutes before the arrival of the
incoming warheads. The President, Defence Secretary and Chiefs
of Staff would go by helicopter to Andrews Air Force Base, outside
Washington DC, and board there the National Emergency Airborne
Command Post (NEACP), a Boeing 747. The other major command
posts would likewise launch command-centre aircraft. If normal
communications were destroyed by the electromagnetic pulse (EMP)
from the exploding Soviet warheads, back-up systems of communication by satellite and an emergency rocket radio communications
system would enable the President to issue orders to the Strategic
Air Command (SAC), which has a facility for airborne launch control
if the underground control centres should be destroyed. See Thomas
Karas, *The New High Ground: Strategies and Weapons of Space
Age war* (New English Library, 1984).
5. See chapters 11 and 12.
6. Chapter 14 discusses these matters further.
7. The death rates at Hiroshima and Nagasaki were highest for people
in the open, less for people in timber-frame houses and less again
for those in concrete buildings, which provided shielding against
thermal and nuclear radiation and to some extent against blast
effects. It is estimated that people in concrete buildings had a 50
per cent chance of survival at only 635 feet from ground zero,
compared with almost half a mile for those in timber-frame school

buildings and more than one and a quarter miles for those out of doors. In other words, the chances of survival were about 11 times as great in concrete buildings, and about 3 times as great in school buildings, as in the open. Among people in the open, those who were lightly-clad (as most people at Hiroshima were) suffered particularly badly from burns (see Glasstone and Dolan, note 3 of chapter 3).

8. See references in F. M. Kaplan, 'Soviet civil defence: some myths in the Western debate', *Survival*, May/June 1978.

9. See also Enthoven and Smith *How Much is Enough?* (note 8 of chapter 2).

10. Edward N. Luttwak (note 1 of chapter 5) pp.8–9.

11. In fairness, Kissinger himself would probably give a similar answer.

9 ARMS CONTROL

1. Thomas C. Schelling and Morton H. Halperin, *Strategy and Arms Control*, (New York: Twentieth Century Fund, 1961), remains an invaluable introduction to the subject, on which the present chapter draws heavily. Other useful sources include John Newhouse, (note 8 of chapter 2).

2. For a fuller discussion, see chapter 13.

3. The United States and the Soviet Union agreed at the SALT 1 summit in May 1982 on a statement of 'basic principles of relations'. In this they undertook to show restraint in their mutual relations, not to seek advantage at each other's expense, to resolve differences by peaceful negotiation and to continue exchanging views on matters of common interest. In the unratified SALT 2 agreement of June 1979 (see note 10 to this chapter) the two sides committed themselves more specifically to strategic equivalence and stability.

4. The first Conference on Security and Co-operation in Europe (CSCE) was held in three stages beginning in July 1973. The final agreement, signed at Helsinki on 1 August 1975 by every European state except Albania and by the United States and Canada, contained a preamble followed by agreements under four headings or 'baskets' which dealt with European security, economic, scientific and technical co-operation, freer movement of people, ideas and literature across frontiers and arrangements for a follow-up conference. In this agreement, and the bilateral 'Ostpolitik' agreements between West Germany and East European countries of the early 1970s which preceded it, the unfinished business from the end of the Second World War was finally completed. The Soviets obtained formal multilateral confirmation of existing frontiers in Europe, thus fulfilling a long-cherished ambition. In return they accepted an agreement requiring each side to notify the other about certain types of military exercises, and they undertook to relax emigration and information restrictions in the Soviet bloc. As part of the preamble to the agreement Eastern governments accepted a general principle

asserting human rights. The follow-up conferences, perhaps inevitably, have achieved much less than the original agreement.

5.   The United States and the Soviet Union concluded an agreement in September 1971 on consultation in the event of nuclear accidents. France and Britain have concluded similar agreements with the Soviet Union.

6.   In the partial test ban treaty (PTBT) of July 1963, the United States, the Soviet Union and Britain agreed that nuclear tests in the atmosphere, in outer space and under water should be banned for an unlimited period subject to the right of any party to withdraw from the treaty if its supreme national interests were at stake – a proviso which has become standard in international treaties. Underground tests were not banned. Other countries were invited to sign the treaty as well. But China, France and other aspiring nuclear powers declined. Tests undertaken since the treaty was signed – underground tests by the superpowers and Britain and tests of all kinds by other countries – have in practice outnumbered pre-treaty tests. But the treaty has contributed to protecting the earth's atmosphere by limiting the testing programmes of the superpowers and Britain to the underground environment.

7.   The quest to prevent the proliferation of nuclear weapons began immediately after the Second World War. On 24 January 1946 the General Assembly of the United Nations, at its first meeting in London, agreed without dissent to a proposal by the United States, Britain, Canada and the Soviet Union for the establishment of an international Atomic Energy Commission charged with making proposals for exchanging basic scientific information, confining atomic energy to peaceful purposes, eliminating nuclear weapons from national arsenals and safeguarding complying states. The American representative on the commission, Bernard M. Baruch, presented proposals for an International Atomic Development Authority which would own and control exclusively all nuclear materials and oversee all activities with nuclear potential. The authority would be responsible for the development and use of atomic energy and have power to inspect all national nuclear activities. The United States offered to transfer ownership of materials and weapons to the new authority as each stage in setting it up was carried out. Once an adequate system for control was in operation with penalties for infringement and no right of veto by any member state, the manufacture of atomic bombs by the United States and other countries would cease and existing stocks would be dismantled. The Soviet delegate, A.A. Gromyko, rejected the American proposals and proposed instead a treaty banning production and use of nuclear weapons, with inspection rights apparently at the discretion of the host country. No agreement was reached, and the commission adjourned indefinitely in 1948.

President Eisenhower proposed a new approach to non-proliferation in his 'Atoms for Peace' speech of December 1953 to the United Nations. He suggested that the United States should provide assistance to other nations wishing to develop nuclear energy for peaceful purposes in return for safeguards which would ensure that these programmes were for peaceful purposes only. President Eisenhower's initiative led to the establishment of the International Atomic Energy Agency (IAEA) in 1956. Almost all nations are members of the agency, which has become the channel for technical assistance by nuclear countries to non-nuclear countries, subject to safeguards.

The non-proliferation treaty (NPT), negotiated between 1965 and 1968, reflected the concerns of the Johnson administration in the United States to secure political commitments to non-proliferation by as many countries as possible and to tighten up the IAEA safeguards – concerns which the Soviet Union broadly shared. Underlying the treaty is a bargain between nuclear weapon states and non-nuclear weapon states. The former undertake to pursue the quest for nuclear disarmament – an undertaking which led to the SALT 1 agreement of 1972 (see note 9 below) – and to make nuclear energy for peaceful purposes available to non-nuclear weapon states. The latter undertake in return not to acquire nuclear weapons and to place all their nuclear activities under IAEA safeguards. The treaty was opened for signature in July 1968 and entered into force in 1970.

At the time of writing 121 countries have signed the NPT. These include most of the major industrialised countries, many of whom could, if they chose, have developed nuclear weapon capabilities. As with the partial test ban treaty, however, France, China and several aspiring nuclear powers including India, Pakistan, Argentina, Brazil, South Africa and Israel have not signed. Since the early 1970s the United States government in particular has made continuing efforts to tighten up the safeguards.

8. The biological weapons convention of April 1972 prohibited the development, production, stockpiling and acquisition of biological agents not justified for peaceful purposes and delivery systems for such agents: existing stocks were to be destroyed within nine months. Also prohibited was the transfer of biological weapons technology. The convention, whose duration is unlimited, went beyond the Geneva Convention of 1925 which forbade the use of chemical and biological agents in war but not their production.

9. The SALT 1 negotiations culminated, after 30 months, in the agreements of May 1972 comprising (a) a treaty limiting defensive ABM systems, and (b) an interim agreement limiting offensive weapon systems in the 'strategic' category, accompanied by a protocol on SLBMs.

In the ABM treaty, each side committed itself to deploy no more than 2 ABM systems – one in defence of the national capital or command authority and the other in defence of a missile silos site. Both systems were to be limited to 100 non-reloadable launchers and interceptor missiles, and limitations were also placed on ABM radars. The number of systems allowed was subsequently reduced by agreement to one for each side. The two sides also agreed not to develop, test or deploy new ABM systems or launchers (research was not prohibited); not to interfere with national technical means of verification (that is, satellite surveillance of the other side's weapon deployments); and not to use measures of deliberate concealment. The duration of the treaty was unlimited. But provision was made for a review every five years and for six months' prior notice of any intention to withdraw from the treaty on grounds of supreme national interest.

The 'interim agreement . . . on certain measures with respect to the limitation of strategic offensive arms' limited the numbers of ballistic missile launcher systems on each side for the five ensuing years to levels close to their existing levels, while allowing for modernisation and replacement. No additional land-based ICBMs were to be built after July 1972, and no old or 'light' ICBMs were to be converted into 'heavy' ICBMs: the United States was thus limited to a maximum of 1054 ICBMs and the Soviet Union to 1618, including no more than 308 'heavy' missiles (a category not precisely defined). An accompanying protocol limited SLBMs and modern ballistic missile submarines to (a) the numbers deemed to be operational and under construction at the time of the agreement plus (b) replacements of old, pre-1964 ICBMs. The United States had 656 SLBMs in 41 submarines at the time. The Soviets were finally deemed to have 740 SLBMs operational or under construction. The agreement did not cover bombers or intermediate-range nuclear forces. It included the same conditions on verification, withdrawal and notice of withdrawal as the ABM treaty.

10.   The unratified SALT 2 agreement provided, like SALT 1, for quantitative limits on strategic offensive arms. The limits were largely agreed between Presidents Ford and Brezhnev at Vladivostok as early as November 1974. The Carter administration then spent a considerable amount of time seeking a more comprehensive agreement which Presidents Carter and Brezhnev finally signed in Vienna on 18 June 1979. Although the United States never ratified the agreement, both sides have broadly complied with it, subject to the qualifications in note 16.

The main quantitative limits related, as in SALT 1, to strategic launchers. But there were two main changes. First, strategic bombers were now included within the limits. Second, the same limits were applied to each side, thus meeting Senator Jackson's criticism of SALT 1. Each side was required to reduce its total launchers to 2400 within six months of the agreement's taking effect. Then, by 31 December 1981, the totals were to be reduced to 2250, and these limits were to remain in force until expiry of the agreement on 31 December 1985. Within the totals there were separate limits, or 'sub-limits', on MIRVed launchers and aircraft carrying air-launched cruise missiles (ALCMs), as follows:

MIRVed ICBM launchers	820
MIRVed ICBM plus SLBM launchers	1200
MIRVed ICBM plus SLBM launchers plus aircraft carrying ALCMs with a range above 600 km	1320

At the time of signing the agreement the Soviets had deployed approximately 2500 strategic launchers. Hence the agreement required them to retire about 250 by the end of 1981. The Americans had deployed only some 2284 launchers; but the sublimits on MIRVs required some adjustment in their MIRVing programme.

The agreement provided also for limits on the number of MIRV warheads carried by each missile (10 for new ICBMs, 14 for new SLBMs), throw-weight (not to exceed the heaviest of existing deployments), and the development of new types of ICBMs (new testings and deployments to be limited to one 'light' ICBM for each side up to the end of 1985). Aircraft carrying ALCMs with a range above 600 km were treated as launchers and included along with heavy bombers in the 2250 over-all limit on launchers. The average number of ALCMs per aircraft was limited to 28.

The agreement grappled heroically with the problem of how to verify limits on MIRVs and bombers, given the Soviets' unwillingness to contemplate on-site inspection. The broad approach adopted was that the 'worst' assumption would be made about all deployments in the absence of 'externally observable differences' to suggest otherwise: that is, missiles and launchers would be counted as MIRVed, and aircraft as heavy bombers, *unless* they were visibly different from MIRVed missiles or launchers or heavy bombers. The SALT 2 limits, like those of the SALT 1 interim agreement, did not cover theatre nuclear systems.

11. The Soviets agreed as a quid pro quo for holding the CSCE Conference (see note 4 above) to participate in talks in Vienna on mutual and balanced reductions of conventional forces in Europe (MBFR). These talks began in October 1973 and progress has been painfully slow. Their existence did, however, enable the United States administration to resist domestic pressures in the mid-1970s for reducing American force deployments in Europe.

The aim of the talks is to limit by agreement the numbers of NATO and Warsaw Pact troops deployed in the central European countries – the Benelux, West Germany, East Germany, Poland and Czechoslovakia. At the time of writing the Warsaw Pact countries have returned to the negotiations after temporarily breaking them off at the end of 1983 in protest at the new NATO deployments of intermediate-range nuclear forces. Provisional agreement has been reached that each side should reduce its forces to 700 000 soldiers (900 000 including airmen and sailors). But there are two stumbling blocks. First, the two sides have still not been able to agree on how to count the troops and in particular on how many troops are deployed in the area at present: in NATO's view Warsaw Pact deployments are substantially greater than the Pact acknowledges. Second, there is no agreement on procedures for verification.

12. The United States tabled at the 40-nation disarmament conference in Geneva in April 1984 a draft treaty which would supplement the Geneva Convention of 1925 by banning the production and retention as well as the use of chemical weapons. The draft provides for international supervision and, by implication, on-site inspection to verify compliance with the treaty. The Soviets have shown their customary reluctance to accept on-site inspection.

13. See chapter 13, note 2.

14. See Christoph Bertram, *The Future of Arms Control: Part I* (Adelphi Papers no.146: IISS, Summer 1978).

15. See Edward N. Luttwak (note 1 to chapter 5).

16. The United States administration has identified the Soviets' development of the SSX-25 in addition to the SSX-24 (see p 78) and their encoding of test missile telemetry signals as treaty violations.

17. For details of the SS-20, see chapter 11, note 6.

18. Page 144 gives details of the proposed deployments, which are due to be made gradually over a period of four or five years.

10 DYNAMIC STABILITY

1. The discussion of escalation in this chapter draws heavily on Thomas C. Schelling, *Arms and Influence* (Yale University Press, 1966). Also on Richard Smoke, *War: Controlling Escalation* (Harvard University Press, 1977).

2. See Shelford Bidwell (ed.), *World War Three: A Military Projection Founded on Today's Facts* (Hamlyn, 1978).

3. See also chapter 14.

4. Clausewitz (note 3 of chapter 5) vol. I, chapter 1, p.23 and vol. III, chapter 6 p.121.

5. For a useful summary of game theory, see Lawrence Freedman, *The Evolution of Nuclear Strategy* (Macmillan, 1981) pp.182 ff.

6. President Kennedy made a significant concession in undertaking not to invade Cuba. But he won universal admiration for his handling of the crisis – the low level 'initial' response of setting an interception or 'quarantine' zone around Cuba, the slow escalation, the firm but reasonable letters to Khruschev, the patient determination to give Khruschev time to decide for himself on a change of course, the decision not to retaliate against the shooting down of an American U2 reconnaissance plane by a Soviet surface-to-air (SAM) missile, and the care which he took to avoid humiliating the Soviet leader, despite the extraordinary succession of lies which he had told about Soviet intentions in Cuba. See Robert F. Kennedy, *13 days* (Macmillan and Pan Books, 1969).

7. See chapter 6.

11 EXTENDED DETERRENCE AND FIRST NUCLEAR USE

1. Compare the argument in chapter 7 about first use of strategic nuclear weapons.
2. I am indebted to Michael Quinlan for the analysis in this and the next sections. For a fuller discussion see chapter 12.
3. Devised by American scientists in the 1970s, the 'neutron bomb' or 'enhanced radiation weapon' is a small, clean fusion weapon (see figure 3.4) designed for use against concentrated enemy armour such as tank formations, while causing a minimum of collateral damage. The weapon's blast and radiation effects (other than neutron radiation) have been reduced to a minimum by use of a very small fission ball or 'primary' and non-radioactive tampers; but the neutron radiation emitted during the first second of the fusion reaction would be capable of penetrating tank armour and concrete buildings and killing the people inside at greater distances than the blast effects.
4. Plutarch, *Life of Caesar*, translated by Dryden and revised by A.H. Clough, (New York: Modern Library, Random House) p.874.
5. See figure 7.2.
6. First deployed in 1977, the SS-20 is a land-based, mobile ballistic missile with a reported range of 2750 miles and CEP of 1300 feet and carrying either a single warhead of one and a half megatons or three MIRVed warheads of 150 kilotons each. About 120 had been deployed at the time of NATO's 'twin-track' decision of December 1979, 360 by the autumn of 1983, and 414 by the spring of 1985.
7. See note 6.

12 LIMITING NUCLEAR WAR

1. The conceptual framework of this chapter is taken from the works of Thomas C. Schelling cited in note 1 of chapter 2 and note 1 of chapter 10. The judgements are the author's own.
2. I owe this way of expressing the role of theatre nuclear weapons to Michael Quinlan.
3. See the discussion in chapter 13 and note 2 of chapter 13.
4. See chapter 7.
5. NATO's ageing ADMs would have to be emplaced before the war began and before the conventional battle was decided, and their effects would, *ex hypothesi*, be felt on NATO territory (see Robert S. McNamara (note 13 of chapter 2)).
6. See chapter 11.
7. See chapter 8 and note 4 to chapter 8.

13 POLICIES TOWARDS THE BALANCE OF TERROR: (1) REJECTION AND ABDICATION

1. This chapter draws on advice from Michael Quinlan and the pub-

lished works of Professor Lawrence Freedman, to both of whom the author is deeply indebted.

2.   The 'nuclear winter' hypothesis first hit the headlines with reports of a 'Conference on the long term worldwide biological consequences of nuclear war' held in the United States on 31 October/1 November 1983. Films offering imaginary reconstructions of a 'nuclear winter' world brought the hypothesis shortly afterwards to the attention of a wider public.

The hypothesis begins from the proposition that a large-scale nuclear exchange involving extensive counter-city strikes would cause many cities to burn, with the emission of millions of tons of sooty smoke. The dust and debris from the explosions and the smoke from the burning cities would form a huge, dark cloud which would (according to the hypothesis) envelop much of the planet for several weeks, possibly including the southern as well as the northern hemisphere. Particularly troublesome would be the smoke, which would remain in the atmosphere over a more extended period and absorb or deflect all but a small fraction of the sun's light. Although these effects would be temporary, so that the sea would not freeze and there would be no Ice Age, land temperatures would drop to sub-zero levels for several months, and the combination of cold and darkness would have profound effects on plants, possibly stopping photosynthesis, as well as killing most farm animals. Many people who survived initially would therefore be likely to starve. Their problems would be compounded in the early stages by radiation from the fall-out of radioactive fission debris and by toxic gases from the burning cities and industrial installations, and in the later stages by increased exposure to ultra-violet light radiation (UV-B) resulting from reductions in the planet's ozone layer. Some scientists have argued that even a smaller-scale nuclear exchange involving (say) 100 megatons could on certain assumptions generate a nuclear winter.

As noted in the main text, the 'nuclear winter' is a hypothesis and is likely to remain so for a long time. Without in any way detracting from the importance of the hypothesis, it is well to remember the points noted in the main text about the type of nuclear conflict assumed and the uncertainties as to whether such a conflict would in fact have the consequences postulated.

3.   I owe most of the argument of this section to Michael Quinlan.

4.   The Charter sanctions the use of force only in self-defence or in defence of the Charter itself.

5.   I owe this formulation to Michael Quinlan.

6.   E.P. Thompson and D. Smith (eds), *Protest and Survive* (Penguin Books, 1980).

7.   See Lawrence Freedman, *Arms control in Europe* (London: Chatham House Papers, no. 11, Royal Institute of International Affairs, 1981).

8.   See Lawrence Freedman, *Britain and Nuclear Weapons* (london: Macmillan, 1980); Norman Polmar, *Strategic Weapons: an Introduction* (Churchill Press, 1975 and Macdonald & Jane's, 1976).

The author is grateful to Michael Quinlan for invaluable advice on this section.

9. The author owes this important point to General Sir David Fraser.
10. The communiqué on Polaris issued after the Kennedy/Macmillan Nassau summit conference of December 1962 stated that:

> The Prime Minister made it clear that, except where Her Majesty's Government decide that supreme national interests are at stake, these British forces will be used for the purpose of international defence of the Western alliance in all circumstances.

The Trident II agreement of March 1982 repeated this language. Mrs Thatcher's letter of 11 March 1982 to President Reagan stated that:

> Like the Polaris force, the United Kingdom Trident II force will be assigned to the North Atlantic Treaty Organisation; and except where the United Kingdom Government may decide that supreme national interests are at stake, this successor force will be used for the purposes of international defence of the Western alliance in all circumstances.

14 POLICIES TOWARDS THE BALANCE OF TERROR: (2) ACCEPTANCE AND IMPROVEMENT

1. See table 14.1.
2. See chapter 13, note 2.
3. See chapter 7.

Index